The Tyndale New Testame

General Editor: PROFESSOR R. V. G. TASKER, M.A., B.D.

THE PASTORAL EPISTLES

THE PASTORAL EPISTLES

AN INTRODUCTION AND COMMENTARY

by

DONALD GUTHRIE, B.D., M.Th.

Tutor in New Testament Language and Literature,
The London Bible College

Inter-Varsity Press,
Leicester, England

William B. Eerdmans Publishing Company
Grand Rapids, Michigan

Inter-Varsity Press
38 De Montfort Street, Leicester LE1 7GP, England
Wm. B. Eerdmans Publishing Company
255 Jefferson S.E., Grand Rapids, MI 49503

First Edition 1957
Reprinted, February 1984

Published and sold only in the USA and Canada by
Wm. B. Eerdmans Publishing Co.

IVP PAPERBACK EDITION 0 85111 863 1
EERDMANS EDITION 0-8028-1413-1

Printed in the United States of America

Inter-Varsity Press is the publishing division of the Universities and Colleges Christian Fellowship (formerly the Inter-Varsity Fellowship), a student movement linking Christian Unions in universities and colleges throughout the British Isles, and a member movement of the International Fellowship of Evangelical Students. For information about local and national activities in Britain write to UCCF, 38 De Montfort Street, Leicester LE1 7GP.

GENERAL PREFACE

ALL who are interested in the teaching and study of the New Testament today cannot fail to be concerned with the lack of commentaries which avoid the extremes of being unduly technical or unhelpfully brief. It is the hope of the editor and publishers that this present series will do something towards the supply of this deficiency. Their aim is to place in the hands of students and serious readers of the New Testament, at a moderate cost, commentaries by a number of scholars who, while they are free to make their own individual contributions, are united in a common desire to promote a truly biblical theology.

The commentaries will be primarily exegetical and only secondarily homiletic, though it is hoped that both student and preacher will find them informative and suggestive. Critical questions will be fully considered in introductory sections, and also, at the author's discretion, in additional notes.

The commentaries are based on the Authorized (King James) Version, partly because this is the version which most Bible readers possess, and partly because it is easier for commentators, working on this foundation, to show why, on textual and linguistic grounds, the later versions are so often to be preferred. No one translation is regarded as infallible, and no single Greek manuscript or group of manuscripts is regarded as always right! Greek words are transliterated to help those unfamiliar with the language, and to save those who do know Greek the trouble of discovering what word is being discussed.

There are many signs today of a renewed interest in what the Bible has to say and of a more general desire to understand its meaning as fully and clearly as possible. It is the hope of all those concerned with this series that God will graciously use what they have written to further this end.

R. V. G. TASKER.

5

CHIEF ABBREVIATIONS

AV   English Authorized Version (King James).

RV   English Revised Version, 1881.

RSV   American Revised Standard Version, 1946.

Abbott-Smith   *Manual Greek Lexicon of the New Testament*, by G. Abbott-Smith, 3rd edition, 1937.

Bengel   *Gnomon of the New Testament*, vol. iv, by J. A. Bengel, translated by James Bryce, 1866.

Bernard   *The Pastoral Epistles* by J. H. Bernard (The Cambridge Greek Testament), 1899.

Dibelius   *Die Pastoralbriefe* by Martin Dibelius, 3rd edition, revised by Hans Conzelmann, 1955.

Easton   *The Pastoral Epistles* by B. S. Easton (S.C.M. Commentary), 1948.

Falconer   *The Pastoral Epistles* by Sir Robert Falconer, 1937.

Harrison   *The Problem of the Pastorals* by P. N. Harrison, 1921.

Horton   *The Pastoral Epistles* by R. F. Horton (The Century Bible), 1911.

James   *The Genuineness and Authorship of the Pastoral Epistles* by J. D. James, 1906.

Jeremias   *Die Briefe an Timotheus und Titus* by Joachim Jeremias (Das Neue Testament Deutsch), 1953.

Lock   *The Pastoral Epistles* by Walter Lock (The International Critical Commentary), 1924.

M & M   Moulton and Milligan's *Vocabulary of the Greek New Testament*.

Parry   *The Pastoral Epistles* by J. Parry, 1920.

Plummer   *The Pastoral Epistles* by A. Plummer (The Expositor's Bible), 1888.

Scott   *The Pastoral Epistles* by E. F. Scott (The Moffatt New Testament Commentary), 1936.

Simpson   *The Pastoral Epistles* by E. K. Simpson, 1954.

Spicq   *Les Epîtres Pastorales* by C. Spicq (Études Bibliques), 1948.

White   *The Pastoral Epistles* by Newport White (The Expositor's Greek Testament), 1910.

CONTENTS

ACKNOWLEDGEMENT

Permission to quote from the RSV has been kindly given by the copyright owners, The National Council of the Churches of Christ in the United States of America.

AUTHOR'S PREFACE

THE Pastoral Epistles have played an important part in the history of the Christian Church and have amply justified their inclusion in the New Testament Canon. Their appeal lies in their blend of sound practical advice and theological statement, which has proved invaluable to Christians both personally and collectively. It is not surprising that the injunctions directed to Timothy and Titus regarding their responsibilities have served as a pattern for the Christian ministry, and have been used so widely in services of ordination.

I have been conscious of many difficulties in approaching my task of commenting upon these letters. Over a considerable period serious doubts have been cast upon their authenticity by many scholars and this has tended to decrease their authority. I have felt obliged to make a thorough investigation of these objections, and the results are given as fully as space will permit in the Introduction. A special examination has been made of the linguistic problem. Because of the technical nature of this study, the conclusions reached are given in an Appendix.

It is impossible to acknowledge indebtedness separately to all those writers who have preceded me in this field and who have contributed to my understanding of these Epistles. There are some, however, who must be singled out for special mention. Among those commentators who have maintained Pauline authorship, Bernard, Lock, Spicq, and Simpson have been specially helpful, while Newport White, Horton, Parry and Jeremias have furnished many useful suggestions. On the other hand, Scott and Easton, who do not favour Pauline authorship, have been constantly consulted, and Dibelius has proved valuable for literary parallels. Harrison's book on *The Problem of the Pastorals* has been indispensable in dealing with the linguistic problem and forms the basis of the investigations given in the Appendix.

It is my sincere hope that this short commentary will stimulate greater interest in and understanding of these concluding Epistles of the great apostle.

DONALD GUTHRIE.

INTRODUCTION

I. THE DESIGNATION AND CHARACTER OF THE EPISTLES

THESE three Epistles have so much in common in style, doctrine and historical situation that they have always been treated as a single group in the same way as the great 'Evangelical' and 'Captivity' Epistles. It was not until 1703 that D. N. Berdot, followed later by Paul Anton in 1726, who popularized it, used the term 'Pastoral' to describe them. While this title is not technically quite correct in that the Epistles do not deal with pastoral duties in the sense of the cure of souls, yet it is popularly appropriate as denoting the essentially practical nature of the subject matter as distinguished from the other Epistles attributed to Paul. The Epistles certainly do not contain a manual of pastoral theology, but their usefulness in the ordering of ecclesiastical discipline was recognized at an early date.[1]

In contrast with the other Pauline letters which are addressed to churches, all three Epistles are directed to individuals, and many of the injunctions are clearly personal. Yet much of the material appears to be designed for the communities to which Timothy and Titus were ministering. Thus they are generally thought to be quasi-public Epistles, although their character as true letters must not be overlooked.[2] The apostle must have written many such letters in the course of his missionary journeys, maintaining in this way not only an interchange of news but an active direction of the many Christian projects

[1] e.g. Muratorian Canon mentions that one Epistle to Titus and two to Timothy are 'still hallowed in the respect of the Catholic Church, in the arrangement of ecclesiastical discipline'. Tertullian and Augustine bear witness to the same fact (see Spicq, *Les Épîtres Pastorales* (1948), p. xxi).

[2] Cf. Spicq, *op. cit.*, pp. xxi-xxxi. Cf. also James, *The Genuineness and Authorship of the Pastoral Epistles* (1906), p. 109, and Ramsay, *Hastings D.B.*, Extra Vol., p. 401.

he had commenced. That these three Epistles alone have survived to be included in the Christian Canon enhances their value as documents throwing light upon the practical problems of early Christianity.

When the literary characteristics of the Epistles are examined, certain features are at once apparent. There is a lack of studied order, some subjects being treated more than once in the same letter without apparent premeditation. The various brief doctrinal statements are intermixed with personal requests or ecclesiastical advice. These letters are, therefore, far removed from literary exercises. They are the natural and human expressions of the apostle's own reflections about the future of the work he is obliged to delegate to others. They reveal, therefore, as much their author's reactions to the situations he faced as contemporary conditions in the Church.

II. THE EPISTLES IN THE ANCIENT CHURCH

In view of the widespread denial of Pauline authorship in modern times, it is necessary to give careful attention to the ancient attestation to these Epistles. It is only against such a background of early Christian opinion that a fair assessment can be made of modern theories unfavourable to Pauline authorship.

There are many traces of these Epistles in the early apostolic Fathers, Clement of Rome and Ignatius, although the evidence is not sufficiently precise to amount to proof. In the case of Clement, Harrison[1] has listed a number of similar phrases and has concluded that the author of the Pastoral Epistles belonged, therefore, to the same period as Clement, a view which had earlier been expressed by Holtzmann.[2] Streeter[3] goes further and argues that the editor of the Pastorals borrowed from Clement's letter. But all these approach the evidence from the standpoint of a definite presupposition, i.e. that the Pastorals belong to the second century and must therefore be later than Clement's letter. The opinion of

---

[1] *The Problem of the Pastoral Epistles* (1921), pp. 177 f.
[2] Cf. Bernard, *The Pastoral Epistles* (1906), pp. xix.
[3] *The Primitive Church* (1929), p. 153.

Falconer, who did not maintain Pauline authenticity, is worth noting on this point. He declared, 'The most probable explanation of the similarities, both in ideas and in language, between the Pastorals and 1 Clement is that the former, as they now are, were known to Clement.'[1] It is only fair to point out, however, that the investigators of the Oxford Society of Historial Theology did not consider that any of the evidence from Clement constituted certain literary dependence.[2] The evidence from Ignatius is equally inconclusive, although Bernard claims that 'the coincidences in phraseology can hardly be accidental'.[3]

The letter of Polycarp shows much closer acquaintance. Six passages are cited by Bernard,[4] some of which would seem to be unmistakable instances of quotation. Jeremias thinks the evidence at least shows that the Pastoral Epistles were known to Polycarp,[5] although this is sometimes disputed by those who deny Pauline authenticity altogether.[6] There are allusions to these letters in Justin Martyr, Heracleon, Hegesippus, Athenagorus, Theophilus, and Irenaeus, which show that they were widely known, while Theophilus definitely believed them to be inspired.[7]

The preceding attestation is as strong as most of the Pauline Epistles, with the exception of Romans and 1 Corinthians.[8] Yet there are two other lines of evidence which are sometimes claimed to make the external attestation as a whole unfavourable to the authenticity of the Epistles.[9] All of them were rejected by Marcion, and are lacking from the Chester Beatty Papyrus (P^{46}). There seems good reason to suppose that Marcion's rejection of them was inspired by dogmatic con-

---

[1] *The Pastoral Epistles* (1937), p. 5.
[2] *The New Testament in the Apostolic Fathers* (1905), pp. 37 ff.
[3] *Op. cit.*, p. xv.
[4] *Op. cit.*, pp. xiv, xv. Cf. also J. D. James, *op. cit.*, pp. 5-24, for a detailed account of the relevant external evidence.
[5] *Die Briefe an Timotheus und Titus* (1953), p. 4.
[6] Cf. Dibelius, *Die Pastoralbriefe*, p. 2.
[7] Cf. Theophilus, *Ad Autolycum*, iii. 14.
[8] Cf. Falconer, *op. cit.*, p. 3.
[9] Cf. Dibelius, *op. cit.*, p. 2.

siderations. James[1] pointed out that Tertullian[2] regarded Marcion's rejection as a strange thing, which suggests it was an innovation. In any case, Marcion would not have liked the Epistles as we possess them.[3] Such statements as 1 Tim. i. 8, vi. 20 and 2 Tim. iii. 16, among others, would have cut right across Marcion's main contentions. If it be argued, on the other hand, that the orthodox party was equally influenced by dogmatic considerations to accept pseudonymous works which supported current ecclesiastical procedure, it must be pointed out that there is no evidence of any struggle in any part of the Church before their unanimous acceptance. Marcion's lone voice, biased as it undoubtedly was, must not be allowed to outweigh the strong attestation from orthodox early Christian writers.

The omission of these Epistles from the Chester Beatty Papyri is considered a greater obstacle to their genuineness, since, if it can be shown that the Codex, when complete, could not have contained them, it must mean that these Epistles were not known in the Pauline Corpus in the third century in Egypt. Many scholars maintain that the closing part of the Codex, which is no longer extant, would not leave room for the inclusion of these Epistles. But Jeremias[4] points out that the Codex shows that the scribe crowded more lines per page into the second half than into the first, and it may well be that he miscalculated the amount of space required. If at the end of his task he required additional leaves it would be necessary to leave the corresponding pages at the beginning blank. This unfortunately cannot be verified, since neither the beginning nor ending of the Codex are now extant, but it seems at least a reasonable explanation of the position.

The conclusion of Salmond,[5] after his careful review of the external evidence, has been often challenged but never disproved. 'If, therefore, the battle had to be fought solely on the ground of external evidence, the Pastoral Epistles would

[1] *Op. cit.*, p. 22.
[2] *Adv. Marc.*, v. 21.
[3] Cf. Spicq., *op. cit.*, Introd., p. c.
[4] *Op. cit.*, p. 4.
[5] *Introduction to the New Testament* (1892), p. 399.

obtain a complete victory.' This will have an important bearing upon our consideration of pseudonymity in relation to these Epistles.

III. THE EPISTLES IN THE MODERN CHURCH

The unbroken tradition of the Church until the nineteenth century was to regard the Pastorals as the work of Paul and therefore authentic. The first determined attack against apostolic authorship was made when Schleiermacher (1807)[1] disputed the Pauline authorship of 1 Timothy on stylistic and linguistic grounds, thus becoming the father of that school of modern criticism which decides questions of authenticity on philological evidence. The main advocates of the non-apostolic authorship of all the Epistles have been Eichhorn (1812), F. C. Baur (1835), de Wette (1844), Holtzmann (1880), who produced one of the most thoroughgoing criticisms of Pauline authorship, Moffatt (1901), Bultmann (1930) and Dibelius (1931, Revised 1955). Many have denied Pauline authorship, but have sought to retain a few genuine fragments. Among these the leading recent exponents have been Von Soden (1893), Harrison (1921), Scott (1936), Falconer (1937) and Easton (1948), of whom Harrison with his book *The Problem of the Pastorals* has undoubtedly been the most influential.

On the other hand, throughout this century and a half of criticism of the Pauline authorship, many careful scholars have maintained the authenticity of these Epistles, among whom the most notable have been Ellicott (1864), Bertrand (1887), Plummer (1888), Godet (1893), Hort (1894), Bernard (1902), B. Weiss (1902), Zahn (1906), J. D. James (1906), Ramsay (1909–11), White (1910), Bartlet (1913), Parry (1920), Wohlenberg (1923), Lock (1924), Meinertz (1931), Schlatter (1936), Spicq (1947), Jeremias (1953) and Simpson (1954). The fact that so impressive a list of scholars can be cited in favour of Pauline authorship serves as a warning against the tacit assumption of some scholars that no scientific grounds

---

[1] In 1804 J. E. C. Schmid had disputed 1 Timothy, but it was Schleiermacher's attack that had the greater effect.

remain for the traditional position, and that all who maintain it are obliged to resort to special pleading.[1] The various problems that have been raised will be dealt with separately in the following sections.

IV. THE PROBLEM OF THE HISTORICAL ALLUSIONS

Many scholars have placed great emphasis on the historical background as weighing heavily against Pauline authorship. Scott, for instance, declares, 'That Paul cannot have been the author is most clearly apparent when we examine the historical framework of the letters.'[2] The evidence must, therefore, be scrutinized with some care and then the various solutions proposed to account for it must be compared.

(a) *The historical allusions in the Pastorals*

These will be dealt with as they occur in the separate Epistles.

1. It seems clear from 1 Tim. i. 3, *as I besought thee to abide still at Ephesus, when I went into Macedonia,* that Paul has either been in Ephesus recently, or else in the near vicinity, and that he is now in all probability in Macedonia. Timothy was left in charge of the Ephesian community, and Paul now writes to instruct him about certain ecclesiastical procedures. No other historical allusions occur in 1 Timothy.

2. In the opening section of the Epistle to Titus, the apostle states *For this cause left I thee in Crete, that thou shouldest set in order the things that are wanting* (i. 5). These words require that Paul paid a personal visit to Crete, and although there is no necessity to demand a lengthy stay in which a series of churches could be established since these may already have existed prior to his visit, the whole Epistle suggests that he was well acquainted with the problems of the Cretan communities and this could hardly have resulted from a fleeting visit.

In closing this Epistle the apostle mentions his determination to spend the winter in Nicopolis where he hopes Titus will be able to join him (Tit. iii. 12). While it is not certain where this

---

[1] Cf. A. M. Hunter's comment in *Interpreting the New Testament* (1951), p. 64.

[2] *Op. cit.,* pp. xvi, xvii.

Nicopolis was situated, it is generally assumed to have been the city of that name in Epirus. But if this is correct it is the only evidence that Paul ever went into this district.

3. It is 2 Timothy that supplies the greatest number of historical details. From the reference to Onesiphorus in i. 17, *But, when he was in Rome, he sought me out very diligently, and found me*, it is a reasonable deduction that Paul is at the time of writing in Rome. It is at least certain he has already been in Rome and equally certain that he is now a prisoner. He mentions that Onesiphorus *was not ashamed of my chain* (i. 16), and he calls himself a *prisoner* (i. 8), while chapter iv contains a clear reference to his trial (iv. 16).

There is a curious request for a cloak left at the house of Carpus at Troas (iv. 13), which would seem to demand a relatively recent visit to make such a request intelligible. The apostle also imparts the news that *Erastus abode at Corinth: but Trophimus have I left at Miletum sick* (iv. 20), which is again only intelligible as a piece of information unknown to Timothy, suggesting that the events related occurred in the recent past.

The problem at once arises whether these historical data can be fitted into Paul's life as recorded in the Acts. The various attempts which have been made to do this may be briefly surveyed according to the imprisonment to which 2 Timothy is attached. Acts mentions only two imprisonments which can be considered in this respect, i.e. Caesarea and Rome. Of recent years, many scholars have also postulated an Ephesian imprisonment and this suggestion will need investigation.

(*i*) *The Caesarean imprisonment.* It is clearly impossible to assign 2 Timothy to any imprisonment other than Rome, if the text of 2 Tim. i. 17 is authentic. Unless this reference is regarded as an interpolation or a corruption, for neither of which the slightest ms evidence exists, the attempt to link the Pastorals as a whole to the Caesarean imprisonment must be abandoned. Quite apart from the reference to Rome, the allusion to Trophimus' illness at Miletus (2 Tim. iv. 20) seems impossible from a Caesarean source, since Trophimus was with Paul in

Jerusalem and was the indirect cause of his arrest (Acts xxi. 29). Furthermore, Timothy also accompanied Paul to Jerusalem (Acts xx. 4) and was not, therefore, left behind at Ephesus.

(*ii*) *The Ephesian hypothesis.* Duncan,[1] who advocates an Ephesian origin of the captivity Epistles, suggests the possibility of assigning the Pastorals to a similar period, but many difficulties beset his proposal. (a) While there may be good grounds for postulating an Ephesian imprisonment, the evidence cannot amount to conclusive proof, and the hypothesis must remain, therefore, largely speculative. (b) It is necessary for Duncan to suggest a textual emendation to eliminate the reference to Rome in 2 Tim. i. 17, a procedure which at once makes the theory suspect. (c) If the Pastorals are treated as a whole the ecclesiastical directions affecting Ephesus would not readily fit into the period immediately following Paul's own ministry there, while room would need to be found for a mission to Crete which would seem to be excluded by Acts xx. 31.[2] Timothy would hardly have needed such explicit instructions had he been working with the apostle so shortly before. (d) Paul mentions a journey from Ephesus to Macedonia (1 Tim. i. 3) which could conceivably relate to Acts xx. 1; but if so it must have taken place after the Ephesian imprisonment suggested by Duncan. Moreover, according to 1 Tim. i. 3, Timothy was left at Ephesus, although Acts xx makes it clear that he soon afterwards accompanied Paul to Jerusalem to deliver the collection for the poverty-stricken Christians there. It is a fair conclusion that, as far as the Pastorals are

---

[1] *St. Paul's Ephesian Ministry* (1929), pp. 184-216. Earlier T. C. Laughlin had attempted to assign the defence mentioned in 2 Tim. iv. 16 f. to an Ephesian trial.

[2] These difficulties would, of course, vanish if part only of the Pastorals are accepted as genuine notes. Duncan admits his approach to these Epistles is 'wholly tentative' ('St. Paul's Ministry in Asia—the Last Phase', *New Testament Studies* (May, 1957), pp. 217, 218). Harrison criticizes Duncan's proposals mainly on the grounds of the 'inherent contradictions' of 2 Tim. iv. But even if these 'contradictions' are not admitted, the evidence of 2 Tim. iv. 6-8 and 16-18 certainly appears to support a Roman rather than Ephesian imprisonment, as Harrison observes (cf. 'The Pastoral Epistles and Duncan's Ephesian Theory', *New Testament Studies* (May, 1956), pp. 250-261).

concerned, the Ephesian hypothesis raises more problems than it solves.

(*iii*) *The Roman imprisonment.* Although some attempts have been made to assign 2 Timothy to the Roman imprisonment mentioned at the end of Acts, and the other two Epistles to earlier periods in the Acts history,[1] it has been generally acknowledged that the three Epistles possess such close affinities that to separate them in this manner is most improbable. As it is obvious that all three cannot belong to this period of confinement, this solution is not regarded with favour.

(*b*) *Proposed solutions*

Since the historical allusions in the Pastorals cannot be fitted into the Acts record, three alternative solutions have been proposed. The 'Fiction' Hypothesis, strongly advocated by Holtzmann,[2] regards all the personalia as fictitious devices to provide an appearance of authenticity. Any particular discrepancies of detail would then be attributable to the author's lack of historical perspective. But this theory may at once be discounted because it fails to account for the obvious realism of the personal allusions. In Harrison's words, 'They have the genuine Pauline stamp. They ring true'.[3] The 'Second Imprisonment' Hypothesis, which assumes that Paul had a period of further activity subsequent to the Acts history, is the traditional explanation of the personalia, and has been embraced by almost all scholars maintaining the authenticity of the Epistles. The 'Fragment' Hypothesis regards the personalia as separate fragments which may be fitted into widely differing situations in the Acts history. This is the solution maintained by the majority of those unable to accept Pauline authorship, and which receives its fullest exposition

---

[1] Cf. the theory of Vernon Bartlet, *The Expositor*, Series VIII, Vol. v. (1913), pp. 28-36, 161-167, 256-263, 325-347. He maintained that 1 Timothy was sent after Paul left Ephesus and that Titus was left at Crete after Paul's visit to Fair Havens.

[2] *Die Pastoralbriefe* (1880).

[3] *Op. cit.*, p. 96.

in Harrison's work. These two latter solutions must both be carefully examined.

The Second Roman Imprisonment Theory. According to Acts xxviii. 30, 31 the apostle spent two whole years in his own hired house, but since nothing is said beyond this, it is as great a possibility that he was released as not. Disputants of Pauline authorship make much of the Acts silence about a release, but this presents a difficulty only if it is assumed that the historian has written a complete history of Paul. But Duncan[1] has demonstrated that Acts contains many lacunae and no confidence can be placed, therefore, in any argument based on its silence. In fact, the extreme leniency of the detention is more suggestive of release than martyrdom. If martyrdom crowned the Acts story it is difficult to see why the historian omitted to mention it.

Another consideration pointing to the probability of release is the terms of Agrippa's declaration, with which the proconsul Festus apparently concurred (Acts xxvi. 32). In his report to the imperial authorities the proconsul could not, in view of this, have been unfavourable to Paul, and this would, in the normal course of Roman justice, have disposed towards a successful trial in the period before Christianity became illicit. The captivity Epistles bear witness to Paul's expectation of release (Phm. 22; Phil. i. 25, ii. 23, 24).[2]

Certain external evidence may be cited in support of a period of further activity, although opinions differ regarding the value of this evidence. Clement of Rome's vague reference to Paul having reached the boundary (*to terma*) of the West can either mean that he had reached his western goal when in Rome, as Harrison[3] interprets it, or that he had reached the western boundary of the Empire (i.e. Spain). Harrison[4] goes to great lengths to disprove the Spanish visit, considering that

---

[1] *Op. cit.*, pp. 95 ff.

[2] Cf. Schlatter's admirably balanced examination of the probability of Paul's release, *The Church in the New Testament Period* (1926, Eng. Trans. 1955), pp. 232-239. Cf. also Spitta, *Zur Geschichte und Litteratur des Urchristentum* (1893), i., pp. 106 f.

[3] *Op. cit.*, p. 107.

[4] *Op. cit.*, pp. 102 ff.

later patristic citations quoted in support of it are explicable as deductions from Rom. xv. 24, 28. But the second imprisonment theory is independent of the Spanish mission, and indeed is almost exclusive of it for it involves considerable further activity in the East. Schlatter's[1] opinion that Paul had already abandoned his Spanish mission by the time he wrote the captivity Epistles[2] is the most reasonable explanation of all the facts.

Eusebius records a report that Paul was sent on a further ministry of preaching after his first defence before ending his life in martyrdom in Rome.[3] But this report could easily be a piece of popular exegesis based on the personalia of 2 Timothy, and is unlikely to have much value as an independent witness. It is nevertheless a valuable indication of fourth-century interpretation of the historical allusions in the Pastorals. Subsequent to Eusebius' time the Release Theory became the accepted explanation, and although Harrison disposes of this evidence on the grounds that later writers have perpetuated an early error,[4] traditional opinion may well preserve more truth than he allows. The absence of any specific early attestation cannot of itself render the hypothesis untenable, while the absence of any contrary evidence leaves a possibility of release. These historical allusions cannot, therefore, weigh against the authenticity while such a possibility remains.

The Fragment Hypothesis. It is the contention of Harrison, however, that the traditional theory is untenable on other grounds, namely, that history would then have repeated itself with a vengeance.[5] Paul again visits Troas with Timothy and Trophimus, again goes to Miletus, is troubled once more by Asiatic Jews, is pursued by the same Alexander, who pursued him even to Rome, and has the same recent prison-companions, Luke, Mark, Timothy, Demas and Tychicus, the latter on both occasions being sent to Ephesus.

[1] *Op. cit.*, p. 236.
[2] If Philippians and Philemon were written from Ephesus, as Duncan suggests, they would, of course, furnish no data for the Roman imprisonment.
[3] *Ecclesiastical History*, ii. 22.
[4] *Op. cit.*, p. 104.
[5] *Op. cit.*, p. 111.

But it is not surprising, if Paul made a second visit to the East after his release, that he again visited Troas and Miletus and was again in touch with many of his former associates. It would be more surprising if it were otherwise. And as for Alexander, there are no grounds for identifying the Alexander of 2 Tim. iv[1] with the would-be spokesman of the Jews in the Ephesian riot, nor is there any suggestion in 2 Tim. iv that the coppersmith's subversive activities were taking place at that time in Rome. These data therefore form a precarious basis for claiming a repetition of history.

Yet it is on the basis of the unlikelihood of such historical repetition that Harrison justifies his Fragment Theory, together with the alleged internal contradictions in the personalia of 2 Tim. iv.[2] Is it probable, he argues, that Paul would have given Timothy careful instructions for the preservation of apostolic teaching and then urged him to come as soon as possible because of the imminence of the apostle's departure? 'If we are to take that noble and impressive farewell seriously, he must have known that it was a physical impossibility for Timothy to carry out these commissions until too late. And if we are to take the commissions seriously, they compel us to suppose that in that farewell Paul exercised a mental reservation which would rob it of half its impressiveness and pathos.'[3] But has not Harrison here misunderstood the purpose of 2 Timothy? As compared with 1 Timothy and Titus there is surprisingly little ecclesiastical instruction. The Epistle mostly comprises personal advice and encouragement to Timothy, and any references to ecclesiastical discipline are so general that it is not at all inconceivable that Paul would touch upon them, aware as he seems to be that this might well be his last communication to Timothy. If there was a considerable delay between the initial examination and the legal trial Paul might well have hoped that Timothy would be able

---

[1] See note in commentary on 2 Tim. iv. 14.

[2] Cf. *op. cit.*, p. 114. Cf. also Harrison's article 'The Pastoral Epistles and Duncan's Ephesian Theory', *New Testament Studies* (May, 1956), pp. 250-261, in which he maintains that Paul could never have written all this material at the same time and place.

[3] Harrison, *op. cit.*, p. 115.

to reach him in time.[1] But if not, Timothy would have in his possession this last precious document from his beloved master. Even if such a solution were to rob the farewell of some of its pathos, is the case to be judged on a preconceived notion of impressiveness? Might not that notion itself be misconceived?

Harrison, however, feels that his case is unanswerable and proceeds to elaborate his theory that all the Pastorals personalia can be fitted into the Acts record, yet at different times and places. His original arrangement[2] of the fragments was as follows:

1. Tit. iii. 12–15. Written from Macedonia to Titus, who is at Corinth, just after Paul's severe letter to the church there. Titus is told to proceed to Epirus.

2. 2 Tim. iv. 13–15, 20, 21a. Again from Macedonia after visiting Troas, as mentioned in 2 Cor. ii. 12 f. Timothy is to join him before the winter.

3. 2 Tim. iv. 16–18a. Written from Caesarea after Paul's first defence.

4. 2 Tim. iv. 9–12, 22b. Paul is in Rome and recalls Timothy to join him there.

5. 2 Tim. i. 16–18, iii. 10, 11, iv. 1, 2a, 5b–8, 18b, 19, 21b–22a. Parts of Paul's last letter to Timothy.

Later Harrison reduced the fragments to three, grouping 2 with 4, and 3 with 5, the former of these two fragments being now assigned to Nicopolis and the latter to Rome.[3] It should be noted that there is no general agreement about these fragments amongst advocates of the theory as a comparison of McGiffert's, Falconer's and Easton's schemes with Harrison's will show.[4] But Harrison's theory is extremely improbable for the following reasons.

1. The disintegrated character of the so-called fragments belies it. It is difficult to see what process of composition the editor of 2 Timothy used in preserving these genuine fragments

[1] Cf. Montgomery Hitchcock, 'The Pastorals and a Second Trial of Paul', *Expository Times*, xli (1930), pp. 20-23.

[2] *Op. cit.*, pp. 115 ff.

[3] *Expository Times*, xlvii (December 1955), p. 80.

[4] These agree only on i. 16-18 and most of iv (except verses 3, 4), but disagree on many other details.

for posterity. He could hardly have mixed them up more than he apparently did in chapter iv had he been completely indiscriminate and lacking not only in historical discernment but also in common sense. Yet the fact remains that chapter iv does not read like a haphazard hotch-potch, and it would be necessary to assume, therefore, on Harrison's view, that the editor must have done his work superhumanly well to have belied all suspicion of disjointedness until nineteenth- and twentieth-century criticism tracked down the muddle.[1]

2. The preservation of these disjointed fragments constitutes another problem, for they are not, for the most part, the type of fragments which normally have much appeal. Even if an early Christian with antiquarian interests had accidently discovered and highly prized these genuine Pauline relics, there would still be need to give an adequate motive for their incorporation so unevenly in Titus and 2 Timothy. But this Harrison and other advocates of fragment theories have not satisfactorily done. It is not enough to state that the Pauline editor composed the Epistles as a means of preserving the fragments or else added the fragments to existing drafts of the Epistles to enhance their authority and to ensure their reception, unless adequate contemporary parallels can be cited as supporting evidence that such a process was normal in early Christian literary practice. But no such parallels are forthcoming.

3. As a process of historical investigation, Harrison's fragment theory is open to further criticism for it is based on the unproved *a priori* assumption that Acts contains the complete history of Paul. It is not scientific method to change the character of historical evidence (as the fragment theory effectively does to the Pastorals personalia) because it does not accord with other accepted historical data.

V. THE ECCLESIASTICAL SITUATION

It has usually been maintained by disputants of Pauline authorship that the ecclesiastical situation reflected in the Pastorals

[1] Cf. Harrison's unconvincing explanation of the editor's procedure of intercalating the various notes, in 'The Pastoral Epistles and Duncan's Ephesian Theory', *New Testament Studies* (May, 1956), p. 251.

is akin to that of the early second century, and therefore is much too developed to belong to the age of Paul. If the evidence supports this claim it would, of course, be impossible to maintain the authenticity of the letters, but an examination of the data shows an entirely different position. Before dealing with the Pastorals data it should be noted that it is quite erroneous to regard these Epistles as manuals of Church order in the sense in which later manuals were used, for there is an almost complete absence of instruction on administration, civil relationships or conduct of worship. The entire ecclesiastical teaching (1 Tim. iii. 1–13, v. 3–22 and Tit. i. 5–9) comprises no more than about a tenth of the subject matter of the Pastorals, and even this is much more concerned with personnel than office. The position may be conveniently summarized as follows:

1. The offices mentioned are those of bishop (*episkopos*), elder (*presbuteros*) and deacon. In both 1 Timothy and Titus certain qualities of a wholly personal character are demanded of bishops, but it is noteworthy that these qualities are quite unexceptional. In fact it is surprising that such low requirements needed to be specified at all. It is significant that in both Epistles the bishops are required to have the ability to teach, but this is no more than would be expected from the more responsible members of the Church. 1 Timothy alone contains instructions for the choice of deacons, but nothing is said about their duties.

2. In both Epistles the terms 'elder' and 'bishop' appear to be used interchangeably. Tit. i. 5–7 is conclusive for the view that these two terms describe the same people, and this fact is now generally accepted among New Testament scholars.[1] In this case the term 'bishop' could not have been used in the Pastorals in the later sense of a monarchical episcopate. There is nothing in these letters, in fact, to suggest that the bishop was in sole charge of any one community, nor that each community was restricted to one bishop. It is true that,

[1] Cf. Hort, *Christian Ecclesia* (1897), pp. 189 ff. Streeter, *The Primitive Church* (1929), pp. 82, 108.

whereas elders are spoken of in the plural, the bishop is mentioned only in the singular. These singular references are, however, to be interpreted in a generic sense, i.e. of the class of bishops, and no deduction can be made from this detail.

3. A group known as 'widows' is specifically mentioned in 1 Tim. v. 3–16, but no other references to these occur in the New Testament. All that this passage states is that a list was to be kept on which the names of widows were enrolled if they were eligible for the Church's support. The evidence is not sufficient to conclude that a distinct order was envisaged.

From this data two opposing deductions have been made. The traditional view is that there is nothing in the Pastorals ecclesiastical situation which necessitates a date later than the time of Paul. At the other extreme is the view, both of those who regard the Pastorals as wholly fictional and of those who maintain genuine fragments, that the ecclesiastical situation is much too advanced for the mid-first-century Church. Let Harrison voice this latter view, 'The whole ecclesiastical situation and atmosphere pre-supposed in these epistles represents a stage of development beyond that for which we have any evidence in the lifetime of Paul or in the Apostolic Age, but entirely in keeping with that of the period to which "Liberal" criticism assigns them'.[1] Now if Harrison is correct in this statement it would be a strong reason for rejecting the authenticity, but can this position be substantiated?

In dealing with this ecclesiastical line of approach the reasons which have led some scholars to deny an early date for the Pastorals on the grounds of the late organization reflected will be enumerated and examined.

(a) *It is maintained that Paul had no interest in Church government.* This idea, current in New Testament criticism since the time of Baur, is based on the assumption that the great evangelical Epistles are the primary criteria for Paul's approach. Since in none of these does he signify any concern about organization within the Church it must follow that he gave it no thought. Indeed, on the contrary, he envisages a charismatic ministry

[1] *Op. cit.*, p. 7.

to be operating in the Corinthian community. There is, however, strong evidence that Paul was not unmindful of church organization where circumstances demanded it. Unless Acts xiv. 23, where Paul and Barnabas are said to have ordained elders in all the south Galatian churches which had been established on the first missionary journey, is an anachronism, as Easton[1] claims, the apostles must have recognized the need for the elder system at the very beginning of the Gentile mission, at least in some communities. It would appear that the only reason for regarding this reference as an anachronism is that it fails to support the theory that the elder-system was a later development to supply the need among other things of tradition-bearers. But only uncritical and unscientific methods could allow such modification of evidence in the interests of a preconceived theory.

A further support for Pauline acknowledgment of established orders within the Church is the address to the Philippian bishops and deacons (Phil. i. 1), who are incidentally mentioned after the rank and file of Christian believers.[2] Whether Paul had anything to do with the appointment of these is impossible to say, but it is, at least, not inconceivable, as this church was founded by the apostle and had had intimate communications with him as the Epistle to the Philippians shows. Yet Easton considers that in this reference (Phil. i. 1) the *episkopoi* cannot mean rule-elders in the later sense of the word, but is a collective word referring to officials, of whatever office or rank. But this again looks too much like a modification of evidence in the interest of a theory to warrant serious consideration. It need only be pointed out that in the case of the Philippian letter, the motive for writing is to express gratitude for a gift sent, and Paul would naturally include in the opening address the officials who had no doubt been responsible for the collection. In no other of Paul's Epistles does such a situation arise and this may possibly account for the lack of allusion to Church officials in the salutations to the other churches. But

---

[1] *Op. cit.*, p. 226.
[2] Cf. Ramsay, 'Historical Commentary on the Epistles to Timothy', *The Expositor*, vii (1906), viii. p. 17.

compare the veiled allusion to 'those over you' in 1 Thes. v. 12.[1]

Another line of evidence comes from Eph. iv. 11 where among the offices mentioned are 'pastors and teachers', which appears to describe one office and not two. Evidently variety of function was fully recognized when this Epistle was written, although this would carry little weight with those who, like Easton, regard Ephesians as a late non-Pauline work.

There is, therefore, considerable evidence to show that Paul was not unmindful of Church organization. The absence of uniformity of government in Pauline churches is capable of other explanations than that Paul was completely disinterested. He appears to have been sufficiently flexible in his approach to allow any system which suited local conditions and was dictated by the Holy Spirit. Perhaps the strongest refutation of the notion of Paul's disinterestedness in Church organization is to be found in his words to the Ephesian elders[2] (Acts xx. 28). 'Take heed therefore unto yourselves, and to all the flock, over the which the Holy Ghost hath made you overseers, to feed the church of God.' Here is an acknowledgment that the Ephesian elder-system was the Holy Spirit's appointment and an indirect confirmation that such a system was fully operative some time before Timothy arrived to take up his duties. It is further significant that Paul addresses these elders as bishops (*episkopoi*).

(*b*) *It is maintained that the Pastorals assume a rule-elder system which could not function in the apostolic age.*

Easton explains the basis of this criticism in the following manner—' "Elders" are, by definition, the guardians and interpreters of the tradition; but they could not function until the tradition itself had been established, until the "faith" had been really "once and for all delivered to the saints" '. But is not Easton's definition of 'elder' too rigid? While there is no doubt that the elder-system was modelled on Jewish precedents, as Easton clearly shows, yet this is no justification for supposing

[1] Hort considers that elders must here be meant. *Christian Ecclesia* (1897), p. 126.

[2] Easton also considers this an anachronism, *op. cit.*, p. 226.

that the Christian conception of the office was strictly limited by its Jewish origin. Even if Easton's limited definition is valid, it does not follow that the system could not have operated until the tradition was fixed, for there was just as much need for the developing tradition to be preserved. There is admittedly some evidence from the Pastorals that local leaders were to be tradition-bearers (e.g. 2 Tim. ii. 2; Tit. i. 9), while Timothy is more than once exhorted to guard the 'truth' committed to him as a trust or deposit, but this seems so elemental a requirement for any church which was to survive that it cannot be thought surprising that Paul should mention it as a requisite for the future.

(*c*) *It is maintained that the Church organization is already established, requiring a considerable time to have elapsed since the apostolic age.* The main evidence brought to support this criticism is 1 Tim. iii. 6 where it is specifically stated that a bishop must not be a new convert (*neophutos*). It may appear at first sight that such a stipulation rules out a church established only a few years earlier by the apostle Paul, but this does not necessarily follow. The church at Ephesus was probably one of the largest churches established by Paul for he spent three years in that city, and consequently after a few years there would be many Christians who had only just come to a knowledge of the faith and many others who had been Christians almost from the start. It would be a policy of natural prudence to exclude the former from eligibility for the bishop's office, but there is no need to visualize the eligible candidates as venerable greybeards who had served a long apprenticeship. As in all primitive communities measures had to be taken at the inception of the church to select some members for special responsibility, and as the membership increased more rigid selection was possible because of a wider choice. In 1 Tim. iii. 6, therefore, the apostle warns only against too rapid promotion.

It is perhaps not without significance that no mention is made of 'neophytes' in the directions to Titus, and this may well be because the Cretan church was of much more recent establishment than that at Ephesus and such a prohibition would therefore be inapplicable. Another point that should not be overlooked is the elder-system which, according to Acts xx, must have been in operation in Ephesus, and which may even have been suggested by the apostle himself and have been instituted immediately after his departure.

The existence of a so-called order of widows is also cited as an evidence of a more fully developed church. But even if 1 Tim. v is understood of a distinct 'order' of widows, which is extremely doubtful, there is no evidence to show when such an order began,[1] and only if such evidence were forthcoming could this passage be used to prove a late date for the Pastorals. Admittedly no other New Testament evidence supports such a women's order, but the balance of probability supports the early use of women for official duties. The reference to Phoebe as a 'deaconess' (Rom. xvi. 1) may be a possible parallel, although the word used there probably denotes service in general and does not refer to a specialized order.[2]

(d) *It is also maintained that the functions of Timothy and Titus are akin to those of an Ignatian type of bishop.*

For this view Easton may be quoted, 'In "Timothy" and "Titus", therefore, the Ignatian bishops are actually found in everything but the title'.[3] He goes on to describe the lack of the title as an intentional avoidance by the pastor of too glaring an anachronism in a Pauline letter. The data upon which he bases his assertion are as follows:—1. 'Timothy' and 'Titus' received the gift of authority at ordination; 2. they are of higher rank than the other elders because their duties are more responsible; 3. they are to appoint elders and are to deal with any charges against elders (this latter point is specially mentioned for Timothy); 4. they are responsible for instruction and discipline. Easton claims that all these functions were exercised by the Ignatian type of bishop and in this he is

---

[1] The earliest unambiguous use of 'deaconess' as a distinctive office appears in the *Didascalia* iii. 12, 13, but a wide gap separates this office from the references in the Pastorals to widows.

[2] Cf. Easton, *op. cit.*, p. 185.

[3] *Op. cit.*, p. 177.

undoubtedly correct. But when he argues that 'Timothy' and 'Titus' must, therefore, be bishops of the same Ignatian type he is guilty of a *non sequitur*, for these functions do not require the monarchical episcopate for their accomplishment. They could just as well be executed by apostolic delegates,[1] as Timothy is portrayed in Acts and both he and Titus in the other Pauline Epistles.

But this line of argument is exposed to other serious objections. First, the writer would certainly have made clear when mentioning the office and duties of bishops that one man only was intended to hold this office in each church, for then the injunctions would have conveyed much greater weight to the second-century church. Second, he would also have avoided using the term 'bishop' indiscriminately to denote 'elders'.[2] Third, he would surely have made some provision for the perpetuation of their office, but this is entirely lacking.

Scott[3] sums up the position of Timothy and Titus in these words, 'Their function is simply to serve as links between Paul and the future church, committing what they have heard from him to faithful men, who in their turn will teach others (2 Tim. ii. 2).' This is a fair statement of the evidence from one who does not maintain Pauline authorship but who clearly sees nothing in the addressees of these letters incongruous with a Pauline situation. The opinion of Lock may be cited in corroboration—'the uncertainty of the exact position held by Timothy and Titus, and the uncertainty of the relation of the *episkopoi* to the *presbuteroi*, and the need of regulating the worship of men and women, are quite different from the situation implied in the letters of Ignatius, and point to a date not later than the first century'.[4] A similar conclusion is mentioned by Clogg who says 'The ecclesiastical organization does not carry us beyond the conditions in a city such as Ephesus, or a missionary province such as Crete, where Christianity had been well established for a few years, and it

[1] Lock calls them 'Vicars Apostolic' (*The Pastoral Epistles* (1924), p. xix).
[2] So Scott, *The Pastoral Epistles* (1936), p. xxix.
[3] *Op. cit.*, p. xxix.
[4] *Op. cit.*, p. xxiii.

would fit any time between about A.D. 60 and 100, that is, it is not inconsistent with authorship by Paul.'[1]

It remains now to gather up the evidence for the ecclesiastical situation underlying the Pastorals when regarded as genuine letters of Paul. At the time of writing there was already a definite system of teaching, apostolically authenticated, committed particularly to apostolic delegates and generally to the church elders. Ordinations were held for church officials, at which laying on of hands was used to symbolize the transference of a special gift to carry out the office. A variety of ministry existed within the churches and great emphasis was laid on the moral qualities of all aspirants for office. Thus the Pastorals ecclesiastical data not only provide a picture of an orderly developing church,[2] but show the apostle in a significant light as an ecclesiastical architect. It is not that orthodoxy and organization have become the absorbing passion in his last days, but rather that sagacious provisions have been made for a time when no apostolic witness will remain, and the Spirit of God will use other means to direct His people.

VI. THE HERESIES REFLECTED IN THE EPISTLES

The treatment of the false teaching current at the time that the Pastorals were written is of first importance to the study of the Epistles, since it was undoubtedly one of the reasons why they were written. Many scholars have maintained that the heresies reflected are akin to those current in the early second century, and therefore the Pastorals must be of contemporary dating and consequently non-Pauline. Easton may again be quoted as representative of this school of thought. 'This common purpose of all three letters, the intensity of the warnings and the elaborate precautions commanded show that the battle was not against error in the abstract nor against more or less academic vagaries on the part of a few individuals (compare on I Tim. i. 4). Christianity was threatened by a coherent and powerful heresy, which was all the more dangerous because it claimed a revelation of divine things more

---

[1] *Introduction to the New Testament,* 3rd edit. (1948), p. 118.
[2] Cf. James' conclusion, *op. cit.,* p. 106.

profound than that set forth in the Church (Tit. i. 16; 2 Tim. iii. 7; 1 Tim. i. 7, etc.)'.[1] The key phrase in this statement of the position is 'coherent and powerful heresy', for if this can be substantiated it would obviously constitute a development beyond anything found elsewhere in the apostolic age. But is such a conclusion supported by the internal evidence? In the following survey each Epistle is treated separately and then an attempt is made to summarize the main features of the evidence to discover whether any coherence is discernible.

In 1 Tim. i. 3–7 Timothy is told to charge 'certain persons not to teach other doctrine, nor to spend time in speculative discussion based on myths and interminable genealogies.' These persons were apparently desirous of being teachers of the law without understanding it. Much discussion has surrounded the meaning of the word 'genealogies' in this passage, but Hort's conclusion[2] that the Pastoral heresies are more closely connected with Jewish legend than Greek speculation seems a reasonable explanation of the scant data available.[3] The interest in the law in this passage would serve to confirm this conclusion.[4]

The next evidence from 1 Timothy is the obscure reference to those who have made shipwreck of their faith, of whom Hymenæus and Alexander are specially mentioned (i. 19, 20). This must presumably be linked with the reference in 2 Tim. ii. 17 ff. to a man named Hymenæus who had swerved from the truth in declaring that the resurrection was already past, but in this latter instance his name is coupled with Philetus and not Alexander. In the former passage it is clear that those mentioned must have caused the apostle considerable and

[1] *Op. cit.*, pp. 2, 3.
[2] *Judaistic Christianity* (1894), pp. 135 ff.
[3] Bernard says 'In the curious production called the *Book of Jubilees* we have a conspicuous proof of the stress laid upon genealogies as the bases upon which legends might be reared' (*op. cit.*, li). N.B. *Jubilees* is thought by some to have originated in the Qumran community—cf. C. T. Fritsch, *The Qumran Community* (1956), pp. 70, 106-7.
[4] Lock considers both Jewish and Hellenistic tendencies coexisted in Ephesus and Crete (*op. cit.*, p. xvii), and Scott remarks that while Gnosticism in its developed state was strongly anti-Jewish, yet at its outset 'it seems to have welcomed Jewish ideas and never ceased to employ Jewish material in the construction of its myths' (p. xxix).

B   33

dangerous trouble for such drastic action to be taken as 'delivery to Satan' (see note on 1 Tim. i. 20). Easton[1] assumes that 2 Timothy must precede 1 Timothy and therefore regards the 1 Timothy treatment of Hymenæus as evidence of a progressively less tolerant spirit in the Church. But it is probable that in 2 Timothy Paul is merely citing these people as examples of godless chatter, in which case no chronological deduction may be made from their incidental mention. On Easton's hypothesis a considerable interval would be required to separate the two Epistles, but this is most unlikely.

There is important data found in 1 Tim. iv. 1–5 which speaks of 'doctrines of demons', specially mentioning such ascetic practices as celibacy and abstinence from food. The latter feature occurs elsewhere in Paul's allusions to false teaching, for in the Colossian heresy there were apparently definite regulations about food (Col. ii. 16, 20–22), while even in the church at Rome there were some who had a lack of balance over food procedure (Rom. xiv). No allusion to celibacy, however, occurs in the Colossian letter. Since Paul's words are here prophetic rather than historic, we may reasonably assume, as Bernard suggests,[2] that this practice had not yet affected the Christian Church. In that case Paul is merely warning Timothy against tendencies which he clearly foresaw, and which in fact were already observable outside the Christian community. It is known, for instance, that the strictest sect of the Essenes practised celibacy.[3] It is interesting to note that Paul gives the Christian answer to abstinence from food, but not to celibacy in 1 Tim. iv. 3–5. This may have been because he was himself attracted to the celibate life, but would not have endorsed the enforcement of it on all Christians.

The only other clear allusions to false teaching are in vi. 3–5, which repeats the warning against controversy and wrangling, and vi. 20 which is closely allied, but which links 'godless chatter' to the much discussed *antitheseis*. This latter word

[1] *Op. cit.*, p. 18.
[2] *Op. cit.*, p. 66.
[3] Pliny's *Natural History* V, xv. Josephus speaks of an Essenic group which allowed a kind of marriage by trial. N.B. Celibacy does not appear to have been enforced in the Qumran community.

occurs frequently in second-century gnosticism, but any specific reference to Marcion's 'Antitheses' is more than doubtful. Easton remarks that 'every orator was equipped with a stock of "antitheses" as part of his common-places',[1] and no more need be implied in this Pastorals occurrence.

In 2 Timothy, apart from the reference to Hymenaeus already mentioned, the main emphasis is again on irrelevant controversies (ii. 14, 16, 23). The apostle proceeds to describe the last days which would be characterized by those *having a form of godliness, but denying the power thereof* (iii. 5). A similar foresight envisages a time when people will have itching ears and will desire teachers to suit themselves (iv. 3). These apocalyptic pre-visions cannot, however, supply specific data for determining the nature of the contemporary errors about which Paul is particularly concerned. The added emphasis on controversies in this more personal second Epistle to Timothy suggests that the apostle is fearful lest his lieutenant should devote too much attention to these futilities, whereas he feels the best policy is to ignore them.

In Tit. i. 10 a significant reference to empty talkers of the circumcision party clearly shows that the heresy in this case had a Jewish origin. This is further substantiated by the specific reference to Jewish myths (i. 14), as compared with the similar but vaguer allusion in 1 Tim. i. 4. A further mention of futile and unprofitable controversies occurs in iii. 9, linked with genealogies and quarrels over the law (cf. 1 Tim. i. 7, 8). From this data it is evident that in Crete some form of Jewish controversies of an entirely speculative and irrelevant nature had arisen.

While there were undoubtedly minor differences between the false teaching in Ephesus and Crete, the major features seem to be common, and there is strong justification for regarding them as separate manifestations of a general contemporary tendency. From the data considered above the following facts may be adduced in summary form. 1. The teaching was dangerous, more because of its irrelevance than because of its falseness. 2. It led to two opposite tendencies;

---

[1] Easton p. 170, and cf. Hort. *Judaistic Christianity* (1894), pp. 138 ff.

asceticism on the one hand (1 Tim. iv. 1–4) and probably licentiousness on the other hand (as 1 Tim. v. 22 seems to suggest). 3. There were many Jewish characteristics as Tit. i. 10, 14, 1 Tim. i. 7 and Tit. iii. 9 show. 4. There was also some kind of all-absorbing interest in genealogies.

Two problems arising from this evidence require discussion. First, what is the relationship of this false teaching to second-century gnosticism? Second, is the manner of dealing with the false teachers consistent with Paul's approach to the Colossian heresy? If the answer to the first question were to show an undeniable connection with developed gnosticism, it would be conclusive against Pauline authorship, as also would a negative answer to the second question. For this reason the importance of these enquiries cannot be overrated.

(a) *The relationship of the false teaching to second-century gnosticism.* To illustrate this relationship the following features which gnosticism has in common with the Pastorals heresy have been brought forward to show a contemporary setting:

1. Gnosticism was fundamentally dualistic, various systems being proposed to bridge the gap between God and the evil world. The fruit of such dualism was seen in rigid asceticism, as for instance prohibition of marriage and severe restrictions on certain foods.

2. There was a general tendency to allegorize the Old Testament, although Marcion, who was not really a gnostic in the fullest sense, rejected the Old Testament altogether.

3. The Christology of gnosticism was generally Docetic, denying the possibility of the incarnation because of a belief in the inherent evil of matter. For the same reason the reality of the resurrection was denied.

4. A spirit of insincerity and, in extreme cases, of bestiality is amply testified.

Undoubtedly a good case can be made out for the supposition that the Pastorals would answer such erroneous tendencies as these. The presentation of Christ as the 'one mediator between God and men' (1 Tim. ii. 5), for instance, could well be the Christian answer to the theory of endless emanations in the more developed gnostic systems. But such a statement would equally well fit any other situation in which the unique mediatorial position of Christ was being challenged, and there is no need to go to gnosticism to find the earliest examples of this. It must have been one of the most primitive crises for Christian apologetics.

Again it might be maintained, as Easton,[1] in fact, suggests, that 2 Tim. iii. 15–17 may reprove the rejection of Old Testament Scriptures and Tit. i. 14 and 1 Tim. i. 7 the allegorizing of Scripture. But this latter tendency was widely found in first-century Jewish speculation, while the former statement need have no reference at all to a tendency to reject the Scripture (see note on 2 Tim. iii. 15–17). The Christology of the Pastorals would certainly be useful in combating Docetism, but no more directly so than that of any of Paul's Epistles, or for that matter, any of the other New Testament books with enough data to set forth a doctrine of Christ's person. The denial of the resurrection, however, is a much closer point of contact.

Gnostic insincerity and bestial practices show a striking similarity with the evil propagated by the Pastorals false teachers; but the key question is whether similar errors do not always produce similar effects, for if they do (and there are strong reasons for believing they do) similarity of effects cannot be regarded as proof of unity of origin.

It will be seen, then, that all that can satisfactorily be claimed is that these false teachers in the Pastorals have a remote kinship with gnosticism; but the evidence is far from conclusive that the writer is, in fact, combating developed gnosticism. It might be maintained, with some reason, that the evidence shows an incipient form of such gnosticism, but no more than this can be claimed. Such commentators as B. Weiss, Dibelius, Wohlenberg and Goguel, some of whom would have found the opposite conclusion more in harmony with their general position, nevertheless frankly admit that to identify the Pastorals heresy with gnosticism is impossible.[2] To this testimony should be added the rejection of the notion that

[1] *Op. cit.*, p. 6.
[2] See quotations in Spicq, *op. cit.*, lxxi.

the Pastorals deal with Marcionism, a view put forward originally by F. C. Baur, but effectively answered by Easton[1] in spite of his acceptance of allusions to gnosticism in general.

(b) The writer's attitude towards false teaching.

The manner in which the writer advises his lieutenants to deal with the false teachers has been strongly urged as evidence against Pauline authorship, for it is alleged that, whereas in the case of the Colossians, Paul refutes heresy, here the writer denounces it. Such a change of attitude is then considered to be evidence of a lesser mind than the apostle's. Both Timothy and Titus are urged to deal strongly with the trouble-makers (1 Tim. i. 3; 2 Tim. ii. 14; Tit. i. 13). But would Paul have refuted such action? The apostle's attitude in this situation can hardly be assessed from his Colossian letter since there he directs his remarks to the church as a whole, a church which, incidentally, he had never visited, and for that reason careful teaching is given to show the nature of the error to be combated. But in the Pastorals the instructions are directed to Paul's special representatives advising what line of action they themselves must take. Is it likely that they also would need an exposition of Paul's method of refutation? It can scarcely be assumed that the apostle had never had to deal with such false teachers while Timothy and Titus were in his company.

Scott[2] thinks it is doubtful whether the writer himself had any real acquaintance with the heresy which he condemns. He is content to ridicule it as 'vain babbling', 'old wives' fables', 'a spreading cancer', 'make-believe knowledge'. But the irrelevance of the teaching was apparent enough to lead the apostle to advise denunciation, while the fruits were of sufficient unworthiness to condemn the system from which they had sprung.

VII. THE DOCTRINAL PROBLEM

Opponents of authenticity have always pointed out with varying degrees of emphasis the theological differences between

[1] *Op. cit.*, pp. 7, 8.
[2] *Op. cit.*, p. xxx.

these Epistles and the other Epistles of Paul. This is certainly one of the strongest contributory factors in the cumulative evidence against Pauline authorship and merits the closest attention.

Not even the strongest critics of authenticity have been able to deny the Pauline basis of the Pastorals theology. Even the radical Tübingen school used this fact in its attempts to create a polemical situation between Peter and Paul as the background of the New Testament literature. It is advisable, therefore, to begin by citing the Pauline parallels of thought. Scott sums up succinctly as follows. The writer 'declares that Christ gave Himself for our redemption, that we are justified not by our own righteousness but by faith in Christ, that God called us by His grace before the world was, and that we are destined to an eternal life on which we can enter even now. These are no mere perfunctory echoes of Pauline thought.'[1] Any attempt, therefore, to assess the allegedly non-Pauline elements of doctrine must be examined against this Pauline background. A common theological background cannot, of course, be conclusive for Pauline authorship, for a secondary work might proceed from the same school of thought bearing upon it the marks of its doctrinal origin. Thus the deniers of authenticity postulate as an alternative solution an earnest devotee of the great apostle, who wrote to represent his master's teaching to his own later age. But the important question is whether such a hypothesis is demanded by the data. To answer this question a survey of the differences between the other Pauline Epistles and the Pastorals is necessary.

To quote Scott again, the writer's 'religious attitude is different from that of Paul, and comes out in the characteristic word *eusebeia* on which all the teaching of the Epistles may be said to turn'.[2] In other words, the writer is supposed to be more concerned with religion than theology, with orthodoxy than formative Christian thought. The age of speculative thinking is over. Indeed, Easton goes so far as to claim that 'gnosticism

[1] *Op. cit.*, p. xxx.
[2] *Op. cit.*, pp. xxx,xxxi.

had taught the Pastor to have a rooted mistrust of all speculative thinking that ministers "questionings" '.[1] Denney had
misgivings about Pauline authorship because it seemed to him
that 'St. Paul was inspired, but the writer of these epistles is
sometimes only orthodox'.[2] But is right belief or 'sound
doctrine', which so dominates the Pastorals, completely out of
the range of the inspired apostle? Is it entirely certain that the
apostle Paul would never have descended from his formative
thinking to consider the need for conservation of doctrine?
The key to the problem may lie in a true understanding of
Paul's theological vision rather than in a bare comparison
between two sets of Epistles. The alleged non-Pauline features,
which must, however, be examined, may be enumerated as
follows:

1. The conception of God is partially Jewish and partially
Hellenistic, according to Easton. Such terms as 'immortal'
and 'invisible' are Hellenistic, but most of the other terms used
as epithets for God are Judaistic (e.g. 'Potentate', cf. 2 Macc.
xii. 15) 'King of kings and Lord of lords' (cf. Ex. xxvi. 7;
2 Macc. xiii. 4), 'unapproachable light' (cf. Enoch xii. 15 ff.).[3]
The problem is not so much the use of terms not found in
other Pauline Epistles but the absence of what is claimed to
be Paul's most characteristic conception of God, i.e. His
Fatherhood. Thus Easton comments, 'But the most truly
Christian title, "Father", appears only in the opening greeting
formulas; there is always a sense of God's remoteness'. Such
passages as 1 Tim. i. 17 and vi. 15, 16 certainly impress the
reader with a great sense of the unapproachable majesty of
God, but it cannot be maintained that such remoteness obtains
in every case. The two passages cited are dominated by a
desire to magnify God and a sense of holy awe is most becoming; but these must be balanced by those setting forth God as
Saviour (1 Tim. i. 1, ii. 3, iv. 10; Tit. i. 3, ii. 10, iii. 4), who
desires the salvation of all (1 Tim. ii. 4), whose saving work is
motivated by goodness and loving-kindness (Tit. iii. 4), whose

---

[1] *Op. cit.*, p. 22.
[2] *The Death of Christ* (1911), p. 147.
[3] Cf. Easton, *op. cit.*, p. 166.

purpose is described as proceeding from grace (2 Tim. i. 9;
cf. Tit. ii. 11), who commissioned Paul to preach the gospel
(1 Tim. i. 1; 2 Tim. i. 1; Tit. i. 3, etc.), and who in Christ
*gave himself for us that he might redeem us from all iniquity, and
purify unto himself a peculiar people, zealous of good works* (Tit. ii. 14).
No one can reasonably charge a writer of words such as these
with being overawed by God's remoteness. If the absence of
the title 'Father' from the body of each Epistle be deemed a
difficulty, it should be remembered that it occurs twice only
in the body of 1 Corinthians (see viii. 6, xv. 24) and of Romans
(vi. 4, xv. 6; but cf. viii. 15).

2. There is an absence of the Pauline teaching of the
believer's mystical union with Christ. The phrase 'in Christ',
so characteristic of Paul, occurs seven times in 2 Timothy
(i. 1, 9, 13, ii. 1, 10, iii. 12, 15) and twice in 1 Timothy (i. 14,
iii. 13), but in none of these cases in a mystical sense (so Easton
claims).[1] Yet a detailed study of these instances does not bear
out Easton's claims, for where qualities are spoken of as 'in
Christ', more is surely intended than merely 'Christian'. It is
difficult to see any difference of approach between 2 Tim. i. 13
in faith and love which is in Christ Jesus, and Col. i. 4 *your faith in
Christ Jesus*. Moreover, if 'in Christ' is generally a synonym
for 'Christian' in the Pastorals, it must also be considered in
the same way in certain Pauline usages (e.g. the saints in
Christ at Colossae, Col. i. 2). True the most frequent Pauline
usage is to describe persons rather than qualities, but where
applied to qualities it is most probable that some mystical
element is intended. Consider for instance 2 Tim. i. 9, *grace,
which was given us in Christ Jesus before the world began*, where the
meaning appears to be that grace was given before the world
began to those who are in Christ, i.e. in a mystical union with
Him (see comment *ad loc*). Easton robs the expression of its
profundity by rendering it, 'assured to us from eternity by the
fact of Christ's existence'.[2]

3. A more serious difficulty is the infrequency of mention of

---

[1] Cf. *op. cit.*, pp. 210, 211. Cf. the writer's Tyndale Monograph, *The
Pastoral Epistles and the Mind of Paul* (1956), p. 25.
[2] *Op. cit.*, p. 211.

the Holy Spirit. This doctrine, although the Pastor accepted it, 'meant very little to him' (says Easton[1]). Of the three times when the Holy Spirit is clearly mentioned distinct from the human spirit (2 Tim. i. 14; Tit. iii. 5 and 1 Tim. iv. 1), Easton regards the first two as citations (i.e. from other New Testament writings) and the third as conventional language when citing prophecy.[2] But to appeal to citation when the wording is too close to Pauline thought rather looks like begging the question.[3] There is nothing in the thought of any of these references which the apostle would not have endorsed. If the absence of further reference to the Spirit's activities be considered non-Pauline, it should be remembered that such references are not evenly spread over all Paul's earlier Epistles, for in the case of Colossians the Spirit is mentioned once only (*your love in the Spirit*, i. 8), in 2 Thessalonians once only (*through sanctification of the Spirit*, ii. 13) and in Philemon not at all.

4. The Pastorals use of the word 'faith' (*pistis*) is said to be non-Pauline, while the characteristic Pauline usage is conspicuously absent. For Paul *pistis* generally denotes the quality of abiding trust in Christ and has passed beyond the root meaning of 'fidelity'. But in the Pastorals the latter meaning is most frequent, together with an objective sense when used with the article representing 'the totality of truths to be believed'.[4] In the Pastorals the objective use with the article accounts for nine out of the thirty-three occurrences of the word (1 Tim. i. 19, iii. 9, iv. 1, 6, v. 8, vi. 10, 12, 21 and 2 Tim. iii. 8), but this in itself presents no great difficulty when Pauline parallels such as Phil. i. 27; Col. ii. 7; Eph. iv. 5, etc. are borne in mind. In many other cases 'faith' is linked with such other virtues as 'love' (2 Tim. i. 13, ii. 22, iii. 10; 1 Tim. i. 5, 14, ii. 15, iv. 12, vi. 11), and 'hope' (Tit. i. 1, 2). But if it be urged that in these cases faith is treated as a fruit of salvation rather than as a

---

[1] *Op. cit.*, p. 22.
[2] *Op. cit.*, p. 234.
[3] For a fuller treatment see the writer's *The Pastoral Epistles and the Mind of Paul*, p. 26.
[4] Easton, *op. cit.*, p. 203. Jeremias considers that the stress on faith-teaching as a fixed norm is explained by the writer's preoccupation with the heresy conflict, *op. cit.*, p. 4.

root from which other virtues spring,[1] comparison with 1 Cor. xii. 9; 2 Cor. viii. 7; Gal. v. 22; Eph. vi. 23; 1 Thes. i. 3, iii. 6; 2 Thes. i. 3, 4; Phm. 5 will supply ample justification from Paul's earlier writings for such treatment of *pistis*, while the great Pauline hymn of 1 Cor. xiii sets love as superior to faith among the three major virtues. A few occurrences such as 1 Tim. v. 12, where *pistis* means 'pledge' (some commentators would also add Tit. ii. 10, where it clearly means 'fidelity', and 2 Tim. iv. 7), are not readily paralleled in other Pauline writings but are quite incidental to the main uses in the Pastorals.

It is still necessary, however, to examine the claim that the most conspicuous Pauline use is absent. Thus Easton comments 'But the full Pauline use of "faith" as the justifying principle is absent from the Pastorals'.[2] It is true that faith is not mentioned in the key passage on justification (Tit. iii. 5–7), but we cannot assume that such faith is excluded. 1 Cor. vi. 11, in fact, furnishes a close parallel in which the same verb is used without mention of faith (cf. note on Tit. iii. 5). It is not unimportant in this connection to observe that the apostle uses this verb *dikaioō* in the theological sense of 'justify' or 'make righteous' only in Romans and Galatians, the two Epistles specifically devoted to this theme. On the basis of Easton's criticism all the other Paulines would be equally deficient, although, of course, the notion of salvation by faith does occur. Admittedly there is an absence of the great Pauline antithesis between faith and works, although Tit. iii. 5 can hardly be understood in any other way, a fact which Easton himself tacitly acknowledges when he admits that the clause is Pauline in substance but the context 'suggests a slightly forced attempt to introduce Pauline language'.[3] Taking the evidence as a whole, the Pastorals use of *pistis* cannot be considered an insuperable obstacle to their authenticity, even though some aspects of Paul's earlier use are missing.

[1] Scott says, 'In the Pastorals faith is not so much a root as a foundation (cf. 1 Tim. iii. 15, vi. 19)—the necessary basis of all right living, though it does not of itself produce it'. *Op. cit.*, p. xxxi.

[2] *Op. cit.*, p. 103.

[3] *Op. cit.*, p. 102.

5. A similar objection has been raised over the Pastorals use of 'grace' (*charis*). Scott expresses it in the following way, 'While the writer thinks of salvation as the free gift of God he allows for a co-operation on the part of men. He describes grace as acting by a process of education (Tit. ii. 11, 12). Through the grace bestowed on us in the gift of Christ we are enabled to master all lower desires and follow the way of godliness'.[1] Nothing could be more Pauline than Tit. iii. 7 *justified by his grace*, which is precisely paralleled in Rom. iii. 24. Easton, however, would distinguish the Titus use as meaning 'power' and the Romans use as 'free and unmerited favour'; but such distinction is wholly unfounded. The expression in Titus is clearly antithetical to verse 5 'not by works of righteousness which we have done', in which case it is the meaning of favour not power which the context demands.

These are the main doctrinal problems advanced against the Pauline authorship of the Pastorals. But certain other considerations need mentioning.

1. The advocates of the Fragment Theory are placed in rather a dilemma over their Paulinist editor for they are bound to maintain *ex hypothesi* that he was well acquainted with the authentic Pauline Epistles, to such a degree, in fact, that his mind must have been soaked in Pauline thought (Harrison). Yet the differences between the Pastoral and Pauline theology force these advocates to admit that 'this disciple of Paul has failed, in not a few respects, to understand him'.[2] In other words, where Pauline parallels can be provided it is evidence of echoes of Pauline thought lodged in another mind, but where deviations are discernible the Paulinist's own thoughts are expressed. Now such a theory is certainly feasible and indeed necessary if the non-Pauline elements are substantiated. But if these elements can reasonably be interpreted in a way consistent with Pauline usage, it is a much more credible hypothesis to regard them as deviations in one mind rather than a mixture of two.

2. A second important consideration is whether Paul can

[1] *Op. cit.*, p. xxxi.
[2] Scott, *op. cit.*, p. xxv.

be conceived of as using stereotyped doctrine. Is not the emphasis on 'sound doctrine', 'the truth', 'the deposit', etc., so frequently met with in the Pastorals, alien to the creative mind of the great apostle? It may seem as if the man from whom the early Church inherited some of its noblest doctrinal thinking has descended to a most uncharacteristic concern for maintaining the tradition; but to conclude that this could not have happened is to beg the question. The only data we have is that the apostle shows little concern for such tradition in his other Epistles, and much concern for it in the Pastorals. Yet it does not follow from this data that different circumstances, particularly the realization that his own work was almost finished, could not have led to a different approach. In addition, the use of stereotyped phraseology would have been much more probable in letters directed to close personal associates than to mixed communities.

Another aspect of the same problem is the citation in these Epistles of such liturgical formulae as the five faithful sayings and the Christian hymn in 1 Tim. iii. 16. Not only is this type of citation entirely unknown in the other Pauline writings, but the use of such formal statements is said to be proof of a later development in the Church, relating to a period when Christian doctrine was reduced to formal statements for catechetical purposes. But the problem is really whether the creative Paul would have cited current formulae, since there is no reason to suppose that such formulae were not used at a very early stage, in the history of the Church.

If it be maintained that the apostle had no interest in conservation of doctrine, it will, of course, be impossible to conceive that he would have cited current formulae. But is it conceivable that Paul had no interest in conservation? Sabatier's oft-quoted statement supplies the answer. 'Paul was an apostle before he was a theologian. To him the need of conservation was more urgent than that of innovation'.[1] It would have been extreme short-sightedness on the part of the apostle if he had neglected to endorse, if not to create some effective means for the propagation of the truths he had

[1] *Paul* (1903), p. 270.

himself helped to formulate.[1] Nor should it be thought strange that the main evidence for such conservative tendencies on the apostle's part should come to us in writings to his closest associates, for their main task seems to have been to ensure the continuity of apostolic teaching. If the latter point be considered an evidence of sub-apostolic dating, it requires only a detailed comparison between the Pastorals and the sub-apostolic Fathers to demonstrate conclusively that the latter failed if they ever attempted to preserve intact the apostolic tradition. No one can deny the gulf which separates the most 'formalized' doctrinal statements in the Pastorals from the most 'inspired' extant utterances of the second-century apostolic Fathers.

VIII. THE LINGUISTIC PROBLEM

It remains to consider what is generally regarded as the most pressing criticism against Pauline authorship and the one which undoubtedly weighs the balance in favour of rejecting the Epistles as authentic in the minds of many scholars. This is the marked difference in language between the Pauline Epistles and the Pastorals, which was first brought into the open as the spearhead of criticism by Schleiermacher (1807) in his work on 1 Timothy. This criticism gradually gained momentum during the nineteenth century, being particularly embraced and enlarged upon by F. C. Baur (1835) and H. J. Holtzmann (1880). It was following P. N. Harrison's treatment of the linguistic data in 1921, however, that many who had hitherto leaned to the traditional Pauline authorship found the position no longer tenable. Even so ardent an advocate of authenticity as Lock showed signs of vacillation in his commentary issued three years later than Harrison's book.

Harrison's presentation of the problem is fourfold: 1. The problem of the large number of words unique to the Pastorals in the New Testament (i.e. 175 Hapaxes). 2. The problem of the large number of words common to the Pastorals and other

---

[1] For a full discussion of this problem and of the use of the faithful sayings, cf. the writer's *The Pastoral Epistles and the Mind of Paul* (1956), pp. 17-29.

New Testament writings but unknown in the other ten Pauline letters. 3. The problem of characteristic Pauline words and groups of words missing from the Pastorals. 4. The problem of grammatical and stylistic differences. He brings a mass of statistics to support his double contention that the Pastorals cannot be attributed to Paul and that they belong to the current speech of the second century. A detailed examination of Harrison's evidence is given in the Appendix[1] and it will consequently be necessary to give here only the conclusions of this linguistic study.

There are certainly many differences between these Epistles and the other ten Paulines, but these differences are not uniform and cannot be held as conclusive evidence of non-Pauline authorship. Such an approach would not only rule out some other Pauline letters but would imply the impossibility of any change in an author's style or language, and this position cannot be maintained. Questions of authorship cannot be decided on numerical data without reference to psychological probability, but Harrison has given no consideration to this latter point. If full allowance is made for dissimilarity of subject matter, variations due to advancing age, enlargement of vocabulary due to changing environment and the difference in the recipients as compared with the earlier letters, the linguistic peculiarities of the Pastorals can in large measure be satisfactorily explained.

The further claim that the language of the Pastorals is the current language of the second century would, if proved, greatly weigh against Pauline authenticity. Harrison appeals to certain similarities with the Apostolic Fathers and Apologists, but on examination his evidence is not as striking as he supposes, and in any case seems to be vitiated by the fact that greater similarities can be shown when the Pastorals are compared with the LXX. Harrison finds it necessary to appeal also to the secular writers of the second century to support his thesis and claims that this evidence proves that words peculiar to the Pastorals in the Greek Testament were in very frequent use in this second-century period. But, in view

[1] See p. 212.

of the fact that all but a small group of these words were known in Greek literature before A.D. 50, Harrison's evidence proves nothing. Only if it could be shown that the language of the Pastorals could not have been used in the first century would there be definite grounds for assigning them to the second century. But none of the linguistic arguments are able, in fact, to establish this position.

IX. THE PROBLEM OF AUTHORSHIP

All the major objections to authenticity having been examined, it is now possible to assess the problem of authorship and to mention the various solutions proposed.

(a) Paul

That Paul himself was the author is supported by the salutation in each of the Pastorals and by the undisputed testimony of the Church. While there are undoubted difficulties in such a view, there are none which make it impossible.

Some scholars, while convinced of the Pauline character of the Pastorals, nevertheless consider some other hand produced the letters. The linguistic and other differences are due to the greater freedom allowed to the amanuensis. Because of the close linguistic affinity of the Pastorals with Luke/Acts, it has been suggested that Luke may have been responsible for the stylistic peculiarities.[1] But it is open to question whether Paul would have allowed such freedom.

(b) Timothy and Titus

A theory has been suggested that the two close associates of Paul edited the Pauline material in their possession and published it in the form in which we now possess it after Paul's death.[2] But there seems no adequate motive for such a procedure unless Paul had left the material substantially in

---

[1] Cf. James, *op. cit.*, pp. 154 f. Holtzmann (*Die Pastoralbriefe* (1880), pp. 92 ff.) drew attention to the remarkable affinities between the Pastorals and the Lucan writings. Moffatt dispensed with the suggestion that Luke was Paul's amanuensis on the grounds that he ignored Titus in his history (*Introduction to the Literature of the New Testament* (1912), p. 414).

[2] Cf. A. C. Deane, *St. Paul and His Letters* (1942), pp. 208-220.

its present form, and if he had there seems little gain, if any, in this hypothesis.

(c) An editor

A modification of the last view is that some other person edited the Pauline material which came into his possession and arranged the notes in their present form shortly after Paul's death,[1] but the problems which are generally claimed to weigh against Pauline authorship are not accounted for by mere arrangement. The editor must in this case have rewritten the material if the objections are to be fully met, although the theory does not suppose this. If the editor did rewrite the material there would seem to be an insufficient motive.

(d) A later Paulinist

It is not enough for any disputant of Pauline authorship to provide an alternative theory. He must be prepared to prove his own hypothesis to be relatively free from the objections on the grounds of which he has denied authenticity. A brief summary is therefore given of the major problems of Harrison's fragment theory.[2]

(i) *The problem of compilation.* First, it is difficult to see why two Epistles were addressed to Timothy and one to Titus if the writer planned to present the Pauline approach to the contemporary situation. That four[3] of Harrison's original five fragments are found in 2 Timothy and the remaining one in Titus provides a major problem, for the Paulinist must have had good reason for his uneven distribution. Yet no adequate explanation of this problem has yet been provided.

2. There is a lack of agreement on the order in which the Epistles were compiled. Some, for example, maintain that

---

[1] Cf. F. J. Badcock, *The Pauline Epistles and the Epistle to the Hebrews in their Historical Setting* (1937), pp. 115-133.

[2] See the writer's *The Pastoral Epistles and the Mind of Paul*, pp. 29 ff. for a fuller discussion of these problems.

[3] Since modified to two out of three, yet the two in 2 Timothy contain far more than the one in Titus (cf. Harrison, *Expository Times*, lxvii, Dec. 1955, p. 80).

1 Timothy and Titus preceded 2 Timothy which was a more direct appeal to Paul, while others, such as Easton, place 2 Timothy first, the success of which spurred the writer to produce the other less obviously Pauline Epistles. Apart from their mutual contradictions, both these suggestions fail completely to account for the Paulinist's inconsistency. Were not all the letters purporting to be direct appeals to Paul?

3. There are personal allusions scattered about in all three Epistles which are not included in Harrison's genuine sections (cf. 1 Tim. i. 3, iii. 14, v. 23; 2 Tim. i. 5, 15; Tit. i. 5), and on the fragment theory it is possible to ascribe these only to the Paulinist's imagination. But is it psychologically probable that any devout disciple of Paul would have thought to invent Paul's concern for Timothy's stomach, or his mention of Timothy's mother and grandmother by name? If the genuine fragments themselves were enough to secure the Pauline imprimatur, why invent others?

4. Another problem is to conceive how the genuine fragments were preserved, for they appear to have been incorporated in a particularly disintegrated manner.[1] Evidently the Paulinist did not notice the historical problems he would create by his reconstruction of these fragments.[2]

5. The Paulinist must either have been an old man himself or else have possessed remarkable insight to portray so precisely the psychological traits of advancing age.[3] But he has also given many indications of the characters of Timothy and Titus, which may reasonably be claimed to accord with what we know of them from elsewhere in the New Testament. It is, of course, open to the defenders of the fragment theory to maintain that this reflects the author's antiquarian interests, but they cannot at the same time charge him with an absence of historical perspective.[4] It seems more reasonable to see in the lifelike portrayals a true record of actual events.

---

[1] For details see p. 23.

[2] Cf. comment on 2 Tim. iv. 16, 17.

[3] Cf. Spicq's excellent discussion of this point, *op. cit.*, pp. lxxxix ff.

[4] For a discussion of Easton's opinion that the author has misrepresented the relationship between Paul and Timothy, see the writer's *The Pastoral Epistles and the Mind of Paul*, pp. 31 ff.

6. There is moreover a real linguistic problem in the fragment theory for it supposes that the Paulinist, thoroughly well versed as he was in the genuine Paulines, must have had frequent lapses when he forgot to give a Pauline flavour to what he was writing.[1] But it is difficult to believe that the Paulinist would write long sections (e.g. 1 Tim. iii. 1–13, v. 14–25) without attempting, according to Harrison's statistics, to give as much as an echo of Pauline phraseology.

7. Arising from the use of Pauline phraseology, the fragment theory, at least as expounded by Harrison,[2] appears to use conflicting canons of criticism. Where passages are thick with Pauline phrases it is evidence of an imitator, for Paul would not cite himself so closely, but where such phrases are lacking it is evidence of genuine Pauline fragments. But this distinction is too fine to be psychologically feasible. It is a purely subjective process to determine when a passage is too much or too little Pauline to be genuine.

8. The fragment theory further presupposes that, in spite of his close acquaintance with Paul's Epistles, the Paulinist often failed to understand Paul's doctrinal point of view,[3] and has in fact missed the major factors in Paul's theology. It has already been demonstrated that no essential contradiction exists between Pauline doctrine and that of the Pastorals, but it would certainly have been more incumbent for an imitator to approximate as much as possible to previous patterns than for Paul himself. A kindred difficulty for this theory is adequately to account for the acknowledged superiority of the Pastorals over all the writer's second-century contemporaries.

(*ii*) *The problem of motive.* It is generally agreed by advocates of the fragment theory that the Paulinist had a genuine desire to represent what Paul would have said had he addressed himself to the contemporary situation. His motives, therefore, were of the highest order, and his use of pseudonymity was

---

[1] Cf. Harrison's argument in *J.T.S.* xlix (1948), p. 209 in reviewing Spicq's *Les Épîtres Pastorales*.
[2] Cf. *The Problem of the Pastorals*, pp. 87–93.
[3] Cf. Scott, *op. cit.*, pp. xxi, xxv.

an evidence of modesty since he had no wish to represent as his own what was in reality his master's thought.[1] But Paul had not given any indication of his approach to a situation in which monarchical episcopacy was either already established,[2] or was, at least, rapidly arising. The Paulinist's difficulties in avoiding anachronisms must have been almost insuperable.

But even if it is possible to conceive of such a purpose, it would still be necessary to conform the author's high-minded purpose with the use of genuine fragments. It is not clear whether the possession, accidental or otherwise, of these fragments prompted him to produce his apostolically-backed ecclesiastical directives, or whether he first conceived the desirability of applying his master's principles to his own generation and the acquisition of the fragments provided the immediate opportunity. But neither of these alternatives seems psychologically probable, for the Pastorals would not have been particularly useful in promoting monarchical episcopacy where the system was not already in existence, and would not have been necessary where it was already an accomplished fact.

A concluding criticism of the theory is based on its use of pseudonymity. Whereas there is a modern fine distinction between imitation and forgery in the approach to the problems of pseudonymity, which may not have as much validity as is often claimed for it, yet it cannot be denied that an hypothesis which requires the postulation of a pseudonymous authorship is at a greater discount than a theory which can explain all the facts, including claims to authorship, without resort to pseudonymity.[3]

X. THE MESSAGE OF THE EPISTLES

Although the Pastorals are directed to meet the contemporary situation in Paul's closing days, they are still relevant to our

---

[1] Cf. Easton, *op. cit.*, p. 19.

[2] As Easton claims (cf. *op. cit.*, p. 177).

[3] Cf. Goodspeed's admission of the difficulty of pseudonymity in separate New Testament writings, *New Chapters in New Testament Study* (1937), p. 172.

modern age. The need for wise dealing with questions of church arrangements and Christian discipline is ever present, and these Epistles have constantly supplied Christian leaders with sober practical advice in these matters. They may lack the profound theological grasp of some of the other New Testament Epistles, but they are not without their theological gems. The diligent student will not only find himself grappling with the practical problems of a developing church, but will find his soul enriched by many flashes of doctrinal insight.

In addition to these valuable uses the Epistles provide an illuminating commentary on Paul's last days. This is particularly true of 2 Timothy, where the apostle's noble example in the face of approaching martyrdom is vividly portrayed. It has been the inspiration of innumerable Christians nearing the end of their course and it will undoubtedly continue to be so.

I TIMOTHY: ANALYSIS

I. THE APOSTLE AND TIMOTHY, i. 1–20.

    (a) Salutation, i. 1, 2.
    (b) The contrast between the gospel and its counterfeits, i. 3–11.
    (c) The apostle's personal experience of the gospel, i. 12–17.
    (d) The apostle's charge to Timothy, i. 18–20.

II. WORSHIP AND ORDER IN THE CHURCH, ii. 1 — iv. 16.

    (a) The importance and scope of public prayer, ii. 1–8.
    (b) The status and demeanour of Christian women, ii. 9–15.
    (c) The qualifications of Church officials, iii. 1–13.
        (i) Bishops, iii. 1–7.
        (ii) Deacons, iii. 8–13.
    (d) The character of the Church, iii. 14–16.
    (e) Threats to the safety of the Church, iv. 1–16.
        (i) The approaching apostasy, iv. 1–5.
        (ii) Methods of dealing with false teaching, iv. 6–16.

III. DISCIPLINE AND RESPONSIBILITY, v. 1 — vi. 2.

    (a) Various age groups, v. 1, 2.
    (b) Widows, v. 3–16.
        (i) Widows in need, v. 3–8.
        (ii) Widows as Christian workers, v. 9, 10.
        (iii) Younger widows, v. 11–16.
    (c) Elders, v. 17–20.
    (d) Timothy's own behaviour, v. 21–25.
    (e) Servants and masters, vi. 1, 2.

IV. MISCELLANEOUS INJUNCTIONS, vi. 3–21.

    (a) More about false teachers, vi. 3–5.
    (b) The perils of wealth, vi. 6–10.
    (c) A charge to a man of God, vi. 11–16.
    (d) Advice to wealthy men, vi. 17–19.
    (e) Final admonition to Timothy, vi. 20, 21.

I TIMOTHY: COMMENTARY

I. THE APOSTLE AND TIMOTHY (i. 1-20)

(a) Salutation (i. 1, 2)

1. Following his general usage, Paul commences with a declaration of his own authority in order to make unmistakable the authority of the message he teaches. His design is semi-official as well as personal, for Timothy himself would need no such reminder of the apostle's authority.

The word *apostle* must be given its more restricted but more frequent meaning of 'membership of the apostolic circle'. It may well be that some at Ephesus had questioned Paul's authority, and his claim to this title would therefore immediately correct any misconceptions about his official position in the Church. The order of the title 'Christ Jesus' (reversed in the AV) may be preferred because for Paul the revelation of the heavenly Messiah was of primary importance. Yet the apostle's usage is far from consistent (cf. Rom. i. 1; I Cor. i. 1).

This idea of authority is intensified by the use of the expression *by the commandment of God*. Paul is more fond of saying 'by the will of God' (as in 2 Tim. i. 1), but he uses the present *kat'epitagēn* in Rom. xvi. 26 to bring out the compulsion of the divine commission (see also I Cor. vii. 6 and 2 Cor. viii. 8). He can never, in fact, forget that he is a man under orders.

It is unusual for Paul to speak of *God our Saviour*, since, apart from the Pastorals, he always attributes the title to Christ. But here his mind dwells on the ultimate source of Christian salvation. The title is fashioned on a familiar Old Testament conception, which would spring naturally from the apostle's theological background. It would also have a contemporary significance in that the term *Saviour* (*sōtēr*)

55

was used in the cult of Emperor worship and was being applied to the infamous Nero. Perhaps an implied contrast may be found in the apostle's use of the possessive *our*. The omission of the article in the Greek may mean the word had by this time become an accepted Christian title.

The linking of *Jesus Christ, which is our hope* (the Greek text does not contain the title 'Lord' and has the reverse order, i.e. 'Christ Jesus', as RV) to the former statement adds weight to the apostle's introduction and throws light on his theological position. As Simpson describes it, this co-ordination of Father and Son as sources of the apostle's authority 'is no slender proof of his conviction of the deity of Christ'. The word *hope* (*elpis*) used in a Christian sense conveys an element of absolute certainty, an element generally lacking in the modern usage of the word.

2. The apostle's description of Timothy as a 'genuine' *son in the faith*, for that is the significance of the Greek word *gnēsios* (translated *own*), is striking evidence of the intimate Christian relationship between the two men. There was nothing spurious about Timothy's standing *in the faith* or 'in faith' (RV; either rendering may represent the Greek *en pistei*, but the former seems preferable as describing Timothy's status in the gospel). He 'was thus a recognized representative of his spiritual father' (Bernard). The father-son terminology to express the master-disciple relationship was widespread in contemporary society, especially in the mysteries, as Dibelius shows. It took on new meaning, however, when related to *en pistei*.

It is interesting to note that Paul uses his fullest formula of salutation, adding to his usual *grace* and *peace* the idea of *mercy*. The same triad is found elsewhere in Paul only in 2 Tim. i. 2 (the occurrence in Tit. i. 4 being a later interpolation). As Bernard well expresses it, 'Even *grace* will not give *peace* to man, unless *mercy* accompany it; for man needs pardon for the past no less than strength for the future'.

As in the opening verse, so here, the source of this triad of blessings is given as God and Christ (*from God our Father and Jesus Christ our Lord*). Christ is the mediator of all the blessings which the Father bestows.

(b) The contrast between the gospel and its counter-feits (i. 3-11)

3. Paul's thoughts flow so rapidly that he forgets to reach the grammatical end of the sentence begun in this verse. The AV completes the sense by adding *so do* at the end of verse 4, but it should be noted that the roughness would not be quite as apparent in Greek as in English. It is not certain if the word *parakaleō* should have its stronger meaning of 'exhort' (RV), or the sense of *besought*. But the idea of request is probably correct. The apostle recalls the commission already given to Timothy for the younger man's encouragement.

The reference to *Ephesus* need not imply that Paul had himself recently been there, since the Greek particle *poreuomenos*, 'when I was going' (not *when I went*) may indicate that he left Timothy en route for Ephesus and charged him to *abide* there. It seems certain that this occasion must belong to the period subsequent to the Acts history (see Introduction, pp. 16 ff). The apostle's words suggest that there was some reluctance on Timothy's part to remain at Ephesus, which was one of the most important of the Asiatic churches, both strategically and culturally. His somewhat timid nature may well have shrunk from so onerous a task.

Timothy is now reminded that he is himself a man of authority. He has a definite commission to hold the false teachers in check, and it is evident that Paul expects him to take a strong line with them, as is shown by the verb *parangellō* (*charge*), a military term which means literally to pass commands from one to the other. *That they teach no other doctrine* (*heterodidaskaleō*) suggests that there was already in existence a recognized standard of Christian doctrine (see Introduction, pp. 44 ff). These words give a timely warning to our modern age against the quest for novelties in Christian teaching.

4. The false teaching is next characterized as *fables* (*muthoi*) and *endless genealogies*. Nothing could be farther removed from the serious content of the gospel. The irrelevance of the spurious doctrine is in direct contrast to the edification which should result from true Christian teaching.

Many scholars see in *genealogies* a clear reference to the second-century gnostic emanations. But there seems stronger reasons to suppose that the anonymous false teachers were members of a sect attracted by the more speculative aspects of Judaism. In Tit. i. 14, where the same word *muthoi* occurs, they are described as Jewish, and there is a strong assumption that Paul has the same kind of people in mind here. An example of the way in which Jewish delight in such speculations led to the composition of mythical histories based on the Old Testament is found in the Jewish book of Jubilees.[1] It was inevitable that methods so unrestrained (*endless*, *aperantos*, may be understood in this sense) would lead to further *questions*, and the whole unprofitable business impressed the apostle with its utter futility. No wonder he contrasts it with *godly edifying which is in faith* (*en pistei*). The Greek word *oikonomia*, rendered *edifying*, is difficult to translate. It means properly 'the office of stewardship' but came to be used in the sense of 'administration', which is the general Pauline usage (cf. 1 Cor. ix. 17; Eph. iii. 2, 9). Moffatt renders the phrase 'the divine order which belongs to faith', but as Scott points out 'the contrast is between two activities, not between two views of the world'. Paul has just stressed the pointlessness of the false teaching and now contrasts this with the discipline which belongs to faith (RSV 'the divine training').

5. The *commandment* or injunction (again a military term *parangelia* is used) could possibly indicate the Mosaic Law, in which case the implication would be that these false teachers had misconceived its true purpose; but it is more likely that the Christian's moral obligations are in mind. By *the end* (*telos*) of this commandment is meant its purpose (RSV 'the aim of our charge'). Certainly for the Christian the goal of all exhortations in practical affairs is love (*charity*)

[1] Cf. Hort, *Judaistic Christianity*, p. 135 ff.; also Dibelius and Jeremias *ad loc.*

which was in all probability conspicuously lacking in these speculative reasoners, whose main purpose was their own intellectual satisfaction.

The apostle then makes clear the source of this love. The preposition *ek* (*out of*) forcibly draws attention to its origin in a threefold aspect.

1. A *pure heart* is a fundamental requisite. Taken over from the Old Testament, the word *heart* stands for the totality of man's moral affections, and without purity there, nobility of character is clearly impossible. Jesus reserved a special promise for the pure in heart (Mt. v. 8) and spoke of the pruning of the vine as an illustration of the cleansing of believers through the word (Jn. xv. 3).

2. *A good conscience.* The Greek word *suneidēsis* indicates self-judgment, the right operation of which was given special prominence in Paul's theology. By way of contrast, Timothy is later reminded that apostasizers are those whose consciences are branded (1 Tim. iv. 2). This conscience-concept was well known in Hellenistic culture, but acquired under Christian usage a broader application (cf. Simpson).

3. *Faith unfeigned.* Faith which is merely a pretence without solid foundation was no doubt all too evident in the false teachers.

This triad of sources for love has caused some scholars to question the authenticity of the passage. Scott, for instance, says, 'For Paul himself faith was sufficient, but this disciple has not fully grasped Paul's conception of faith'. Easton also objects that Paul would not use faith in this way. It may be true that no precise parallel is extant in Paul's writings, but there can be no doubt that Paul would have endorsed the statement that love proceeds from faith. In his great hymn of love, he links love with faith and hope, although subordinating the latter two to the former. In any case, his use of faith there is closely allied to the use here.

6. This Christian triad has clearly been neglected by certain people. They have *swerved* and *turned aside.* The two vivid verbs imply that having missed the mark (*astocheō*), they inevitably turned off their course (*ektrepō*). By losing their Christian bearings they drifted into a trackless waste, for life without this triad of virtues not only lacks love, but produces no more than meaningless chatter. The word *vain jangling* (*mataiologia*) sums up the irrelevance which formed one of the main features of the false teaching.

7. The desire *to be teachers of the law* is a mark of the Jewish character of these men, whose main interest seems to have been to rival contemporary Rabbinical exegesis, rather than to expound the gospel. Paul brings a scathing indictment against instructors so unfitted for their task; they are both unintelligent and ignorant. They have no grasp of the sacred content of the text, and when they speak, their words are as meaningless to themselves as to others. The profundities of Christian truth must never become muffled in meaningless subtleties, a fault which those who indulge in allegorical interpretations do not always succeed in avoiding.

8. The mention of law in verse 7 leads the apostle to discuss the law and its purpose. He grants it possesses certain useful functions when used lawfully (*nominōs*). This adverb, found only here and in 2 Tim. ii. 5 in the New Testament, furnishes the key to the statement concerning the law. The law must be restricted to its primary purpose—the restraint of evil-doing. In this sense it may be described as 'good', and it is significant that the Greek word used is *kalos* rather than *agathos*, since the former draws attention, not only to excellence of intrinsic quality, but also to beauty of outward form. The apostle is far from decrying the noble precepts of the Mosaic law, but is emphatically opposing the futilities of much Pentateuchal speculation. He goes on, in fact, to describe the various classes for whom the law is especially designed.

A question arises whether this approach to the law is irreconcilable with Paul's doctrine. Easton thinks it is, and even finds the statement in these verses irreconcilable with 2 Tim. iii. 16, 17. But Jeremias is surely correct in appealing to Rom. vii. 12, 16 to prove that the approach here does not differ from Paul and does not conflict with 2 Tim. iii. 15–17.

9, 10. Paul's proposition is stated both negatively and positively. Negatively, law has little relevance for law-abiding people. When Paul outlines the positive function of the law he appears, at first sight, to restrict himself to gross evil-doers. Yet, in enumerating extreme examples, the apostle indicates the limit of the law's restraining and condemnatory purposes. Lesser crimes are naturally included within these limits. Scott points out the significance of the order; first offences against God, then crimes against fellow-men as listed in the ten commandments.

It is further significant that nothing in this list corresponds with the law's condemnation of covetousness; this raises a difficulty for Easton, who points out that Paul especially appealed to it in Rom. vii. 7 in referring to his own experience of law. But his purpose is very different for he is obviously concerned here with the external function of the law in the restraint of evil-doers. Bernard says 'Only those sins have been enumerated of which human law can take cognisance'. There is no necessity to suppose that this statement excludes every other function of the law. Since its supercession by the gospel, the Decalogue still retains its value as an external instrument of justice, but for the *righteous man* (*dikaios* here being used in its widest sense, but probably intended to represent the Christian) it can no longer apply as a positive standard of conduct. It was not designed (*ou keitai*, not laid down) for that purpose. It is designed, however, for the *lawless* who ignore law; for the *disobedient* or insubordinate (*anupotaktos*), who are not amenable to discipline; for the *ungodly* who have no reverence for God and *sinners* who oppose Him; and for the *unholy* and *profane* who deny sacred things.

The reference to *murderers of fathers* and *murderers of mothers* should perhaps be understood as smiters of parents, an extreme violation of the fifth commandment. *Whoremongers* (RSV 'immoral persons') and *them that defile themselves with mankind* (*arsenokoitai*, RSV 'sodomites') are perhaps similarly regarded as extreme violations of the command not to commit adultery.

The list of offences is rounded off with a proviso for anything else *contrary to sound doctrine*, which comes as a surprise after an inventory of criminal offenders against the law. Easton suggests that the use of the word *doctrine* in this context is almost grotesque to modern ears. But the word *didaskalia*, which is more frequent in the Pastorals than anywhere else in the New Testament, shows a transference of thought from teaching mainly designed for criminals to teaching intended as the normal rule of life. Hence the description of the *didaskalia* as 'sound' (*hugiainousa*), another word which frequently recurs in the Pastorals (but nowhere else), and which denotes the wholesomeness or healthiness of true Christian teaching. As Scott says, 'Law is a sort of medicine, only to be applied where the moral nature is diseased; Christian teaching is a healthy food for healthy people, a means of joy, freedom, larger activity'. However unexpected, the conclusion of the list suitably shows the ascendancy of the gospel and leads the apostle to make a further statement about it.

11. This verse sums up the section from verse 8 onwards. Paul has been speaking of law not according to his own opinion but *according to* the gospel. The Greek means literally 'the gospel of the glory of the blessed God'. The AV *glorious gospel* expresses a partial truth but misses the full grandeur of the original by transferring the glory from the central figure in the drama to the drama itself. The word is similarly found as a genitive of content in 2 Cor. iv. 4–6, where it describes the gospel as a manifestation of the glory of God in the face of Jesus Christ.

Except here and vi. 15 nowhere in the Bible is *makarios* (*blessed*) applied to *God*, but the usage is frequent in Philo. It describes God not as the object of blessing, but as experiencing within Himself the perfection of bliss. Such a thought accords well with the splendour which He radiates through the gospel.

The phrase *committed to my trust* applied to the gospel is

characteristically Pauline (cf. 1 Cor. ix. 17; Gal. ii. 7). The agent, though unexpressed, must clearly be God.

(c) **The apostle's personal experience of the gospel (i. 12–17)**

This section appears to be a digression, but is nevertheless necessary to the argument. As Easton aptly puts it, 'If Christ could change Paul, the greatest of sinners, into an Apostle, there is no limit to His transforming power. So let no man say that his duties as a Christian are beyond his abilities'. By a natural association of ideas, the thought of the magnitude of the gospel committed to him (verse 11) leads the apostle to marvel at his own experience of God's enabling power.

12. The sudden outburst of thanksgiving which now follows is thoroughly typical of Paul, who never ceased to marvel at the gospel. The enabling power of God is a constant theme of the apostle. The aorist tense of the participle, *endunamōsanti* (*who hath enabled*, RSV 'given me strength') indicates a past reality. In an alternative but less well attested reading the present participle *endunamounti* lays emphasis on Christ as the constant enabler (cf. Phil. iv. 13). Both readings express a profound truth, but since Paul is here in reminiscent mood, the past tense, in addition to being the better attested, accords better with the context.

The apostle next expresses the reason for his thankfulness, i.e. that he was accounted *faithful*, which should here be understood in the sense of 'trustworthy'. That he makes this statement without boasting is evident from the term *diakonia* used to express his *ministry*, and from the self-revelations that follow. This term, a favourite Pauline expression, lends support to an early date for the Pastorals, since in second-century times the risk of confusion with the established order of deacons would make the term inapplicable to an apostle.

The words *putting me into the ministry* draw attention to the divine initiative, which provided Paul with the ground of assurance throughout his varied service (cf. 1 Cor. xii. 28).

13. It is not surprising that Paul's reminiscences lead him to consider his pre-Christian state, for reflection upon Christ's enabling power only magnified his own sense of unworthiness. His self-condemnatory description of himself as *blasphemer* and *persecutor* must, therefore, be given full force, while the word rendered *injurious* should be much stronger, for *hubristēs* signifies a violent insolent man, in short, a thoroughly objectionable character. Yet such a man as this *obtained mercy*! The passive verb, meaning 'to have mercy shown to one', is characteristic of Paul (Rom. xi. 30, 31; 1 Cor. vii. 25; 2 Cor. iv. 1), whose previous state of wretchedness compelled him to acknowledge the sovereign character of God's merciful provision. But the apostle perceives a reason for the mercy. It was, he says, *because I did it ignorantly.* Unlike that wilful ignorance which increases guilt (cf. Rom. x. 3), Paul's ignorance was linked with a 'pure conscience' (2 Tim. i. 3), marred only by *unbelief.* His misguided pre-Christian career had been the object of pity rather than judgment in the sight of God, who recognized in Saul of Tarsus a servant of mighty potential when once he was enlightened.

14. Paul could never write for long without bringing in *the grace of our Lord.* For him it was no mere abstract concept, but an operative and formative force dominating both thought and action. His words here recall those of Rom. v. 20, for in both cases verbs compounded with *huper* are used in an attempt to express the super-abundance of divine grace. A difficulty is felt by some scholars over the way the Christian qualities are combined in this verse. Scott, for instance, declares, 'Paul himself would not thus have described faith and love as separate from grace, and given in addition to it'. Easton also objects that Paul 'saw in faith something very much more than one of the fruits of conversion'. But there is no need to suppose that any un-Pauline distinction between *grace* and *faith* and *love* finds expression in this verse. In fact, the preposition *meta* (*with*) indicates the closest connection between the grace of God and the two co-ordinate Christian virtues. Paul would readily agree that apart from the operation of divine grace, love and faith would be impossible, yet without the latter there would be no evidence of the former. Nor is there substance in Easton's opinion that grace is here used as 'power' as distinct from 'pure favour' (cf. Rom. v. 20), since the word is clearly an enlargement of the mercy mentioned in verse 13. The same virtues, faith and love, qualified by *in Christ Jesus* are found in 2 Tim. i. 13. (See note there.)

15. The striking formula, *This is a faithful saying*, meets us nowhere else in the New Testament apart from four other occurrences in the Pastorals. This is alleged to present a problem for Pauline authenticity, but there is no reason to suppose that Paul could not, or would not, have appealed to such sayings.[1] In the present context, he seems to be citing, in rhythmical form, a statement current in the churches and acknowledged as a 'sure word'. It may seem strange that he should use the formula when writing to Timothy, but he probably wishes to remind his younger associate of the fundamental character of the statement to which he is about to appeal.

The additional words *worthy of all acceptation* are found only here and in iv. 9 in the New Testament, but became a regular formula in the Greek vernacular (see M & M on *apodochē*).

Christ Jesus came into the world to save sinners epitomizes the cardinal fact of Christian truth. To quote Simpson, it 'breathes the very soul of the gospel'. The emphasis on the incarnation and its purpose is more Johannine than Pauline, and this adds further weight to the view that Paul is here quoting a current statement of the gospel. Because of its content the words may perhaps be directly traceable to the words of Jesus, contained in the source which formed the basis of the fourth Gospel (cf. Lock).

Paul never got away from the fact that Christian salvation was intended for *sinners*, and the more he increased his grasp of the magnitude of God's grace, the more he deepened the consciousness of his own naturally sinful state, until he could write *of whom I am chief* (*prōtos*). This is not an expression of

---

[1] See the writer's monograph, *The Pastoral Epistles and the Mind of Paul*, pp. 18-21.

formal devotion, as Easton supposes, but a mark of sincerest humility. Paul sees himself in the vanguard of those whose sins have called forth the resources of God's mercy. It is Paul's way to use superlatives of himself, whether ranking himself as least of the apostles (1 Cor. xv. 9) or less than the least of all saints (Eph. iii. 8) or chief of sinners. We need not feel, as Scott does, that Paul's 'self-abasement is morbid and unreal', any more than we need conclude the same about John Bunyan for writing *Grace Abounding to the Chief of Sinners*.

16. The thought of having received mercy is repeated from verse 13, but here the specific purpose is given. Paul conceives of his own striking case as a special example of what Christ could do with other human lives. Though the same Greek word *prōtos* is rendered 'chief' in verse 15 and *first* in verse 16, it seems better to understand the latter in the same sense as the former. Mercy shown to the foremost sinner must provide a superlative example for subsequent centuries, especially as Paul's case had elicited so clearly the *long-suffering* of Jesus Christ.

The Greek word rendered *pattern* (*hupotupōsis*) may be understood either as an outline sketch of an artist, or as a word-illustration expressing an author's burning purpose (cf. Simpson). In a sublime sense Paul's experience was to serve as a compelling example to countless numbers who *should hereafter believe*. The construction (*epi* with the dative) after the verb *believe* indicates that Christ is the firm basis of faith. Such unshakable assurance serves not only in this life but in eternity.

17. A typical Pauline doxology is called forth by these moving reflections on the mercies of God. New features not found in earlier examples admittedly appear, but there is the same all-absorbing adoration of God and the same sense of the majesty of God. Nowhere else does Paul use the phrase 'King of the ages' (*basileus tōn aiōnōn*, AV *the King eternal*), which occurs in fact only in Tobit xiii. 6, 10 and Rev. xv. 3 in the Greek Bible. It was probably current in Jewish circles and springs out of the Jewish view of the two ages, the age that is and the age to come. God was King in both spheres, and indeed of the 'ages of the ages' as the phrase *for ever and ever* (*eis tous aiōnas tōn aiōnōn*) suggests.

The ascription *immortal* (*aphthartos*) appears to be more Hellenistic than Jewish, yet Rom. i. 23 supplies a Pauline parallel. Similarly the adjective *invisible* (*aoratos*) applied to God finds a Pauline parallel in Col. i. 15. There seems little doubt that instead of the AV *only wise God* we should read 'only God'; the adjective *wise* has been borrowed from Rom. xvi. 27. The omission of the adjective here provides a more emphatic expression of Jewish monotheism.

(d) The apostle's charge to Timothy (i. 18–20)

These verses are a resumption of verses 3-5, and state precisely the purpose of the apostle's writing.

18. Paul uses the same word *parangelia* to indicate the *charge* laid upon Timothy as he used in verse 5 to denote the Christian injunction to love. As often in military contexts (e.g. in Xenophon and Polybius) it conveys a sense of urgent obligation. Timothy is solemnly reminded that the ministry is not a matter to be trifled with, but an order from the commander-in-chief. It is significant that the verb *commit* (*paratithēmi*), used of the entrusting of the charge to Timothy, is used also in 2 Tim. ii. 2 of Timothy passing it on to others.

According to the prophecies which went before on thee must be understood in the sense of predictions in some way granted to Paul concerning Timothy before his call to the ministry. It may be parallel to those given to the Antiochene church regarding the missionary vocation of Paul and Barnabas. In any case the words testify not only to the complete confidence of Paul that Timothy was God's choice as his successor, but to the endorsement of that choice by the Christian communities with which Timothy was associated.

Paul continues the military language, *war a good warfare*, as he assures his young lieutenant that the several prophecies confirming his calling will provide inspiration for the conflict that lies ahead (RSV 'inspired by them' brings out the meaning better than AV *by them*).

19. Whereas in Eph. vi. 10–17 Paul describes in detail the Christian's armour, he confines himself here to two items of equipment which embrace the fundamental aspects of doctrine and practice. *Faith* and *a good conscience* are three times conjoined in this Epistle (cf. i. 5 and iii. 9), showing the inseparable connection between faith and morals. We need not restrict *faith* here to 'right belief' as Easton does, although that aspect is undoubtedly included. It appears to epitomize the spiritual side of the Christian warrior's armour.

In the next clause *put away* relates to *conscience*, which, if once ignored, is bound to affect the *faith*. Scott rightly says 'More often than we know, religious error has its roots in moral rather than in intellectual causes'. The converse is equally true, for faulty belief not infrequently leads to moral disaster. But Paul's chief concern is to warn against the peril of neglect of conscience. The verb *put away* (*apōtheō*) implies a violent and deliberate rejection.

With the word *shipwreck* the military metaphor turns into a nautical one. As Lock cryptically remarks, 'The Christian teacher must be good soldier and good sailor too'.

20. *Hymenæus* (mentioned again in 2 Tim. ii. 17) and *Alexander* are cited as samples of shipwrecked believers. As to the identity of Alexander, the details available are insufficient to conclude that he is the Alexander mentioned in Acts xix. 33 and 2 Tim. iv. 14. Whoever these men were their case called for strong disciplinary action, described in the figurative words *delivered unto Satan*. The same expression is used in 1 Cor. v 5 and both cases must be understood in the same way. If the 1 Corinthians passage is interpreted as implying excommunication, Paul means no more than that they are put out of the Church into Satan's province (i.e. the non-Christian world). But Easton objects that 'excommunication would heighten blasphemy instead of deterring it' and he prefers therefore to understand the expression to mean the infliction of physical disaster. The instances in Acts v. 1–11 and xiii. 11 of discipline having physical results and the more obscure allusion in 1 Cor. xi. 30 support the latter idea, but a combination of both may be the correct view. Probably Hymenæus and Alexander should be regarded as exceptional cases.

The concluding clause *that they may learn not to blaspheme* shows clearly that the purpose was remedial and not punitive. However stringent the process the motive was mercy, and whenever ecclesiastical discipline has departed from this purpose of restoration, its harshness has proved a barrier to progress. But this is no reason for dispensing with discipline entirely, a failing which frequently characterizes our modern churches.

II. WORSHIP AND ORDER IN THE CHURCH
(ii. 1–iv. 16)

The main business of the Epistle now begins, and in the opening words of this section Paul appears to continue the theme of i.3. He deals with several subjects directly concerned with the organization of the Church.

(a) The importance and scope of public prayer (ii. 1–8)

1. The words *first of all* relate not to primacy of time but primacy of importance. It is essential, at the outset, to ensure the noblest approach to public worship. While the verb translated *exhort* (*parakaleō*) can bear the sense of 'entreat' or 'encourage', the more martial meaning is probably intended in view of its association with the stronger verb *parangellō* in i.3.

It is not possible to distinguish precisely the provinces covered by the four words here used for prayer. The first three have so much in common that little useful purpose is served in defining their respective meanings; yet there may be significance in the fact that *deēseis* (*supplications*) brings out a clearer sense of need than *proseuchai* (*prayers*), the more general word for prayer, while *enteuxeis* (*intercessions*) is a regular term for petition to a superior. The very variety of terms serves to emphasize the richness of this spiritual exercise. *Giving of thanks*, as in Paul's earlier Epistles, is regarded as an integral part of prayer, yet it is an element which has been too often in the background in modern Christian devotions. The reminder that prayer is *for all men* is timely in view of the temptation to confine our prayers to our own narrow interests. The wider the subjects for prayer the larger becomes the vision of the soul that prays.

2. Examples of the universal scope of prayer are limited to prayer for the ruling classes, perhaps because of the tendency for Christians to leave these out of their devotions, especially when rulers are openly hostile. The plural *kings* need not imply a time when co-emperors shared the imperial throne, for a general principle is being stated, applicable at all times. This Christian attitude towards the State is of utmost importance. Whether the civil authorities are perverted or not they must be made subjects for prayer, for Christian citizens may in this way influence the course of national affairs, a fact often forgotten except in times of special crisis.

The purpose, rather than the content, of such prayer is now stated. *That we may lead a quiet and peaceable life* means that government may achieve conditions of peace and security, enabling the Christian and his fellow-men to pursue their own lives. The twin synonyms *ēremos* (*quiet*) and *hēsuchios* (*peaceable*) both mean 'quiet' and 'tranquil' and seem to be linked here to emphasize the importance of calmness and serenity in social affairs.

The next two words denote the character that can best be developed in an atmosphere of calm. The first *eusebeia* (*godliness*) is a general word for religious devotion, while the second, *semnotēs* (*honesty*) denotes the Christian's dignity of demeanour, or seriousness of purpose. For their fullest expression both require conditions of external peace, although they may often be intensified in circumstances of stress.

3. It is questionable whether *for* belongs to the text since the manuscript evidence for it is mostly late. With its omission the connection of thought with the preceding verse is less clear, but *this* (*touto*) appears to refer to verse 1, i.e. to the idea of universal prayer. The two parts of this verse should be taken separately: (a) universal prayer is *good;* (b) it is *acceptable in* *the sight of God.* This latter proposition presents the ultimate standard for all Christian worship.

The title *God our Saviour,* already used in i. 1, has special significance here, as it relates prayer for all men to the saving character of God. There is point in praying on all men's behalf to One whose nature it is to save, a thought developed in the next verse.

4. The words *who will have all men to be saved* became a centre of controversy between the Calvinists and Arminians of the seventeenth century, owing to their implied universalism. Bernard considers the verb used (*thelō,* 'to desire') represents the general purpose of God as distinct from a single volition. It speaks, therefore, of God's consistent mercy towards all, without distinction of race, colour, condition or status. There may have been a tendency towards exclusiveness on the part of some, who were influenced perhaps by the same urge that drove the later Gnostics into their own exclusive circles of initiates, and Paul, to provide an antidote, may here be stressing God's universal compassion. Even if it is difficult to reconcile this statement with Paul's teaching elsewhere regarding the sovereignty of God, no one would deny that these words fairly represent the magnanimity of the divine benevolence. The words *all men* must be linked with the 'all' of verse 1. Intercession for all men could be justified only on the ground of God's willingness to save all (cf. Jeremias).

Simpson suggests another line of interpretation, in which the verb 'to save' (*sōzō*) is understood in its weaker sense of 'preserve' or 'protect'. After quoting Deissmann in support he comments, 'The ordination of prayer for rulers accords with the divine willingness that all men should be preserved from lawless misrule'. But the passage as a whole seems too theological to be taken in this sense, and the concluding part of this verse, *to come unto the knowledge of the truth,* accords better with spiritual salvation than natural preservation, unless it means that peaceful conditions assist the propagation of the gospel.

The phrase *knowledge of the truth* is reminiscent of John and is not found in Paul outside the Pastorals. It should be understood as the whole revelation of God in Christ, to know which must be the ultimate aim of Christian salvation.

5. Both Moffatt and Easton treat this verse as a quotation. Scott prefers to regard the words as the writer's own comment, probably influenced by a knowledge of the Epistle to the Hebrews. But Paul himself would certainly have agreed with both statements in this verse. He reasoned from the unity of God to the universalism of his mission in answering Jewish exclusivism in Rom. iii. 29, 30. Here the appeal to the doctrine of the unity of God common to Judaism and Christianity links up with the divine desire that all should come to a knowledge of the truth.

The second part of the verse adds an exclusively Christian element. The doctrine of Christ as *mediator* (*mesitēs*) is more fully expounded in the Epistle to the Hebrews in connection with the covenant. That no bond between God and man was possible apart from *Christ Jesus* is also fundamental to Paul's thought. It is because a mediator must be representative that the humanity of Christ, *the man Christ Jesus*, is also brought into prominence.

6. Thinking of Christ as mediator leads Paul to make a more precise declaration regarding the atonement. The mention of a *ransom* (*antilutron*) echoes the words of Jesus, 'the Son of man came . . . to give his life a ransom (*lutron*) for many' (Mk. x. 45). The addition of the preposition *anti*, 'instead of', is significant in view of the preposition *huper*, 'on behalf of', used after it. Christ is conceived of as an 'exchange price' on behalf of and in the place of *all*, on the grounds of which freedom may be granted. Yet not all enjoy that freedom. The ransom, it is true, has infinite value, but the benefits require appropriation. The apostle is implying here that since the ransom is adequate for all, God must desire the salvation of all.

The precise meaning of the last phrase, *to be testified in due time* is obscure owing to its compressed character. Since the words follow immediately the profound statement about

Christ's saving work, it is best to assume that 'the testimony' intended is God's act in sending His Son at the appointed time (cf. Gal. iv. 4).

7. The opening words may be paraphrased, 'To spread this testimony I was appointed *a preacher* (or herald) and *an apostle*'. Paul had not appointed himself to so great and hazardous a task; it was laid upon him by God (cf. 2 Tim. i. 11). The emphatic *I* expresses the sense of personal wonder. But why need Timothy be reminded of the divine character of Paul's vocation? Surely of all people he should have been well aware of it? And why the strong asseveration, *I speak the truth in Christ, and lie not?* Many scholars (e.g. Harrison, Easton) find genuine difficulty in believing that Paul would ever have expressed himself in this manner to the real Timothy, but strong asseverations of this nature may be paralleled in Paul (Rom. ix. 1; 2 Cor. xi. 31; Gal. i. 20). Admittedly these parallels were written in circumstances where Paul's authority had been disputed by some, and this was not the case with Timothy. But if the Pastorals are regarded as semi-public it may well have been necessary for Timothy to possess the strongest possible assertion of Paul's true apostleship to combat some at Ephesus who denied it (cf. Jeremias). Timothy's own commission would clearly be implicated in the authenticity of his predecessor's call. In any case, Scott agrees that 'whether borrowed or not, the strong assertion of veracity is quite in place'. No less an issue was at stake than the veracity of the Gentile mission.

Bernard links the strong assertion with the following rather than preceding words, giving veracity to Paul's claim to be especially appointed *a teacher of the Gentiles* rather than his claim to apostleship. But the two claims are inseparable. *In faith and verity* (the same word as 'truth' in verse 4 and to be understood in the light of it) shows the sphere of the teaching, embracing both the spirit of the teacher and the content of the message, though the latter seems more in prominence.

8. Paul now resumes the subject of prayer. The authority which he has just vindicated shines out in the opening verb *boulomai* (*I will*) which should be regarded almost as a command. Scott likens it to a royal decree.

Presumably the singling out of *men* as subjects for prayer in this verse must be taken in conjunction with what is afterwards said about women (verse 9). In using the phrase *every where* (lit. 'in every place'), Paul may be echoing Mal. i. 10, 11, but the phrase is characteristically Pauline (cf. 1 Cor. i. 2; 2 Cor. ii. 14; 1 Thes. i. 8), while the practice of *lifting up . . . hands* was common among Jews and pagans as well as Christians when in the attitude of prayer (cf. Lock). Although constant prayer is here regarded as a matter of Christian obligation, the gesture mentioned is incidental to the qualifying adjective *holy*. Worshippers with hands stained by unworthy deeds must first be cleansed before approaching God in prayer (cf. Ps. xxvi. 6). The closing words of this verse are aptly rendered by Moffatt, 'free from anger and dissension'. This brings out the more probable meaning of the last word *dialogismos*, translated *doubting*. Such attitudes of mind are as alien to the holy place of prayer as sullied hands. Not merely pure actions but pure motives are essential in Christian worship.

(b) The status and demeanour of Christian women (ii. 9-15)

9. Grammatically this section continues the injunction in verse 8, i.e. it gives observations on women's conduct in public prayer. But it seems most unlikely that Paul intends to restrict himself in this way, for no clear distinction can be drawn between what is fitting for public worship and what is fitting at other times. The advice given seems to be general and we must therefore suppose that Paul turned from his immediate purpose in order to make wider observations about women's demeanour.

The word translated *apparel* (*katastolē*) probably refers to demeanour as well as attire. *Modest* (*kosmios*, lit. 'orderly, decent') demeanour alone accords with the spirit of Christian worship. It reflects a right attitude of mind, for Paul was shrewd enough to know that a woman's dress is a mirror of her mind.

Outward ostentation is not in keeping with a prayerful and devout approach.

The words *shamefacedness and sobriety* may be rendered 'modesty and self-control', indicating dignity and seriousness of purpose as opposed to levity and frivolity. Paul leaves no doubt as to what he means, by adding a list of prohibitions relating to outward adornments.

The plaiting of the hair was a usual feature of Jewish women's hairstyle, and in the more elaborate types the plaits were fastened with ribbons and bows (cf. Strack-Billerbeck). Such tendencies to ostentatious adornment must be resisted by Christian women, and the same applies to the use of jewelry and costly clothing. In all these injunctions the one dominating idea is the avoidance of anything designed merely to promote ostentation, with all its accompanying dangers.

10. Paul hastens to add that women are not denied all adornment, but that the greatest asset a woman possesses is a devout and godly life. He makes it clear that he speaks only for Christian women, those *professing godliness*, whose standards must always be higher than those of non-Christians. There is particular stress here and elsewhere in the Pastorals on the necessity for *good works*, probably because current speculations tended to divorce doctrine and practice. The idea of 'good works' as an adornment is suggestive, for a life of selfless devotion to others may well enhance the appearance. A woman's adornment, in short, lies not in what she herself puts on, but in the loving service she gives out.

11. That women should *learn in silence* is in full accord with 1 Cor. xiv. 34, 35, although in the latter case the reference is specifically to public worship. It may be that Paul's present stricture is to be taken with the same proviso, and was designed to curb the tendencies of newly emancipated Christian women to abuse their new-found freedom by indecorously lording it over men. Such excesses would bring disrepute on the whole community, as had probably happened at Corinth, and called for firm handling. When taking part in public worship the woman's share is to *learn*, or at least to 'listen quietly' (Moffatt).

The equality of the sexes, so much in the forefront of modern thought, received little recognition in ancient times. Not only was the prevailing Greek attitude against it, but Hebrew thought was equally unsympathetic.[1] The entire subjection (*en pasēi hupotagēi*) mentioned by Paul relates primarily to public worship as it was then enacted, and reserve must be exercised in deducing universal principles from particular cases. The idea, however, of woman's subjection is not only engrained in the conviction of the mass of mankind (which would not in itself, of course, be a justification for it), but also appears to be inherent in the divine constitution of the human race. Paul mentions this latter aspect in verse 13.

12. A woman is apparently encouraged to learn yet not allowed to *teach*. There may have been local reasons for this prohibition of which we know nothing. It is noteworthy that no such specific injunction is found in 1 Corinthians, although 1 Cor. xiv. 34, 35 forbids a woman to be heard in church. If the present prohibition is restricted to public teaching (as seems most probable) it accords perfectly with the 1 Corinthians passage. Paul cannot be accused of being a woman-hater, as is sometimes alleged, on the strength of this evidence, since he acknowledges some women among his own fellow-labourers, such as Priscilla (Rom. xvi. 3–5) and Euodias and Syntyche (Phil. iv. 2, 3). The prohibition may have been due to the greater facility with which contemporary women were falling under the influence of impostors (cf. Falconer).

Rabbinic prohibitions were much more severe than Christian, since a woman, although theoretically permitted to read the Torah in public, was in practice not allowed to teach even small children.[2] The teaching of Christian doctrine, nevertheless, is confined by Paul to the male sex, and this has been the almost invariable practice in the subsequent history of the Church.

The word rendered *usurp authority over* (*authenteō*) means 'have the mastery of' or more colloquially 'lord it over'. In

[1] Cf. Strack-Billerbeck, III, pp. 428 ff.
[2] Cf. Strack-Billerbeck, III, p. 467.

public meetings Christian women must refrain from laying down the law to men and hence are enjoined to silence. It may be that Paul has married women mainly in mind and that 'man' should here be understood as husband, although this would not be so relevant if church meetings are mainly in view. Indeed, the concluding injunction to silence could not apply to the Christian home and the whole verse must therefore relate to the community.

13. In 1 Cor. xi. 9, Paul had already made use of the argument that the priority of man's creation places him in a position of superiority over woman, the assumption being that the original creation, with the Creator's own imprimatur upon it, must set a precedent for determining the true order of the sexes. Their relationship, as Simpson points out, was 'not competitive, but concordant and counterpart.'

14. Another reason why woman must submit to man is now added, *Adam was not deceived, but the woman*. Whereas Eve was deceived or beguiled, Adam sinned with his eyes open. As Bengel says: 'The serpent deceived the woman; the woman did not deceive the man, but persuaded him' (cf. Gn. iii. 17). Logically this should make Adam more culpable, but Paul is concerned primarily with the inadvisability of women teaching, and he may have in mind the greater aptitude of the weaker sex to be led astray. The concluding words, *was in the transgression (en parabasei gegone)*, are well rendered in RSV 'became a transgressor', the Greek perfect expressing an abiding state. That Paul did not absolve Adam from responsibility in the *transgression* is evident from Rom. v. 12 ff. where the entry of sin into the world is attributed to Adam, as representative man, and Eve is not even mentioned.

15. From the allusion to Eve, Paul seems to pass to women in general, by making a statement *she shall be saved in child-bearing (dia tēs teknogonias)* which must rank among the most difficult expressions in the whole of the Pastorals.

1. Moffatt translates the words 'woman will get safely through childbirth', understanding them as conveying to women encouragement in their natural sphere. This certainly

accords well with the Genesis story which pronounces on Eve the doom that in sorrow she shall conceive, adding the assurance of safe delivery if the conditions are observed. It is probable that the duty of child-bearing is emphasized to offset the unnatural abstinence advocated by the false teachers (cf. Jeremias).

2. Chrysostom takes the verb 'save' in its spiritual sense, but to avoid the manifest absurdity of making the statement suggest that child-bearing is a woman's means of salvation, as if unmarried or childless women are *ipso facto* excluded, he understands the word 'child-bearing' as equivalent to child-nurture, and supplied 'children' as the subject of the verb *continue*. But this would make women's salvation a matter of good works of a particular kind, and it is inconceivable that Paul meant this.

3. Another equally improbable suggestion is that the words should read as in RV 'she shall be saved by means of the child-bearing' (i.e. the Messiah). For if that were the writer's intention he could hardly have chosen a more obscure or ambiguous way of saying it. That Paul would have left the words 'the child-bearing' without further definition is highly improbable. The Greek article is generic, describing the whole process of child-bearing, rather than definitive of one particular instance.

4. Scott proposes a fourth possibility, taking the words to mean 'she will be saved even though she must bear children', that is to say, she shall be linked with man in salvation, in spite of the penalty for her misdemeanour imposed on her. Scott concludes, 'The writer, in fact, is making a sort of apology for what he has said about women'. This view has the advantage of showing to Christian women the way in which the original curse upon their race is mitigated by Christian salvation, but it imposes an unnatural meaning on the Greek preposition *dia*.

In this verse the verbs change from singular *she shall be saved* to plural *if they continue* and it can only be assumed that the latter part of the verse refers to Christian women in general. Indeed, it is not too much to claim that the former part of the verse must be interpreted in the light of the latter half. Christian women are exhorted to continue exercising a quartet of Christian virtues—*faith, charity* (love), *holiness* and *sobriety* (i.e. self-control). Moffatt renders these as adjectives, 'faithful and loving, and holy as well as unassuming', suggestively bringing out their qualitative character, but the Greek preposition *en* implies that woman's proper sphere, as contrasted with the teacher's office, is in the manifestation of these Christian graces, a sphere in which she has, in fact, shone more eminently than man.

(c) The qualifications of Church officials (iii. 1–13)
(i) Bishops (iii. 1–7). There is some question whether the initial formula should be attached to the preceding words, as the statement about a bishop's office seems to lack sufficient theological weight (so Parry). Since, however, in all probability this was a popular or proverbial saying, it is more likely to have referred to a bishop's office than the obscure allusion to Eve in the previous chapter. In the opening formula Moffatt prefers the alternative reading 'popular', *anthrōpinos*, in place of *faithful* or 'true', but this is not strongly supported and looks like a scribe's attempt to lessen the problem of the more usual formula being applied elsewhere to religious truth rather than a mere proverbial statement. Probably Paul cites it here because it aptly epitomized what he intended to say about the dignity of a bishop's office.

It is important to notice that the modern word *bishop* does not represent the Greek word *episkopos*, which properly means 'overseer'. In its original usage, at least until the time of Ignatius, it was restricted to those who exercised oversight in the local church. In the proverbial saying in this verse, the office referred to is quite general and might encompass any position, secular or ecclesiastical, where 'oversight' was necessary. Nor is there any hint here or elsewhere in the Pastorals of the monarchical episcopacy so much lauded by Ignatius (see Introduction, pp. 30 ff). Simpson's suggestion that Paul is using in this saying the words of some proposition submitted for his adjudication has much to commend it.

Moffatt well renders the latter part of the sentence 'is set upon an excellent occupation'. Wherever spiritual values have been rightly assessed there has always been a high estimate of the Christian ministry.

The first verb translated *desire* is *oregomai*, 'to stretch oneself out', hence 'to aspire to', but not in a bad sense; the second verb, *epithumeō*, expresses strong desire, 'to set one's heart upon'.

2. With precise detail Paul proceeds to list the qualities required in an overseer. Easton, following Vögtle, has shown that parallel ethical lists were current in Greek circles designed for various occupations, e.g. king, general, midwife, etc. The qualities required for Christian rulers are strikingly similar in many particulars. It is surprising that the required standards, particularly the negative ones (e.g. *not given to wine, not a brawler*, etc.), do not lead us to suppose that the usual aspirant for office was of a particularly high quality, since no exceptional virtues are demanded. Yet this in itself accurately reflects the earliest state of the Christian Church, when the majority of converts probably came from a background of low moral ideals.

There seems to be no special reason for the order in which the qualities are mentioned, a lack of system which also pervades the Hellenistic lists. *Blameless* or 'without reproach' (*anepilemptos* means not only of good report but deservedly so; cf. Abbott-Smith) nevertheless suitably stands first, as being indispensable to the Christian minister's character. The next words, *husband of one wife*, have been variously interpreted. Some have understood them as a prohibition of second marriages (e.g. Tertullian), supported by the parallel phrase in v. 9. Others have suggested that they enforce monogamy for Christian ministers as opposed to the polygamy often practised in the contemporary heathen world, but, as Bernard argues, no Christian, whether an overseer or not, would ever have been allowed to practise polygamy. The only occasion for such an injunction would be to exclude any who before their conversion had been polygamists. A third suggestion is that the words mean simply that 'a bishop must show an example of strict morality' (Scott).

The next virtues may be suitably rendered 'temperate, self-controlled, well-behaved, hospitable, competent to teach'. The first three are closely akin and describe an orderly life, while the fourth would have particular point in the early Church, since without the willing hospitality of Christian people expansion would have been seriously retarded. The fifth quality describes mental achievement, for an overseer must certainly have the propensity to pass on advice and doctrine to enquirers.

3. Some of the qualities here required amount to denials of extreme cases of excess; e.g. *given to wine* implies drunkenness, a *striker* violence and a *brawler* contentiousness. Such excesses are clearly quite alien to the Christian spirit, which is particularly exemplified by contrast in the sole positive quality in this verse, *epieikēs*, translated *patient*. Simpson gives as its English approximation 'gracious, kindly, forbearing, considerate, magnanimous, genial'. (Cf. Tit. iii. 2 and Phil. iv. 5.) The derived noun is used in 2 Cor. x. 1 of Christ, who provides *par excellence* an example of this quality.

4, 5. A most important principle, which has not always had the prominence it deserves, is next propounded. Any man unable to govern his children graciously and gravely by maintaining good discipline, is no man for government in the Church. The principle is universal, for potential skill in a larger sphere can only be indicated by similar skill in a lesser sphere (cf. the rewards granted in the parable of the talents, Mt. xxv. 14 ff.). The parallel between Church (in the expression *church of God* the local community is clearly in view) and home brings impressive dignity to Christian home-life, a dignity as imperative in the twentieth century as in Paul's day. The apostle is here dealing with Church officials in whom such worthy home-life is indispensable (cf. verse 12). Yet his words must not be taken to mean that the same standards are not expected of Christians generally (cf. Eph. v and vi and Col. iii and iv).

The Greek phrase rendered *with all gravity* (*semnotēs*) is better translated 'with complete dignity' (as Easton), avoiding the suggestion of sternness yet retaining the idea of natural respect. The parenthetical question in verse 5 is in complete accord with Paul's style (cf. the three examples in 1 Cor. xiv. 7, 9, 16), giving rhetorical support to the point just made. It is significant that the same verb (*proistēmi*) is used here for fathers ruling their children as later for elders ruling the Church (v. 17; cf. also 1 Thes. v. 12 and Rom. xii. 8).

6, 7. The aspirant to office must not be a *novice* (*neophutos*), a word apparently used here of one recently baptized. It is often supposed that such a proviso must indicate a late date for the Pastorals, since in a recently established church all the members would necessarily be recent converts. In a church the size of Ephesus, however, a few years would suffice for converts to be regarded as established in view of the constant flow of new converts. It is significant that this particular feature is omitted from the directions for the Cretan church, whose more recent establishment no doubt rendered it inappropriate. In itself this provision is most reasonable, as too rapid promotion may easily lead to excessive pride and instability. The Greek word *tuphoō* translated *lifted up with pride*, means literally 'to wrap in smoke' (Abbott-Smith) and suggests that a new convert would find himself 'in a cloudland of conceit' (Horton). Pride gives a false sense of altitude, making the subsequent *fall* seem all the greater.

It is not clear what is meant by falling *into the condemnation of the devil*. It may mean (a) the condemnation reserved for the devil, i.e. the judgment meted out for the sin of pride; or (b) the condemnation wrought by the devil, i.e. the condemnation brought about by the further intrigues of the devil when a man is once lured into his grasp through pride; or (c) the condemnation of the slanderer, taking *devil* in its original sense, and understanding by the phrase the malicious attacks to which an arrogant neophyte is subjected as a result of his vanity. The use of the word in 2 Tim. ii. 26 in the sense of 'devil' and the rarity with which *krima* (judgment, condemnation) means 'slander' (as Calvin noted) makes the third suggestion improbable, while of the other two the more natural interpretation seems to be the first, since pride is clearly a pressing danger for a promoted neophyte.

The next requirement, a *good report* among non-Christians (*them which are without*), may at first sight seem impossible in view of the lack of favour shown towards Christianity in the contemporary world. Yet the injunction was essential to protect the Church from unnecessary abuse, for the non-Christian world has generally respected the noble ideals of Christian character, but has persistently condemned professing Christians, particularly ministers and leaders, whose practice is at variance with profession. It is not that outsiders are arbiters in the Church's choice of its officers, but that no minister will achieve success who has not first gained the confidence of his fellows.

The snare of the devil is again ambiguous, for it may either mean the trap laid by the devil into which a man unpopular among non-Christians will easily fall; or it may refer to the devil's sin of pride. The mention of *reproach* suggests the former as the more probable interpretation, although the latter forms a better parallel with the previous verse.

(ii) Deacons (iii. 8-13). The earliest allusion to *deacons* is found in Acts vi, where the purpose of their appointment is mainly practical. Since they were particularly concerned with the distribution of the Church's charities it was as essential for them as for the presiding elders to be morally equipped for the task. There is no need to suppose that the office of deacon was a late development in view of Phil. i. 1. There deacons are specially linked with bishops, probably because a gift is under consideration, for which no doubt they had been mainly responsible.

The list of qualities specified is closely akin to the preceding, but there are significant variations. Once again an element of seriousness is prominent, for such a quality would naturally call out a due measure of respect. The word *doubletongued* (*dilogos*) could sustain the meaning 'tale-bearer' suggesting the idea of gossipers, a tendency which would be all too easy yet damaging for the holder of the deacon's office. The meaning may, however, be *doubletongued*, i.e. speaking one thing to one person and something different to another.

The two further comments forbidding wine addicts and men with insatiable appetites for base gain are both expressed in stronger terms than in the case of the overseers, no doubt because their house-to-house visitation would expose them more pointedly to these evils.

9. The deacons are to be men not merely of practical acumen, but also of spiritual conviction. They have a possession described here as *the mystery of the faith* which must be tenaciously held. *Mystery (mustērion)* is a common Pauline expression denoting, not what is beyond knowledge, but what, being once hidden, is now revealed to those with spiritual discernment. Some scholars see a difference here from Paul's normal usage, assuming that *mystery* has now become a conventional term. 'It is assumed that although men cannot understand the gospel, they must accept it with implicit faith as given by God' (Scott). But we are not committed to this interpretation of the word, for it is difficult to see how anyone can hold with *a pure conscience* what he fails to understand. To Paul the word always conveys a sense of wonder at God's plan of salvation (Rom. xvi. 26), and he cannot conceive of other Christians lacking the same realization. The whole phrase might mean (a) the mystery, the substance of which is the Christian faith (the use of the article supports this); or (b) the mystery appropriated by faith. In view of other occurrences in the Pastorals of *the faith* representing a body of doctrine, the former interpretation seems most consistent. But Lock prefers the meaning 'holding their own faith, the secret of their allegiance to Christ, secure under the protection of a good conseience'.

10. The testing which is here regarded as necessary must be understood rather as an examination of the required qualities than as a period of probation. The verb *dokimazō* means to test in the hope of being successful (cf. Abbott-Smith). Appointment of deacons, as of every officer in the Church, demands careful scrutiny. Spicq rightly appeals to Acts vi. 3

to show that the proving is carried out by the assembly of believers. Only when adequate testing has been made and the man is found to be *blameless*, (*anenklētos*, irreproachable), may he exercise his office.

11. In this special injunction to women, some understand a reference to the deacons' wives and there is much to be said for this in view of the probable share such a wife would have in her husband's visitation work. Others have postulated an order of deaconesses, but there is difficulty in view of the special section later in the Epistle devoted to women workers. Yet the word *hōsautōs* translated *even so* shows a close connection between the women and the deacons, and would support the contention that a new class is introduced analogous to the preceding order of deacons. Another argument in favour of deaconesses is that no special requirements are mentioned for the wives of bishops (cf. Spicq). The truth probably lies between these two views. The reference is too general to postulate with certainty a distinct order of deaconesses, but some feminine ministration was necessary in visitation and in attending to women candidates for baptism. For such work certain moral qualities would be essential whether for deacons' wives or for deaconesses in their own right. These qualities all contain a serious note, befitting the character of their task. The last condition *faithful in all things* is aptly phrased by Moffatt as 'absolutely trustworthy', an exacting yet necessary demand.

12, 13. Domestic orderliness and parental control are as necessary in a deacon as in an overseer and the requirements stated are in this respect identical with the previous list. A different reason, however, is given, perhaps by way of encouragement to the lesser officials of whom so high a standard is demanded. It is not quite clear what the words *purchase to themselves a good degree* mean, but three different suggestions have been made. The word rendered *degree* (*bathmos*) literally means 'a step', and is taken to mean (a) a step in promotion to a higher office; (b) 'standing', or 'vantage ground', relating to the influence gained in the esteem of the Christian community (so RSV)[1]; (c) 'standing in the sight of God'. The first seems quite out of harmony with the context and, as Scott rightly points out, it would make the previous instructions ridiculous if this were the main aim of the deacon's office, i.e. to provide a stepping stone to the elder's office. The second makes good sense and fully accords with the context, for as Simpson remarks 'Influence is a by-product of character'. But the third possibility cannot be ruled out in view of the concluding phrase, *great boldness in the faith*, which is co-ordinate with *bathmos* as object of the same verb 'to gain for oneself'; both parts may therefore legitimately be understood in a spiritual sense. Yet the transition of thought from moral qualifications to spiritual status is more difficult than that required for solution (b). Boldness seems primarily towards man, though it could include the notion of boldness in approach to God.

The expression *in the faith which is in Christ Jesus* has been much discussed. It is objected that this application of the usual Pauline phrase *in Christ Jesus* is in fact un-Pauline, because Paul uses it almost without exception to describe persons and not qualities. Easton[2] claims the writer here uses the phrase as synonymous with 'Christian'. Admittedly this particular application is unusual for Paul, but it is surely not inconceivable that the apostle should use his favourite expression when describing *faith*, since he is here concerned with the exercise of faith and not the body of Christian doctrine.

(d) The character of the Church (iii. 14-16)

This section marks a pause in the apostle's instructions in order to put them in a right perspective, to give the reason for them, and to give a reminder of the wonder of the Christian revelation which must never be divorced from practical arrangements. 'The writer is no mere ecclesiastic, more concerned with the mechanism of the Church than

[1] Cf. Hort, *Christian Ecclesia*, p. 202.
[2] *Op. cit.*, p. 210.

with its spiritual life' (Scott). Spicq is probably right in considering this the culminating doctrinal point and indeed the key to the Pastorals.

14. Although the apostle hopes soon to meet Timothy he writes the preceding instructions in case of delay. The major problem is why the apostle did not give Timothy the necessary instructions before leaving him at Ephesus. It might appear on the one hand that Paul lacked sufficient foresight to prepare his deputy, and on the other hand that 'Timothy's immaturity is so extreme that even these elementary instructions are indispensable' (Easton), neither of which propositions seems likely from what we know of the two men from other sources. If, however, we assume the semi-official character of the letters, there is no necessity to suppose these instructions were entirely new to Timothy (cf. Jeremias). Indeed the explanation may well be that the present Epistle is confirmatory of oral advice given to Timothy on Paul's departure and is sent before Paul's arrival to buttress the authority of his deputy. It is also possible that Paul was obliged to leave Ephesus hurriedly, and for this reason has had to supply Timothy with authorized instructions. Easton seems to overstate the case in proving Timothy's immaturity from the elementary character of the instructions, for such an argument would mean that the Pastorals would have increasingly less to say to a developing church. Naturally the instructions seem more elementary to the twentieth century than to the first.

15. In the Greek text, except for a few Western authorities, the subject of *behave* is omitted and could, therefore, refer to men generally or to Timothy himself. It probably refers to Timothy since he is the subject of the main verb, but it has been contended that a general reference is more in keeping with the preceding injunctions. On the other hand these injunctions are directed to Timothy to ensure that suitable appointments are to be made, and an allusion to his own official behaviour cannot be deemed alien to the present context. The Greek verb *anastrephō, behave,* means 'to conduct oneself', and could well apply to the discharge of official duties.

The idea of the *church* as a household has already been introduced in verse 5. The *house of God* is defined precisely as *the church of the living God*, which is clearly no material building but a spiritual assembly. The image is a favourite one in Pauline thought. The absence of the article before *ekklēsia* in the Greek (as in verse 5) suggests that the local community is again primarily in mind, yet conceived of as part of a larger whole.

The phrase *pillar and ground of the truth* has caused difficulties, mainly because it appears to give greater eminence to the Church than to the truth. The uniform New Testament teaching is that the Church is grounded on the truth, not vice versa. To avoid the difficulty the following suggestions have been made.

1. The whole phrase relates to Timothy and not to the Church. But Timothy could hardly be described as a *pillar* or prop of the *truth*, and in any case the Greek construction would not naturally suggest such an antecedent.

2. By rendering the word *hedraiōma* 'bulwark' instead of *ground*, the major difficulty disappears, for the Church has in varying degrees been the custodian of spiritual truth, and was in any case intended to be so.

3. A third suggestion that the phrase should be attached to the subsequent words and be regarded as a description of the *mystery of godliness* (Bengel) is ruled out by the awkwardness of such a construction in the Greek and the anticlimax involved in the thought (Scott). It is important to notice that no articles are used with either *pillar* or *ground* in the Greek and this must be considered intentional. A building needs more than one pillar, and undoubtedly Hort is right in supposing that 'each living society of Christian men' is here in view.[1] There may also be the idea that other agencies are used equally of God in the preservation of the gospel (e.g. Scripture, conscience).

[1] *Christian Ecclesia*, p. 174.

16. The Christian hymn contained in this verse is introduced by a formula intended to intimate something of the grandeur to follow. The adverb *homologoumenōs*, translated *without controversy*, means 'by common consent'. The phrase *mystery of godliness* calls for some comment since it occurs nowhere else. Mystery has already been met in verse 9 with the genitive *of faith*, but here it is qualified by a word which in ii. 2 appears to denote religion in general, although clearly the Christian religion is in view. But why does Paul use this unusual expression here? Perhaps the answer may be found in the implied comparison between the practical godliness previously enjoined on Church officers and the inner character of its revealed secret (*mustērion*) described here.

The AV, based on the Received Text, reads *God was manifest in the flesh*, but all modern editors reject this reading in favour of 'Who was manifest', the masculine relative evidently referring to Christ, who was no doubt mentioned in an earlier part of the hymn which was omitted from the citation. It was evidently well known and its application to Christ would be beyond dispute.

The lyrical quality of this hymn is missed in the English translation, but is most impressive in the Greek. The first phrase celebrates the incarnation and presupposes the pre-existence of Christ, a magnificently succinct statement of a most profound Christian truth. The mystery has been made known, yet how incomprehensible we discover it to be! The next expression, *justified in the Spirit*, may be regarded as parallel to the previous phrase, in which case since *in the flesh* (*en sarki*) denotes the sphere of operation of the verb 'manifest', so *in the Spirit* (*en pneumati*) must denote the sphere of the verb *justified*. If this is a correct assumption, *in the Spirit* would refer to Christ's human Spirit (paralleled in Rom. i. 4), and the meaning would then be that Christ was vindicated by God in the spiritual realm, i.e. when He declared Him to be His Son. On the other hand, if the parallelism is not enforced, the Greek preposition *en* could be understood instrumentally in which case the Holy Spirit would be declared as agent in vindicating the cause of a crucified, rejected Messiah, and this idea would connect well with the first phrase. But the former interpretation on the whole seems preferable.

The next phrase, *seen of angels*, is obscure, for it is not certain in what sense *angels* is to be understood. If the reference is to the principalities and powers believed to rule the unseen world (cf. the word 'elements' used in Gal. iv. 3, 9 and Col. ii. 8, 20 and cf. also Col. ii. 15 and Eph. vi. 12) the idea would be that the triumphant Christ showed Himself to His spiritual enemies. But the words may also be taken as a reference to the hosts of unfallen angels, which seems to be supported by such statements as 1 Pet. i. 12 and Eph. iii. 10. The hosts of heaven are depicted as eager to receive back the exalted Son of God, but this latter thought is more clearly gathered up in the sixth phrase. At the same time the idea of angelic worshippers of the Son was a popular theme among primitive Christians as the book of Revelation shows.

Bernard considers that an emphatic antithesis exists between the third and fourth phrases, between the revelation to *angels* and to *Gentiles*, both together indicating the extent of Messiah's manifestation. But it is probably better to link the fourth and fifth phrases as parallel. The universalism of the gospel is classed next among the wonders of this *mystery*, and this factor would have special point for Paul, the apostle to the Gentiles. It must never be forgotten that a Hebrew Christ had become a Christ for the nations. As this expression focuses on earth so does the next, which celebrates the response to the preaching *in the world*. Some understand the words to mean 'throughout the world' and take them as indicating the consummation of gospel preaching as the previous phrase shows its commencement. But they may indicate no more than the fact that the proclaimed Messiah is received by faith in the sphere of the world (here used without moral connotation) as contrasted with the ascension in glory with which the hymn concludes.

The refrain *received up into* (*en*, 'in') *glory* may be regarded as parallel to *seen of angels*, or if the first refrain is understood as referring to hostile agencies, this contrasting reference to the ascension would mark a fitting climax to the whole hymn. In any case there seems to be some thread of thought linking the fifth and sixth phrases, for Christ's triumph on earth (in the faith of His people) is concluded by His triumph in *glory*. The hymn could not close more suitably than with the humiliated Messiah's exalted entry into His heavenly sphere. It is noticeable that nowhere in the hymn is the death or resurrection of Christ mentioned, a surprising thing if this letter is Paul's own work. But if he is here citing a current hymn and citing only a part, it is at least possible that the part not cited contained these great truths. The part preserved can hardly represent a complete Christian creed, and indeed is not intelligible apart from some doctrine of the cross and resurrection being assumed.

(e) Threats to the safety of the Church (iv. 1-16)

Having pointed out the exaltation of Christ and the future prospects of the Church, the apostle next comes to opposing elements. Whenever truth flourishes error will raise its head, and the apostle is concerned that Timothy should deal rightly with this insidious opposition.

(i) The approaching apostasy (iv. 1-5). The ministry of the *Spirit* in apocalyptic revelations is emphatically brought out by the word *expressly* (*rhētōs*, 'in specific terms'), indicating that these elements of future events have been distinctly made known. At the same time no precise citation can be identified, and it is necessary, therefore, to apply the words to the general tenor of apocalyptic passages, especially in the teaching of Jesus (as e.g. Mk. xiii. 22). Paul himself has more than once prophesied such risings of false teachers (e.g. 2 Thes. ii. 1-12; cf. Acts xx. 29).

In the latter times (*en husterois kairois*) is a phrase which suggests a more imminent future than 'in the last days' (used in 2 Tim. iii. 1). Here the apostle is thinking of times subsequent to his own, but he foresees that Timothy needs to be cognisant of them. Indeed, as often in prophetical utterances. what is predicted of the future is conceived of as already operative in the present, so the words have a specific contemporary significance.

The apostasy is specified in a twofold manner. On the one hand the apostates are *giving heed* (or devoting themselves) *to spirits* that lead astray. These are evidently supernatural evil spirits whose existence and influence Paul has vividly described in Eph. vi. 11 ff. Such spirits of error are contrasted with the Spirit of truth. In addition, reference is made to *doctrines of devils*, which probably means doctrines taught by demons. Although closely akin to the first description, *seducing spirits*, it differs by putting the emphasis on the teaching rather than on the teachers. This has particular point as a contrast to the 'sound' doctrine of the Pastorals.

2, 3. The main elements in their character and teaching are now brought out in order to leave no doubt in Timothy's mind about the precise nature of the heresy. The Greek construction demands that the words *speaking lies in hypocrisy* be understood of the human agents of the demons, i.e. 'through the hypocrisy of men that speak lies' (RV). Grammatically the phrase itself could describe the hypocrisy of the demons, but this is impossible in view of the following two clauses. The meaning seems to be that the demons and seducing spirits find particular allies in hypocritical liars. These people have no sense of the wrongness of their actions for *their conscience* is *seared*, or 'cauterized', according to one possible meaning of the word *kauteriazō*. The apostle's description of people 'past feeling' in Eph. iv. 19 supports this medical understanding of the term, but it might mean that their consciences are branded with a hot iron to show their true owner to be Satan (cf. Lock).

The false teaching comprised two prohibitions: marriage and the eating of certain foods. There is no doubt that these point to an incipient gnosticism with its dualistic view of matter, which found its climax in the heretical teachers of the early second century (cf. Introduction, pp. 36 ff). The apostle's strong opposition to these practices is due to their dangerous implications. He argues that prohibitions such as these are in conflict with the divine ordinance. Here he strikes at the roots of dualistic gnosticism, which denied that God created matter.

To insist on the reception of God's gifts *with thanksgiving* is a typically Pauline theme. Such a note must never be absent from the believer's attitude either to material or spiritual realities. As Scott rightly remarks, 'the question at stake is that of our whole conception of God. Are we to think of Him as grudging us our earthly life, or are we to find in it a continual proof of His presence and goodness?'

The concluding words of verse 3 are not to be taken as promising any special material benefits for Christians (i.e. those who *believe and know the truth*), but as demonstrating that what was created for all men must therefore be legitimate for Christians.

4, 5. The apostle next supplies a reason for his previous statement. It involves a fundamental principle that what a good Creator creates must be *good*. The word *apoblētos* (*to be refused*), which occurs nowhere else in the New Testament, means literally 'to be thrown away', and is here used in the sense of 'tabooed' as Moffatt suggestively renders it. Such taboos should have no place in an intelligent Christian's approach, in strong contrast to the many systems of taboo in heathen cults. Note the repetition of the demand for *thanksgiving* (cf. verse 3).

There is some obscurity about the meaning of verse 5. Whatever is received with thanksgiving is *sanctified*, i.e. it becomes 'holy' to the user as contrasted with heathen taboos. The Christian concept of holiness embraces such mundane matters as 'meats', the least obvious subject for sanctification. But the precise means of this sanctification is not so clear. *The word of God and prayer* are clearly distinguished and yet closely allied. Bernard discusses the possible meaning of the former phrase and comes to the conclusion that it points to the use of Scripture in the 'grace' before meals. This seems more probable than the interpretation which maintains that *the word of God* stands for 'the divine revelation'. If it is correct, it draws attention to the practice of prayer before partaking of meals, and gives a timely reminder to modern Christians who tend either to neglect altogether the practice of 'grace' or else minimize its significance. The *word of God* could perhaps refer to Gn. i. 31 (as Easton maintains), although a difficulty arises in the use of the present tense *is sanctified*. It is also extremely awkward to construe in this way because of its close connection with *prayer*, which seems clearly to refer to those partaking of the meal. Whichever view is held it is evident that the sanctifying power of God's Word has a dominant influence over the apostle's thought, reminding us of the words of Christ in Jn. xv. 3.

(ii) Methods of dealing with false teaching (iv. 6–16). The apostle now begins a personal directive to Timothy, which serves at the same time all ministers of the gospel who are called to deal with similar situations. It is significant that the approach is not mere denunciation, as so often alleged, in contrast to Paul's constructive approach in Colossians. In fact the word *hupotithēmi* translated *put . . . in remembrance* means no more than 'suggest' which in many cases would carry more weight than 'command'. It literally means 'to place under', and Scott makes the interesting suggestion that *these things* (i.e. those mentioned in the previous verses) are like stepping stones over treacherous ground.

It is a sign of *a good minister of Jesus Christ* to lay before his people the positive answer to negative doctrine, and anyone who fails in this respect forfeits the right to be accounted worthy of the ministry. The present participle *entrephomenos* suggests a continual process of being *nourished up in the words of faith*, i.e. as the Greek article implies, in the body of Christian doctrine. There is no better means of spiritual nourishment than a constant dwelling upon the great truths of the faith, which Timothy had had the inestimable privilege of receiving at first hand from the apostle.

In the concluding phrase *whereunto thou hast attained*, the verb *parakoloutheō* suggests as the meaning either 'which you have closely investigated' or 'which you have followed as a standard'. The former is paralleled in Lk. i. 3 and might very well fit Timothy's position. In 2 Tim. iii. 10, however, the alternative sense of the same verb seems more probable. Both interpretations have this in common, that they focus attention on a pursuit of *good doctrine* as contrasted with false doctrine. That the best refutation of error is a positive presentation of truth is a principle which the Church in every age constantly needs to learn.

7, 8. By way of contrast to the 'good doctrine' the apostle describes the false teaching as *profane* (*bebēlos*), a word already used in i. 9 in the list of law-breakers coupled with 'unholy men'. The use of this word to describe professedly religious people shows the utter bankruptcy of their religion. The addition of the epithet *old wives* brings out forcibly the frivolous character of the false teachers' *fables* (*muthoi*) well paraphrased by Moffatt as 'drivelling myths'. There can be no compromise with these. They must be rejected (*paraiteomai* suggests a strong refusal; cf. Tit. iii. 10 and 2 Tim. ii. 23).

Again the apostle is quick to balance a negative with a positive injunction. He turns to athletics for his illustration, probably to emphasize the contrast between manly exercise and *old wives'* tales. There is a further comparison between physical and spiritual discipline. The apostle admits a place for the former but sets a strict limit upon its exercise. It profits only a *little*. Spiritual training on the other hand is profitable *unto all things*, or better 'in all directions' (Moffatt). Its range is immeasurably greater for it embraces not only this life but the life to come. The *promise* of *life* is not an equivalent for worldly prosperity, but sums up the blessedness of godliness. Irrespective of his present earthly circumstances, a Christian may fairly be said to have the best of both worlds.

9, 10. There is some doubt whether the *faithful saying* formula of verse 9 relates to the statement in verse 8 about godliness, or to the following statement giving the reason for our present toil. Many commentators prefer the former alternative because verse 8 sounds more like a proverbial saying than verse 10, and because the conjunction *for* (*gar*) gives the reason for the worthiness of the saying. Yet the subject matter of verse 10 is more theologically weighty than verse 8 and would therefore be admirably adapted for current catechetical purposes, while the use of the conjunction is by no means conclusive since a parallel occurs in 2 Tim. ii. 11, where the same conjunction forms part of the saying. It seems preferable, therefore, to connect the formula to the subsequent verse.

The word *kopiaō* rendered *labour* suggests strenuous toil, and is used by Paul in Phil. ii. 16 to describe athletic fatigue. The idea is therefore a continuation of the metaphor in verses 7 and 8. The reading of the AV *and suffer reproach* (*oneidizometha*) is probably incorrect. The alternative reading *agonizometha*, 'and strive', not only has the weightier manuscript support, but also accords better with the context. This race of godliness demands every ounce of energy a man possesses.

The reason given for this perpetual striving is the constancy of the believer's hope. The Greek *ēlpikamen* means more than *trust*. The perfect tense implies a continuous state of hope, i.e. 'because we have fixed our hope'. The ground of hope (*epi* with the dative) is given as *the living God, who is the Saviour of all men*, in which expression *Saviour* must be understood in its common meaning of 'Preserver', although, as Simpson points out, 'Christianity raises the word to a higher plane'. In fact the last part of verse 10, which singles out believers as special objects of God's saving power, suggests that the word *Saviour* is here used in a double sense, so much so that Easton considers these words are 'by no means a graceful addition' to the original citation. But there is a clear development in the thought, since the believer's special confidence in God is reinforced by the knowledge that the divine mercy is universal in its scope (cf. ii. 3, 4).

11, 12. The next injunctions are more directly concerned with Timothy himself. There is to be a note of authority in Timothy's teaching, as *parangelle, command*, shows: and the apostle's purpose is clearly to inspire his timid representative to display such firmness. The reference to Timothy's youthfulness has led many scholars to imagine him as a mere stripling, but *neotēs* may indicate any age up to forty years old (Lock). It must therefore be regarded relatively. Many of the Ephesian Christians, and especially the elders, were almost certainly of maturer years; and if for some time they had served under the leadership of the veteran missionary apostle Paul, it is by no means inconceivable that some would look with disfavour and contempt on the younger Timothy. As a counter-balance to contempt Timothy is to live in an exemplary manner (for the use of the same word *tupos* for Paul's own ethical example, cf. Phil. iii. 17; 2 Thes. iii. 9). 'Although a young man, he was to excel in those very qualities in which youth is wont to be deficient—gravity, prudence, consideration for others, trustworthiness, mastery over the passions' (Scott). In this way it would become evident to the believers that in Christianity authority is contingent upon character and not age. Every young man called to the ministry or to any position of authority in the Church would do well to heed Paul's fivefold enumeration. The words *in spirit* of the AV should be deleted, for they have very slight MS support and are clearly an interpolation. *In word* and *in conversation* (*anastrophē*, 'behaviour') apply to Timothy's public life, while the other three are concerned with inner qualities which nevertheless have a public manifestation.

13. The three pursuits to which Timothy is bidden to devote himself until the apostle's arrival are concerned with his public ministry, although the verb *prosechō* (*give attendance*) implies previous preparation in private. *Reading* is generally understood as 'reading aloud' to the people under his charge, and there is little doubt that the reading of the Old Testament is here in mind. The Church carried on this synagogue practice and made it a basic element of Christian worship. As in the synagogue so in the Church, the reading of Scripture was followed by an *exhortation* (*paraklēsis*) based upon it, but in Christian worship a special place was reserved for *doctrine* (*didaskalia*) which consisted of instruction in the great truths of the Christian faith.

14. *The gift* (*charisma*) which Timothy must not *neglect* appears to be the spiritual equipment received at the time of ordination (cf. Calvin). This use is thoroughly Pauline and draws attention to the most primitive stage in Church development, when charismatic ministry was of greater importance than official positions. Scott unsuccessfully attempts to circumscribe this evidence of early tradition by maintaining that *charisma* here means 'office' and not 'gift'. Although the word 'gift' draws attention to the part played by the Holy Spirit in Timothy's ministry, the exhortation not to neglect it brings out equally emphatically the human responsibility. God's gifts, like the talent, must never be left unused.

There were two distinct yet complementary confirmations of Timothy's commission. The first, *prophecy*, has already been mentioned in i. 18, where it refers to some prophetical indication of Timothy's call, and undoubtedly it must be here understood in the same sense. This was accompanied by an outward indication in *the laying on of the hands of the presbytery*. No difficulty need be entertained over the fact that in 2 Tim. i. 6 Paul speaks exclusively of his own part in such a ceremony, for there are two possible solutions: either the elders were associated with Paul in the ceremony, and are specifically mentioned here to draw attention to the corporate attestation of Timothy's commission; or else the two references to laying on of hands may refer to different occasions (cf. White). The former, on the whole, seems the more likely explanation. The idea of the impartation of the gift of the Spirit through the laying on of hands is frequently found in the Acts (e.g. viii. 17, ix. 17, xix. 6), and provides a significant object lesson in the divine-human co-operation in the early Church.

15, 16. The methods by which the gift may be nurtured are carefully delineated. The first requisite is either to 'practise' or to *meditate* (*meletaō* can mean either). If the former, which has the support of general Greek usage, is the meaning, the athletic metaphor must still be in the writer's mind; but the latter sense is perhaps more suited to the context, since *these things*, relating to verse 13, would need to be constantly in Timothy's mind. Whichever was Paul's intention, it is clear that Timothy is to become so closely acquainted with these injunctions that they become second nature to him. He is to *give* himself *wholly to them* (*en toutois isthi*, 'be in them', a construction expressing absorption in anything), a fitting reminder of the exacting nature of the Christian calling. The mind is to be as immersed in these pursuits as the body in the air it breathes.

The Christian minister's 'progress' (*prokopē*) as on a journey (AV wrongly *profiting*) is under public observation (note the significance of the *all*) and for that reason demands most careful thought. Timothy is to ensure that what most impresses other people is his true Christian development, and not some lesser thing such as brilliance of exposition or attractiveness of personality.

It is significant that in the next injunction the teacher and his teaching are intimately linked. He must first *take heed*, i.e. keep a strict eye on himself, and then on his teaching. Moral and spiritual rectitude is an indispensable preliminary to doctrinal orthodoxy. Timothy must also have continually in mind either the advice just given, or the more general injunctions of the letter, according to the interpretation given to the words *in them*.

In following out the previous advice Timothy will achieve a double purpose. He will not only be working out his own salvation (in the sense of Phil. ii. 12), but will also be assisting others to do the same. The danger of neglecting one's own salvation is greater in the Christian minister than in others, and even the apostle Paul himself could fear lest he became a castaway after preaching to others (1 Cor. ix. 27). Calvin suggestively comments that although salvation is God's gift alone, yet human ministry is needed, as is here implied.

III. DISCIPLINE AND RESPONSIBILITY
(v. 1—vi. 2)

Almost the whole of the remainder of the Epistle contains specific directions to Timothy to assist him in dealing with various classes of people within the Church. It may seem surprising that so much attention is given to the problem of widows, but no doubt this was a constant source of anxiety in the early Church as Acts vi shows. Since they were recipients of the Church's bounty it was fitting that careful regulations should govern their selection.

(a) Various age groups (v. 1, 2)

1, 2. The term *elder* (*presbuteros*) used here applies not to the Church officials of that name, but to older members of the congregation. The verb *epiplēssō*, used for *rebuke*, is a strong one meaning 'censure severely', and those advanced in years should be spared such treatment. If correction is necessary Timothy is to *intreat*, or, as RV, 'exhort' (*parakaleō*). The same applies to older women. Towards the younger members there must be true fraternity, but a special word, *with all purity* (*hagneia*), is added to safeguard Timothy's relations with the younger women.

(b) Widows (v. 3-16)

(i) Widows in need (v. 3-8). *Honour* (*timaō*) appears to convey not only the normal idea of respect, but also of material support (cf. Mt. xv. 5) in view of the subsequent passage. Easton points out the graceful character of this word. 'Treat poverty not as something contemptible but as deserving honour'. *Widows indeed* means widows with no other means of support, i.e. genuinely destitute. It was a Christian duty to care for these.

4. The apostle makes it quite clear that where widows have close relatives, these relatives must relieve the Church of the responsibility to support them. The expression translated *requite*, *apodidonai amoibas*, means to make a worthy requital (cf. M & M). Such an essentially practical procedure is nevertheless linked with spiritual example, since to *shew piety* implies a religious attitude towards God. *Ekgona* translated *nephews* is a general term denoting 'descendants' and would be better rendered 'grand-children', while the word *progonoi*, *parents*, is equally general for 'progenitors'. Responsibility for parents, which is carried over to the second and even third generations, has the divine endorsement. It *is acceptable before God* in view of the fifth commandment (cf. 1 Tim. ii. 3). *Let them learn* may refer to widows or to their descendants, but the context favours the latter.

5–8. The characteristics of a true widow are next specified. (a) She is *desolate* (*memonōmenē*, 'left entirely alone'); (b) she *trusteth in God* (*ēlpiken*, lit. 'has fixed her hope in the direction of God'), which distinguishes her from non-Christian widows; (c) she is a woman of constant prayer, the expression found here being strongly reminiscent of Anna (Lk. ii. 37), while the tense as well as the meaning of the word *continueth* (*prosmenō*) serves to emphasize a prevalent attitude rather than a series of definite actions.

In the contemporary world many widows were tempted to resort to immoral living as a means of support, and that is probably in the apostle's mind when he uses the verb *spatalaō* (*liveth in pleasure*). Moffatt paraphrases it as 'plunges into dissipation'. To be dead while still living is a thoroughly Pauline paradox (cf. Rom. vii. 10, 24), and Timothy is here reminded that widows supporting themselves illicitly are attempting to support what is already dead ('a religious corpse'—Simpson). Such people have clearly no claim on the Church's care.

These things which Timothy is to *give in charge*, i.e. 'command', must refer to the responsibility of children to support their forbears (verse 4), and the responsibility of widows to fulfil the requirements mentioned in verse 5. By so doing he would assist them to be irreproachable (*anepilēmptos*; cf. iii. 2).

Provision for one's *own* relatives and especially for one's *own house* (probably referring to one's immediate family circle) is an indisputable Christian duty. To deny this is to deny the essence of the Christian *faith* and puts one in a worse position than an *infidel* who in the contemporary world generally acknowledged his obligation to parents (cf. Scott). It was unthinkable that Christian morality should lag behind general pagan standards.

(ii) **Widows as Christian workers** (**v. 9, 10**). Whether there was at this time a distinct order of widows performing functions among women members, comparable to those of the elders, is a much disputed question (cf. comment on iii. 11). While the following passage clearly points to some kind of register with a specific age qualification, there is not sufficient data to conclude for an 'order of widows' as Bernard does.

9, 10. The proviso of so high an age as sixty presents a difficulty as to whether *widow* should be understood in the same sense as in verses 3–8 (i.e. of genuinely destitute Christian widows) or in the sense of widows belonging to an order. In the former case it is inconceivable that the Church would set an arbitrary age in dispensing help to destitute widows, while in the latter case it is difficult to believe the entry age to an official ecclesiastical order would be as high as sixty, in the contemporary world a relatively more advanced age than in our own. It seems preferable, therefore, to suppose that special duties in the Church were reserved for some of the old widows receiving aid, and some official recognition of this fact was given. Although the verb *katalegō*, translated *taken into the number*, is used in Greek literature of the enrolment of soldiers, it can also mean 'reckon', a sense which would support the explanation given above.

In addition to the age-restriction there are two further requirements. (a) The widow must be *the wife of one man*, which can only mean that she has not remarried after her husband's death; (b) she must also be well reported for her conduct in the home and elsewhere. The order in which the *good works* are mentioned is significant: child-care ranks first, hospitality next, humble service towards fellow-believers third, and general sympathy and benevolence fourth. All these *good works* are not only essentially practical, but are even commonplace in character. A Christian woman well versed in these would be of inestimable value in caring for orphans, entertaining visiting Christians, attending to the many practical details, some very menial, such as feet-washing (a reminiscence of the Lord's own action, Jn. xiii. 1–7) and visitation work among needy people. Moreover, the widow to be chosen must have *diligently followed* these pursuits.

(iii) Younger widows (v. 11–16). *Younger widows*, who would presumably be eligible for relief when in genuine distress, are not, however, to be allowed to discharge any official function, because of the strong possibility of re-marriage. The word *katastrēniazō, wax wanton against,* occurs only here in the New Testament and suggests the metaphor of young oxen trying to escape from the yoke. The younger widows would not wish to be tied to Church duties if further opportunity came for marriage. That some official functions must here be meant is evident from the fact that the wanton-ness is regarded as directed *against Christ* Himself, by which the apostle implies that any widow who has undertaken special Church duties would be disloyal to Christ if she ever wished to marry.

12. *Damnation* is rather too strong a translation of *krima* which denotes 'judgment'. The meaning is that the widows who forsook their sacred obligations in order to marry would be deserving of censure, for such action would amount to casting aside (*atheteō,* 'to regard as void') their *first faith,* i.e. their pledge of service.

13. An awkward Greek construction makes the meaning of the first part of this verse uncertain. If *they learn to be idle* is the correct interpretation, the idea seems to be that such widows, having disregarded their pledge, become increasingly idle. Another possible interpretation is that 'they learn by idleness', but this does not seem to fit the context so well. The use of the verb to *learn* disproves any suggestion that the idleness comes on unconsciously. The idleness produced two unpleasant fruits. The widows were *wandering* (RSV 'gadding') *about from house to house,* which may mean that younger widows were misusing their opportunities in visitation, an interpretation borne out in the second result—that they become 'tale-bearers and scandal-mongers, saying indecent things' (Easton). The phrase *speaking things which they ought not* may however mean that they gossip about private matters and cannot be trusted with confidences. It is not particularly evident, at first sight, why the younger widows would be more susceptible to this danger than the older, but the apostle clearly thinks that women of maturer years would be the less liable to gossip.

14. In order to avoid such problems the apostle urges the *younger women* to marry. As this is clearly a continuation of the preceding section as *therefore* shows, it must apply to widows and not young women generally. No contradiction with 1 Cor. vii. 25 f., where Paul states a definite preference for the unmarried state, need be supposed, for the widows under review are those whom he would class as 'incontinent'.

Rather than become idle scandal-mongers these women should devote themselves to the bearing of children and the managing of homes (*guide the house*, but *oikodespoteō* means properly 'to rule a household'). This common-sense advice is in striking contrast to the rage for celibacy which developed in the later history of the Church. The apostle is once again most anxious that unnecessary reproach from any non-Christian opponent should be avoided. The word *occasion* (*aphormē*) is a military term for 'a base of operations', a favourite Pauline metaphor (cf. Rom. vii. 8, 11; 2 Cor. v. 12, xi. 12 and Gal. v. 13).

15. The apostle's injunctions to strict discipline are occasioned by the example of some who have already *turned aside* from their true course and have followed *after Satan*, by which is probably meant 'given themselves to immoral conduct'.

16. Some difficulty arises here over the Greek text for the best attested reading has 'If any woman believer has widows', but the alternative reading *any man or woman* would seem to accord better with the sense, for it is difficult to believe that the exhortation to relieve the Church of its responsibility to care for widows would be confined to women. The verse is closely parallel to verses 4 and 8 but Paul is here particularly concerned with widows not eligible to be enrolled.

(c) Elders (v. 17–20)

17. Attention is next focused on the officials of the Church with special advice about their remuneration. There is no doubt that *honour* (*timē*) should be understood in this sense, in view of verse 18. The adjective descriptive of this honour, *double*, would appear to have the sense of ample or generous provision, but this would depend on their efficiency, as the adverb *well* indicates. It has been suggested that *double* refers to both age and office, or that it shows an advance on the honour due to widows; but the interpretation adopted seems preferable. The word for *rule* (*proistēmi*) means general superintendence, and describes the duties allotted to all presbyters. But special consideration is due to those who *labour in the word and doctrine*, i.e. preach and teach, suggesting a special class within the presbyterate.

18. The proposition is supported by two citations linked together under the formula *For the scripture saith*, precisely in the Pauline manner (cf. Rom. iv. 3, xi. 2; Gal. iv. 30, etc.). The first citation is from Dt. xxv. 4, and the second is exactly paralleled by Lk. x. 7, where the words are attributed to Jesus. The same passage from Deuteronomy is cited by Paul in 1 Cor. ix. 9 under the caption, 'For it is written in the law of Moses'. With this the apostle links the Lord's command (1 Cor. ix. 14), but does not as here cite His words. The two sayings were evidently closely associated in the apostle's mind, and there is no need to suppose that he is quoting from the canonical Gospel, although that cannot be entirely ruled out. He may be citing from a collection of the words of Jesus, and if so it is clear that such a collection was placed on an equality with the Old Testament, at least as far as the authority of each was concerned. To the apostle the words of Christ would naturally assume an importance proportionate to his conception of Christ's Person. It cannot be maintained, on the contrary, that both Jesus and Paul cite from a current proverb, for Jesus did not describe it as such and Paul here classes it as Scripture, which he could never have confused with a proverbial saying. Scholars who maintain the non-Pauline authorship of the Pastorals claim that their position presents less difficulty, for the later writer might actually be using Luke's Gospel (cf. Scott), which could not be said of Paul if the prevailing estimate of the date of Luke's Gospel is correct (i.e. A.D. 80–85).

Whatever the apostle is here citing, he intends Timothy to understand that a divine sanction underlies the principle of fair provision for those who serve the Church. Too often a niggardly attitude has been maintained towards faithful men who have laboured for Christ in the interest of others. The apostle has already deplored money-grubbing (iii. 3), but he equally deplores inadequate remuneration. If God ordained ample provision for oxen treading out corn, it is incumbent upon Christian communities to see that those who devote time and energy to their service are adequately rewarded.

19, 20. It was of utmost importance to safeguard innocent men from false accusation, and as Jewish law required the agreement of two witnesses before a man might be called upon to answer a charge (cf. Dt. xix. 15) so it must be in the Church (cf. Mt. xviii. 16; 2 Cor. xiii. 1), especially when *an elder* is implicated. He must be protected against malicious intent; but if there are real grounds for accusation, then disciplinary action should be taken before the whole Church (unless *all* here means all the elders). Such action could not fail to have a salutary effect upon the community (*that others also may fear*) by drawing attention to the need for Christian purity. The abuse of discipline has often led to a harsh and intolerant spirit, but neglect of it has proved a danger almost as great. When faced with sinning elders a spineless attitude is deplorable.

(d) Timothy's own behaviour (v. 21–25)

21. The sudden and solemn charge delivered to Timothy

at this juncture throws a flood of light on the young man's character. He needs stiffening up and the apostle finds it necessary to use a strong expression—*I charge thee* (*diamarturomai*, 'solemnly protest') *before God, and the Lord Jesus Christ, and the elect angels.* A similar adjuration is used in 2 Tim. iv. 1, but without reference to angels. The mention of these *elect angels* is surprising, but may be due to the belief that they are commissioned to watch over men's affairs. There may also be an eschatological reason, reminiscent of the Lord's words in Lk. ix. 26. The same phrase occurs in the apocalyptic book of Enoch xxxix. 1.

These things, that Timothy must *observe,* are all the careful instructions already given. RSV suggestively translates 'keep these rules'. In so doing Timothy must be both unprejudiced and impartial, never allowing personal inclination to bias his judgment.

22. There is difference of opinion whether the ordination ceremony is here in view, or the restoration of penitents after due discipline. Easton objects to the former on the grounds that Timothy would not alone be responsible for the ordination of elders (cf. iv. 14), yet the directive given to Timothy may be intended also for the elders. If he presided it would fall to his lot to exercise restraint. Such an interpretation certainly suits the context better if the whole section from verse 19 onwards concerns elders, but there is much support for the contrary opinion. The second half of this verse, *neither be partaker of other men's sins* seems to mean that whoever lays hands upon an unworthy man must take responsibility for the man's sins. It is difficult to believe, however, that this could apply generally to penitents, although it would have some relevance to penitent elders. It seems preferable, therefore, to take the act of laying on of hands in the sense of setting apart for specific service, as elsewhere in the Pastorals (cf. 2 Tim. i. 6). Undue haste in Christian appointments has not infrequently led to unworthy men bringing havoc to the cause of Christ.

The rather abrupt personal charge to Timothy, *keep thyself pure*, must primarily be understood in the general sense of honourable and upright behaviour. It is as if the apostle had said—make sure you appoint 'pure' men and keep yourself 'pure' in the process.

23. Expositors who look for some close connection between this verse and the preceding are faced with a knotty problem, but the solution might lie in the precise meaning of 'pure' in verse 22. It may be that the apostle feared lest his injunction 'keep yourself pure' might be interpreted too rigidly as an exhortation to ascetic practices, and he wished to make clear that 'purity' was not synonymous with abstention. Possibly Timothy was naturally inclined towards asceticism. On the other hand there may be no connection with the previous verse intended, and this advice may be interjected because the apostle calls to mind Timothy's weak health, and thinks it helpful to draw attention to the medicinal value of wine.

Drink no longer water means not that Timothy is to abstain altogether from water-drinking, but is to cease from doing so exclusively. It may be that contaminated water had contributed to Timothy's indigestion and so the apostle suggests a remedy. The verse shows Timothy to be a man of delicate health, and is one of those incidental touches which help the modern reader to feel greater sympathy with him. It is an intimate touch quite natural to the apostle when writing to a close associate, but strange indeed if written by a later pseudonymous writer.

24, 25. It is best to regard verse 23 as parenthetical and to make these last two verses resume the thought of verse 22. A distinction is drawn between men whose sins are clearly evident (*prodēlos*, not *open beforehand*) and those whose sins are not immediately apparent but who will ultimately be pursued by them (*they follow after*). The *judgment* could be the estimate of Timothy and his associates, but more probably the judgment of God is in mind. This seems even clearer from verse 25 where conspicuous and concealed good works are set side by side, the latter, however, ultimately becoming known. These parallel observations, viewing human potentialities both negatively and positively, bring out forcibly the complexities involved in selecting suitable candidates for God's work. Hasty action relies on first impressions, but these impressions are often deceptive. Unworthy men might be chosen, whose moral culpability lies deeper than the surface; and worthy men, whose good actions are not in the limelight, might easily be overlooked. The whole situation demands extreme caution.

(e) **Servants and masters (vi. 1, 2)**

In communities where the membership included numerous slaves together with some of their masters, the relationship between them was a pressing problem. Slaves enjoyed equality of status within the Church, but a decided social inferiority in their respective households, an irreconcilable antithesis which found its only solution in the ultimate abolition of slavery. But since the time was unpropitious for overturning this deeply rooted system, interim Christian rules were indispensable.

1. The apostle envisages two kinds of situation. In this verse Christian slaves (as *douloi* should be rendered rather than *servants*) who belong to non-Christian *masters* are in mind, while in verse 2 the *masters* are specified as *believing*. The resultant dangers in each case differed. A Christian slave who had found liberty in Christ might be tempted to maintain less respect for his master than he ought, particularly if the latter were harsh and tyrannical. But in such circumstances the cause of Christ is served best by an attitude of respect.

Servants . . . under the yoke is not pleonastic, but draws attention to the non-Christian approach to slaves who were regarded as little more than cattle. The expression strongly brings into focus the servile social conditions of the contemporary world. In such conditions it was more important where possible to avoid reproach against *the name of God and his doctrine* (i.e. the Christian faith) than to make an abortive revolutionary attempt to undermine the social structure.

2. A danger to which Christian slaves with believing masters were particularly exposed was to neglect their obligations. They must not *despise* masters whose discipline has become less taxing, because it has been tempered by the love of Christ, and because they are prepared to regard their own slaves as *brethren* for Christ's sake. Rather should the slaves render better *service* to such masters in return for the better treatment received. The *partakers of the benefit* may refer to the masters or the slaves. The grammatical construction favours the former, in which case the reference is to the advantage gained by the master in the increase of the slave's goodwill. To apply the phrase to slaves would mean that they reap the benefit of having a master *faithful and beloved.* Perhaps the ambiguity was intentional to remind both masters and slaves that the *benefit* which would accrue if both were 'faithful and beloved' was mutual.

IV. MISCELLANEOUS INJUNCTIONS (vi. 3–21)

The concluding portion of the Epistle contains no clear sequence of thought, and it is best therefore to deal with it in self-contained sections. There are further reflections about false teachers, and two separate passages dealing with wealth enclosing a personal note to Timothy, concluded by a majestic doxology. The letter then ends with another exhortation telling Timothy how to deal with the heresy, almost like a postscript adding weight to what has already been given in the earlier part of the letter.

(a) More about false teachers (vi. 3–5)

3. The words *these things teach and exhort*, which in the AV are attached to the end of verse 2, could refer to what precedes, but seem more illuminative when regarded as introductory to what follows (as RSV). Timothy is to stand out in obvious contrast to those who *teach otherwise* (the same word *heterodidas-kaleō* as in i. 3). The *things* intended are probably all the subjects mentioned in the Epistle.

The verb *proserchomai* translated *consent* (a meaning for which no parallel exists) literally means 'approach'.with the derived sense of 'attaching oneself to' (cf. Simpson's lexigraphical discussion). The true teacher is to adhere to *wholesome words* (cf. i. 10), which are further defined as *the words of our Lord Jesus Christ*. But the definition may itself be understood in two ways: (a) it may refer to the sayings of Jesus, or (b) it may indicate words about Jesus, descriptive of Christian truth. The latter is more in keeping with the context and with the general usage in the Pastorals. It is further supported by its connection with the concluding clause, i.e. *doctrine which is according to godliness*, although this could also apply to some sayings of Jesus to bring out their essential contrast to the ungodliness characteristic of the false teaching. Spicq, who considers that Luke's Gospel is here meant, cites Schlatter's opinion that it is difficult to believe that Paul could so speak of the words of Jesus if no Gospel existed in the community, Acts xx. 35 furnishing an illuminating parallel.

4, 5. The description of a teacher throws revealing light on the nature of his teaching, a principle applying as much to true as to false doctrine. The characteristic of these false teachers make an unenviable list. For a comment on *tetuphōtai, proud*, see iii. 6. The true state of these puffed-up teachers is nothing short of abysmal ignorance, as the apostle points out.

The next words are not easy to represent clearly in English. *Doting* seems too strong to render *noseō*, which literally means 'to be sick' and is obviously intended as a pointed contrast to the 'healthy' words of verse 3. Controversies and arguments (*questions and strifes of words*) have impaired their mental health to such a degree that they have become diseased. Easton's 'having a morbid craving for arguments' probably catches the true meaning. This is a noteworthy example of the processes by which intellectual wrangling so often ends in moral deterioration.

All the evil results mentioned are mental activities, with some discernible progression, for dissension is bound to follow *envy*. In fact, on every occasion except one where *eris*, the Greek word here rendered *strife*, is used in the New

Testament, it is conjoined with a word for *envy* (three times with *phthonos* as here and elsewhere with *zēlos*). It is significant that Paul alone uses *eris* and includes it in all his lists of the works of unrighteousness. *Railings*, i.e. slander, and *evil surmisings* are inevitable concomitants, while *perverse disputings*, i.e. mutual irritations, are inseparable from 'men depraved in mind' (Moffatt): for when reason is morally blinded, all correctives to unworthy behaviour are banished, and the mind becomes *destitute* (RV 'bereft') *of the truth*. The concluding clause should read 'supposing that godliness is a way of gain', or as Moffatt translates it, 'they imagine religion is a paying concern'. But true godliness must never be commercialized for it is a matter of the heart and not the pocket. Whether the meaning is that these false teachers charged high fees for their specious teachings, or used their garrulous religious profession as a cloak for material advancement is not clear. The reading *from such withdraw thyself* has less weighty MS support than that which omits the words (as in RV).

(b) The perils of wealth (vi. 6–10)

Because money was a chief concern of the false teachers the apostle proceeds to deal with some of its dangers and lays down principles of universal significance.

6. The dictum of the false teachers is first of all admitted, yet with an all-important proviso. The notion of self-mastery inherent in the word *autarkeia* translated *contentment* is singularly Pauline (the noun occurs elsewhere only in 2 Cor. ix. 8 and the adjective in Phil. iv. 11). Godliness will only be true *gain* when independent of circumstances, and the apostle himself provides an admirable pattern of this in Phil. iv. 11. To the Stoic notion of self-mastery Christianity brings the essential quality of a contented mind.

7, 8. The thought contained in verse 7 has many parallels both biblical and classical and is cited here as axiomatic (cf. Jb i. 21; Ec. v. 15). The wording in the AV does not precisely represent the best supported Greek reading, which requires the rendering 'because (*hoti*) we can take nothing out', but it does give what appears to be the true sense. The veracity of the first part of the verse does not seem to depend on the truth of the second clause as would be the case if the reading 'because' be maintained. Rather does the apostle wish to point out that material possessions are equally irrelevant at our entrance into and our exit from the world. Yet it may be that the correct reading shows that the controlling factor is exit rather than entry. Such a thought would emphasize more strongly the transitory character of life's journey (cf. Spicq).

Verse 8 gives a definition of Christian contentment. If we have no more than the bare necessities such as *food and raiment* (*skepasma*, lit. 'covering material', which may represent shelter as well as clothes) contentment should result. Stoic parallels to this idea are cited by Lock, and it is not inconceivable that the words echo a current proverb. They provide a timely reminder of the futility of the mere pursuit of wealth.

9. Strong words are used in the description of those whose desires are set upon the acquisition of wealth. The words apply to all whose aims are controlled by the passion to increase material possessions, yet there is here no condemnation of such possessions in themselves. The apostle is not so much thinking of those already rich, as of those ever grasping to become so. On the two other occasions in the Pastorals where *snare* is used, it is described as the devil's, and this is suggested here by its close association with *temptation*. Three clear steps of decline are discernible, first the lure, then the lust, and finally the total moral ruin. The verb *buthizo* (*drown*) vividly represents the desire for wealth as a personal monster, which plunges its victim into an ocean of complete destruction (both *olethros*, *destruction*, and *apoleia*, *perdition*, probably in the sense of ruin, suggest irretrievable loss).

10. A well-known maxim is next quoted to justify the strong language just used. The Greek does not contain an article before *root*, and it is therefore a problem to decide the correct meaning. Even without the article the position of the words in the Greek throws emphasis on *root*, and parallels could be found to justify the article in English. This makes the expression more sweeping, but the apostle's mind is so absorbed with the snares of riches that he addresses himself to extreme cases. Certainly for those mentioned in verse 9 the root of all their evils was *love of money*, but it must not be deduced from this that love of money is the sole root of all evils, for the New Testament does not support this. Such graspers have been led to take a wrong turning (*they have erred from the faith*) and the Greek passive, *apeplanēthēsan* (lit. 'were led astray') suggests that they are helpless dupes in the grip of a merciless deception. At the same time the process of piercing is laid to their own charge for they *pierced themselves through* with self-inflicted pangs of disillusionment.

(c) A charge to a man of God (vi. 11–16)

11. The apostle addresses Timothy as a *man of God* in striking contrast to the previous description of a man of material desire (*thou, su,* is emphatic). Yet the things which Timothy is to *flee* must be given a wider connotation than the dangers of wealth. There is probably an extended reference to all the vices mentioned from verse 4 onwards.

The antithesis in the words *flee . . . follow after* is in the characteristic manner of Paul. It is repeated exactly in 2 Tim. ii. 22. Of the objects of pursuit the first two describe a general religious disposition, *righteousness* being used in its widest sense of conformity to what is right towards both God and man, and *godliness* of general piety. This double pursuit is also found in Tit. ii. 12. The two following virtues, *faith* and *love*, are fundamental to Christianity and cardinal in Paul's teaching. Scott supposes a difference from Pauline usage, because for the apostle *faith* and *love* are all-inclusive not needing to be linked with other virtues. But Gal. v. 22 provides a sufficient answer to such a criticism, since there the same two virtues are linked with other virtues similar to those mentioned here.

The concluding virtue, *meekness*, denotes 'gentleness of feeling' (*praüpatheia*), a rarer quality than *patience*, but a precious target for the man of God.

12. The command to *fight* (*agōnizō*, lit. 'to contend for a prize') is generally supposed to be an allusion to the Olympic Games and this seems supported by the cognate use of the noun *agōn*. White thinks the expression had by now become stereotyped as an athletic metaphor, but Simpson claims that a military meaning is also present. Whether in contest or in conflict, the verb implies a disciplined struggle (cf. Col. i. 29), and its tense shows that the striving is a continuous process. Timothy is to carry on a struggle already begun, but the following verb (*epilabou*, *lay hold on*) denotes a single complete event. This thought does not exclude the idea of *eternal life* as a present possession in the Johannine sense, but points to its perfect appropriation.

The *good profession* (better 'confession' as in verse 13 where *homologia* is again used) is taken by most commentators to refer to Timothy's baptism, although some have seen an allusion to ordination, but the close link with the quest for eternal life suits the former occasion better than the latter.

13. Timothy's own confession is compared with Christ's before Pilate, and a solemn charge is delivered, conditioned by the character of the witnesses (i.e. the quickening God and the confessing Christ). The reason for describing God in this context as the God *who quickeneth all things* is to bring out the ever-present character of the divine witness. The notion of Christ as a witness is more characteristic of the Johannine writings (cf. Rev. i. 5 and Jn. xviii. 37) than Paul's, but the latter often invokes God as witness (cf. Rom. i. 9; 2 Cor. i. 23; Phil. i. 8; 1 Thes. ii. 5, 10).

14. *The commandment* which Timothy is urged to keep spotless is probably Timothy's baptismal commission. It may, however, refer to the charge in verses 11 and 12, which is invested with sufficient solemnity to be termed a *commandment*. This latter seems more in keeping with the context especially if Meinertz's view that verses 12, 13 refer to ordination is correct. It is strange to find such words as *without spot* and *unrebukeable* applied to a *commandment* and some scholars therefore construe it with the subject of the verb (i.e. Timothy), but this latter suggestion involves an awkward Greek construction. Nevertheless the context seems to demand the application of the words to Timothy himself and it is preferable to understand them in this way.

There is a distant forward look in this verse, which may mean that the coming (*epiphaneia*) of Christ was no longer considered imminent. The coming is envisaged as a definite historical event still in the future (cf. 1 Thes. iii. 13, v. 23; 1 Cor. i. 8; Phil. ii. 15, 16 for the Pauline idea of blamelessness at the coming of Christ, or in the day of Christ).

15, 16. It is not unlike Paul to launch suddenly into a magnificent doxology, but some (e.g. Scott) have questioned whether the doxology itself is not more like a Christian hymn than a spontaneous Pauline production. The titles used of God cannot be precisely paralleled from Paul's writings, while the ascription of the adjective *blessed* to God is exclusive to the Pastorals in biblical Greek, although Hellenic parallels exist (see note on i. 11).

Lock suggests that this doxology may be reminiscent of a formula in use in synagogue worship because of its strong Jewish flavour. If so it may well have been a doxology which sprang readily to the lips of the apostle when his mind was centred on God's sovereign disposition of the events of time. The word *Potentate* (*dunastēs*) in contemporary usage meant a prince or a chieftain as distinct from a king exercising sovereignty in his own power. But the description *only* makes clear that the apostle was not referring to a delegated authority (which in God is inconceivable), but a unique and princely dignity. The title *dunastēs* is applied to God in Ecclesiasticus and 2 Maccabees, but in the New Testament it is found elsewhere only in the Lucan writings (Lk. i. 52; Acts viii. 27) where it applies to human officials.

In the Apocalypse (xvii. 14, xix. 16) the double title *King of kings, and Lord of lords* is twice used of Christ, which suggests that it was probably an accepted Christian ascription. There are parallels in the Old Testament (Dt. x. 17; Ps. cxxxvi. 3; Dn. iv. 34, LXX) and in the Apocrypha (2 Macc. xiii. 4).

Already in i. 17 *immortality (athanasia)* is ascribed to God, although there the adjective *aphthartos* is used. Both words are found in parallel clauses in 1 Cor. xv. 53, 54 with apparently no difference of meaning. The expression *who only hath immortality* does not deny it to any other, but brings out the uniqueness of the divine immortality in that God alone inherently possesses it, being Himself the source of all life. Linked with this characteristic of eternity are two qualities which equally distinguish God from all others, His transcendence (*dwelling in the light which no man can approach unto*) and His invisibility (*whom no man hath seen, nor can see*). Undoubtedly the background of the apostle's thought is Exodus xxxiii. 17–23 which graphically portrays the awful majesty of God. The more usual conclusion of a doxology is an ascription of glory (*doxa*) to God, but here the words *honour* (*timē*) and *power* (*kratos*) are probably called forth by the present use of *Potentate*. Other Pauline uses of the word *kratos* in the sense of God's power are found in Eph. i. 19, vi. 10 and Col. i. 11.

(d) Advice to wealthy men (vi. 17–19)

The preceding section was parenthetical for the theme of riches is now resumed, although with a different purpose. The earlier section concerned those aspiring to be rich, whereas this deals with those already rich. It should be noted that such digression is characteristic of Paul's style.

17. The approach to wealth is strikingly moderate. There is no suggestion of denunciation. Rich men must carefully avoid two perils: (a) loftiness of mind, and (b) too much dependence on wealth. Scott suggests that the parable of the man who built his house on the sand may lie beneath this warning. In face of the increase in materialism the reminder of the uncertainty of riches is apposite to our modern age. To many the advent of the Welfare State may provide a parallel danger to trust in material security instead of in God, the Giver of all things. These words would incidentally provide an answer to excessive abstinence, for if God has ordained everything for enjoyment (*who giveth us richly all things to enjoy*) the ascetic approach cannot be right.

18, 19. Positive and practical demands are made upon rich men. Their actions are to be characterized by goodness and generosity, both of which are described actively and passively. They are to *do good* and to *be rich in good works*. They are, further, to be generous and to share with others.

Because of the mixture of metaphors involved in *laying up in store . . . a foundation*, some scholars prefer the suggested emendation of the text, translated by Moffatt 'amassing right good treasure' (reading *thēma lian* for *themelion*). But because the emendation not only lacks any MS support but also involves an awkward and unusual Greek construction, it is better to assume a mixture of metaphors. The thought at least is clear, and is reminiscent of the words of Jesus (Mt. vi. 20 and Lk. xviii. 22).

The concluding clause (*that they may lay hold on eternal life*) is closely linked with the similar phrase in verse 12, but with an interesting variation. The Greek *tēs ontōs zōēs* must be rendered 'life which is life indeed' (as RV), bringing out vividly its contrast with life propped up by so uncertain a support as riches.

(e) Final admonition to Timothy (vi. 20, 21)

20. The Epistle closes with another exhortation urging Timothy to *keep* (or better, 'guard' as RV, the same verb *phulasso* being used as in v. 21) the faith as a fixed deposit, *parathēkē*, a word which occurs only here and in 2 Tim. i. 12, 14 in the New Testament. This deposit cannot be distinguished from the frequent objective use of the terms 'the faith', 'the commandment', etc., but its particular significance is found in the preciousness of what is to be guarded. It is like treasure deposited in a bank for safe keeping. The metaphor must not, of course, be pressed too far, for the minister of the gospel does not keep the 'deposit' from others, but encourages them to come and share in its precious secrets. Timothy is to guard the deposit by deliberately turning away (the same verb *ektrepomai* as is applied in i. 6 to the false teachers' defection from truth) from the false teaching, here described as *profane babblings* and *oppositions*. The meaning of the first expression is clear from parallels in the Pastorals (e.g. 1 Tim. iv. 7; 2 Tim. ii. 16), throughout which the futility of the false teachers' jargon is frequently stressed. The second word has occasioned much discussion because of Marcion's use of the term *antitheseis* as a title for his Gnostic speculations based on the alleged opposition between the Old Testament and the Christian gospel. Only scholars who date the Pastorals very late can claim that Marcion's work is here specifically referred to, but there is no evidence to show that Marcion was the first to use the word in this sense, nor is there sufficient support in the scattered references in the Pastorals to prove that Marcion's teaching is in mind. (For further discussion see the Introduction, pp. 34 ff).

The pseudonymous knowledge that Timothy must shun should be understood in the light of the profane babble and empty chatter of which the apostle has already spoken. The false teachers were claiming quite naturally that their teaching was the true *science* or knowledge (*gnōsis*), a characteristic certainly not confined to second-century gnosticism. It is evident in all the modern cults which claim an exclusive grasp of true 'knowledge'.

21. This parting shot at the false teachers significantly uses the same word *astocheō* (*have erred*) to describe their defection as was used at the beginning of the Epistle (i. 6).

The concluding benediction is interesting because *with you* is in the plural. This may mean that the Epistle was designed for others beside Timothy, although examples in the papyri of the plural used for individuals are not uncommon (cf. Moulton, *Expositor*, 6th Series, VII. 107). Both 2 Timothy and Titus close with the same plural greeting, while the conclusion to the Epistle to the Colossians furnishes an exact parallel from Paul's earlier letters.

II TIMOTHY: ANALYSIS

I. SALUTATION, i. 1, 2.

II. THANKSGIVING, i. 3–5.

III. ENCOURAGEMENT FROM EXPERIENCE, i. 6–14.
   (a) The gift of God, i. 6–10.
   (b) The testimony of Paul, i. 11, 12.
   (c) The charge to Timothy, i. 13, 14.

IV. PAUL AND HIS ASSOCIATES, i. 15—ii. 2.
   (a) The Asiatics, i. 15.
   (b) Onesiphorus, i. 16–18.
   (c) Timothy, ii. 1, 2.

V. DIRECTIONS TO TIMOTHY, ii. 3–26.
   (a) The basis of encouragement and exhortation, ii. 3–13.
      (i) Various examples, ii. 3–6.
      (ii) Further reminiscences, ii. 7–10.
      (iii) A Christian hymn, ii. 11–13.
   (b) Methods of dealing with false teachers, ii. 14–26.
      (i) Positive action: what to promote, ii. 14, 15.
      (ii) Negative action: what to shun, ii. 16–18.
      (iii) Ultimate certainties, ii. 19.
      (iv) Degrees of honour, ii. 20, 21.
      (v) The teacher's behaviour, ii. 22–26.

VI. PREDICTIONS OF THE LAST DAYS, iii. 1–9.

VII. FURTHER EXHORTATIONS TO TIMOTHY, iii. 10–17.
   (a) An historical reminder, iii. 10–12.
   (b) An exhortation to steadfastness, iii. 13–17.

VIII. PAUL'S FAREWELL MESSAGE, iv. 1–18.
   (a) The final charge, iv. 1–5.
   (b) A triumphant confession, iv. 6–8.
   (c) Some personal requests, iv. 9–13.
   (d) A particular warning, iv. 14, 15.
   (e) The first defence, iv. 16, 17.
   (f) The forward look, iv. 18.

IX. CONCLUDING SALUTATIONS, iv. 19–22.

I. SALUTATION (i. 1, 2)

1. As in the other Pastorals, Paul claims the title *apostle of Jesus Christ* (cf. note on 1 Tim. i. 1). The formal opening to this Epistle, although in conformity with ancient practice, seems rather stiff when addressed to Paul's closest associate. Easton, in fact, considers it unthinkable that Paul would use such solemn formality to his tried lieutenant, but he is clearly not informing Timothy of his apostleship or even reminding him. He can never forget the noble work to which he was so impressively called. The phrase *by the will of God* reflects Paul's deep consciousness of the divine purpose for his life, and springs from his constant wonder at the catastrophic encounter near the gates of Damascus.

Unlike the opening of 1 Timothy, the phrase *by the will of God* is here qualified by the words *according to the promise of life*, which give the purpose of Paul's apostleship. He is sent to proclaim a gospel of life, and Timothy is reminded at the commencement of this Epistle of the apostle's high calling.

The concluding words, *which is in Christ Jesus*, qualifying *life*, conceive of the Christian's life being centred in Christ, an idea reminiscent of Gal. ii. 20, where Paul says: 'I live, yet not I, but Christ liveth in me'. This use of the formula *in Christ* accords therefore with Pauline thought.

2. A greater intimacy is introduced in the description of Timothy as his *dearly beloved son*, and there can be no doubt that this young man was held in the most affectionate esteem by the great apostle. As in the salutation in 1 Timothy, *mercy* is added to the more usual *grace* and *peace* (cf. 1 Tim. i. 1).

II. THANKSGIVING (i. 3-5)

Here only in the Pastorals does Paul follow his frequent

procedure of including thanksgiving and intercession immediately after the salutation, a practice which had become an
accepted convention in contemporary letter-writing.

3. The same formula is used to denote thanks as in 1 Tim.
i. 12 (cf. note there), although it is not the usual Pauline
formula. The apostle mentions his service to the same God
as his ancestors, in order perhaps to draw attention to what
he is about to say concerning Timothy's own forbears. The
words *from my forefathers* must be understood to mean that Paul
thought of Judaism in such close connection with Christianity
that his present worship of God is in a sense a continuation of
his own Jewish worship. Although possessing such firm
convictions about the superseding of the Jewish law, he never
speaks of it with disrespect and sometimes even expresses
pride in its observance (cf. Rom. vii. 12; Phil. iii. 4–6).

This service must be carried out with a *pure conscience* (an
expression parallel to that occurring in 1 Tim. i. 5). As a Jew
the apostle would know that morality and worship and
service go hand in hand. When worshipping God the believer
must have no ulterior motives, his mind and purpose must
be untainted.

The Greek *hōs* is best rendered 'as without ceasing I remember you' rather than *that without ceasing*, which suggests
that the content of thanksgiving was his constancy of prayer.
But the meaning is that 'as often as' (so Lock) Paul remembered Timothy in his prayers he gave thanks. His constancy
in prayer for the Christian communities whom he served
may be amply illustrated from Paul's other letters (cf. Rom.
i. 9; Phil. i. 3; Col. i. 3), and he would be even more diligent
in praying for his closest associates.

The mention of *night and day* brings out the seriousness of
the apostle's purpose, reminiscent of Acts xx. 31. The same
expression, applied to prayer, is found in the directions to
genuine widows in 1 Tim. v. 5, and since in that case it
concludes the clause, there is justification for the AV connecting it with the preceding words in this case. It stresses
continuity of prayer and gives added strength to the words

without ceasing (*adialeiptos*, an expression found elsewhere only in Rom. ix. 2 in the New Testament). The RV, however, connects the words with the next clause, 'night and day longing to see thee,' and this is favoured by RSV and many commentators. In either case the frequency of prayer for Timothy would intensify the longing to see him. Such expressions as these illuminate the spiritual stature of the apostle who in constant and hazardous journeyings could so maintain an attitude of continuous intercession. His practice provides an example for all servants of the gospel.

4. The apostle's intensity of feeling frequently comes to the surface in his letters, and the words *greatly desiring to see thee* are reminiscent of the strong yearning found in Rom. i. 11; 1 Thes. iii. 6; Phil. i. 8, where the same verb *epipotheō* is used. A particularly intimate touch is the memory of Timothy's tears (*being mindful of thy tears* is better rendered 'as I remember your tears' RSV), which appears to be a reference to their last time of meeting (cf. Acts xx. 37). In modern times convention restrains men's tears, but in Paul's time the expression of strong emotion was less inhibited. Timothy, who seems to have been a sensitive type of man and who was deeply attached to the apostle, obviously felt the parting keenly.

The apostle does not disguise his own pleasure at the prospect of seeing his friend. As Easton says 'in the Gk. "tears" and "joy" are tellingly juxtaposed'. Though partings are often painful their very tears are a pledge of greater joy at the possibility of reunion. The words used to express the purpose of his longing, *that I may be filled with joy*, are characteristic of the apostle's wholeheartedness, for he uses the verb *plēroō* (to fill) no less than twenty-three times.

5. *When I call to remembrance* commences a new sentence in AV, and this is probably correct, although the RV connects with the preceding words. Since the expression *hupomnēsin labōn* literally means 'having received a reminder', it was suggested by Bengel, and the suggestion is favoured by many commentators, that Paul had just had news of Timothy. RSV has rightly, 'I am reminded'. It is striking to note that four different expressions are used in verses 3–6 to denote memory. To *have remembrance* (verse 3) is paralleled in 1 Thes. iii. 6; to be *mindful* (verse 4) is used in 1 Cor. xi. 2; to *call to remembrance* or 'be reminded' (verse 5) is not used elsewhere by Paul (but cf. 2 Pet. i. 13); and to *put in remembrance* (verse 6) is paralleled in 1 Cor. iv. 17. This rich variety of wording emphasizes the apostle's reminiscent mood, and his desire that Timothy himself should have stores of memory on which to draw.

It is Timothy's *unfeigned faith* which prompts some further reflections. A similar description of faith has already been met in 1 Tim. i. 5, although it is not found elsewhere in Paul. Scott supposes that 'faith' here means no more than religious feeling, since no question of sincerity could arise over the inner relation of the soul to God. Yet a profession of such faith could certainly be unreal, and where the sincerity of faith is transparent there is good reason for its special mention. It may be, as White suggests, that Timothy was deficient in other aspects of his conduct, but 'his unfeigned faith made up for much'.

The indwelling of faith is paralleled by the Pauline ideas of the indwelling God (2 Cor. vi. 16), the indwelling Spirit (Rom. viii. 11; 2 Tim. i. 14), the indwelling word (Col. iii. 16) and indwelling sin (Rom. vii. 17). The metaphor of a building and its inhabitants was well suited to express this inner character of Christianity.

The thought of Timothy's faith stimulates the memory of his grandmother's and mother's faith. But there is difference of opinion among commentators whether the Christian or Jewish faith is here meant. The use of the word *first* (*prōton*) in this context has been supposed to indicate that Lois was a devout Jewess and was the first to inculcate religious faith in Timothy; in other words, 'he had been subject to religious influences as far back as he could remember' (Scott). Yet if Christian faith is intended, *prōton* may mean that Lois was the first to become a Christian, followed by Eunice and her son. The reference to Timothy's parents in Acts xvi. 1 is little help in solving this question since the word 'believer'

used of Eunice could apply equally to both Jewish and
Christian believers. Since by her marriage to a Greek Eunice
cannot have been a strictly orthodox Jewess, it seems more
probable that Christian faith is meant (cf. comment on iii. 15).
The lack of mention of Timothy's father, who according to
Acts. xvi. 1 was a Greek, was probably because he was not a
Christian (Jeremias). Such personal details bear a genuine
stamp and some scholars who dispute the authenticity of the
Pastorals as a whole list this passage among the genuine
fragments (e.g. Falconer). It is difficult to believe that a
pseudonymous writer would have thought of mentioning
Timothy's forbears by name if the Epistle was directed to
some 'Timothy' of a later age.

The apostle was not only deeply conscious of the powerful
home influences which had shaped his own career, but was
impressed by the saintly atmosphere of Timothy's home.
Lois and Eunice were perhaps well known in the Christian
Church for their domestic piety. The apostle closes this
personal reminiscence by the assertion of a strong conviction
(*and I am persuaded that in thee also*), in thoroughly characteristic
style, the verb *peithō* being used twenty-two times in Paul's
writings. There is no doubt in his mind about Timothy's faith.

III. ENCOURAGEMENT FROM EXPERIENCE (i. 6–14)

There is no real break between this section and the last, for
it is thankfulness over Timothy's faith that leads Paul immediately to give his first personal charge to his lieutenant.
The terms of this passage suggest that Paul recognizes that
Timothy's character requires some moral stiffening.

(a) The gift of God (i. 6–10)

6. The opening word *Wherefore* (an unusual Greek expression
for Paul) connects with the apostle's assurance regarding
Timothy's faith. Because of this Timothy is first encouraged
by being reminded of God's commission to him. For his heavy
responsibilities he needs no new gift but a rekindling of that
already received. The Greek *anazōpureō* (*stir up*) means either

'to kindle afresh' or 'to keep in full flame'.[1] There is no necessary suggestion, therefore, that Timothy had lost his early fire, although undoubtedly, like every Christian, he needed an incentive to keep the fire burning at full flame.

As in 1 Tim. iv. 14, *the gift* (*charisma*) is certainly more than natural ability and has the character of a supernatural operation of the Spirit. In both cases the endowment is connected with the laying on of hands, and must be understood in the light of the special tasks to which Timothy was commissioned on that important occasion. It is noticeable that the *charisma* is specified as being *in* (*en*) Timothy, making quite clear that the true gift of God is an internal grace and not an external operation. Every Christian minister needs at times to return to the inspiration of his ordination, to be reminded not only of the greatness of his calling, but also of the adequacy of the divine grace which enables him to perform it. Indeed, every Christian worker engaged in however small a task requires assurance that God never commissions anyone to a task without imparting a special gift appropriate for it.

7. The gift is now defined more precisely, since the connecting particle *for* links this verse closely with verse 6. The words *hath not given* are a translation of the Greek Aorist and point to a specific occasion. RSV has 'God did not give us' and this correctly focuses attention on the event when it took place. This may indirectly refer to the outpouring of the Spirit on the Christian Church at Pentecost, as White suggests, in view of the collective *us* (*hēmin*). But it seems better to assume that the plural is here used to soften a direct personal criticism and that the occasion of Timothy's own commissioning is in view. It may be that his besetting sin was timidity, and this was Paul's tactful way of dealing with it.

The negative statement, *not . . . the spirit of fear* (RSV 'of timidity'), serves to heighten the positive. The word for timidity or cowardice (*deilia*) is used here only in the Greek Testament, although frequently in the LXX. The statement is reminiscent of Rom. viii. 15, but Easton claims that the writer 'turns triumphant ecstasy into moralistic exhortation'.

[1] So Abbott-Smith.

Yet the purpose of each statement is clearly different. That Timothy received a spirit of cowardice at ordination was unthinkable to the apostle. The Christian gospel could never be furthered by men of craven spirit. Instead, the Christian minister receives a triad of graces, i.e. *power, love* and *a sound mind*. The spirit of *power* means not that the servant of God must of necessity be a powerful personality, but that he has strength of character to be bold in the exercise of authority. The power of the Holy Spirit within him has enabled many a naturally timid man to develop a boldness not his own when called in the name of God to fulfil a difficult ministry. The Spirit of *love* is to all Christians indispensable, most of all to the chosen ministers of Christ, and none understood its power more clearly than the apostle who wrote the incomparable hymn of love in 1 Cor. xiii. The third feature is *a sound mind*, or more literally 'self-control' (RSV), for no one can have mastery of others who has not first subdued himself. Yet the apostle has more in mind than stoical self-effort, for this self-mastery is described as a divinely bestowed gift.

8. In virtue of these special endowments Timothy is told, *Be not thou therefore ashamed.* There is no need to suppose that Timothy had already shown symptoms of shame, but the apostle is evidently intent on strengthening his mind should the temptation arise. Natural timidity quickly breeds shame; and calls to courage are not out of place even to many who have proved the stalwartness of their faith. *The testimony of our Lord* may mean either 'testimony about our Lord', or 'testimony borne by our Lord'. The former has the support of 1 Cor. i. 6 and is favoured by most commentators. It amounts, as Easton says, to 'the Christian message as a whole', a message which inevitably brought ignominy to its preachers, especially in a Greek environment where the preaching of the cross was foolishness (1 Cor. i. 23). Timothy might also be tempted to be ashamed of Paul's bonds, since imprisonment for the sake of the gospel carried with it a social stigma. The apostle is so deeply conscious of the Lord's purpose in his present affliction that he can describe himself as *his prisoner*, as in Eph. iii. 1 (cf. also Phil i. 12-14). Men might imprison his body, but they could never enslave his spirit. To Christ alone he acknowledged himself a captive.

The exhortation to be *partaker of the afflictions of the gospel* is a development of the previous prohibitions. It denotes a readiness to share, if need be, the same afflictions that others have endured for the sake of the gospel. A new word seems to have been coined to express this thought, *sunkakopatheō*, which means 'to take one's share of ill-treatment'[1] (cf. also ii. 3). Lock thinks the prefix *sun* means that Timothy is called upon to share in the apostle's sufferings. The evil treatment meted out to Christ's ministers is a recurring theme in this Epistle, for the uncompounded verb is also used twice (ii. 9, iv. 5).

The concluding words, *according to the power of God* are intended to assure Timothy that the sharing of suffering for the gospel's sake is never undertaken in one's own strength. 'Stronger than all suffering is the power of God' (Jeremias). This is the complement of verse 7 where a spirit of *power* is included in God's gifts.

9. This verse and the next are considered by some scholars (e.g. Easton) to be cited from a Christian hymn, but if so the language and thought are thoroughly Pauline, and it would be necessary to suppose that the apostle had himself adapted his own teaching to a suitable liturgical form.[2] First he makes a double assertion about God's relation to us. God *hath saved us, and called us*. His saving activity is prominent in the Pastorals, especially in the sixfold use of the title 'Saviour', and although this designation is nowhere else found in Pauline writings, the idea of divine agency in human salvation is more prominent in Paul than in any other New Testament writer (cf. 1 Cor. i. 21).

The Christian's vocation is attributed to God, as usual in Pauline writings (e.g. 1 Cor. i. 9; Gal. i. 6; Rom. viii. 28). There is a close connection between salvation and vocation.

---

[1] So Abbott-Smith.

[2] See the writer's Tyndale monograph *The Pastoral Epistles and the Mind of Paul*, pp. 17-29 for a fuller discussion of this point.

Christians are saved not only from a life of sin but to a life of holiness. As Spicq well puts it, 'The consequence of salvation is a consecration of Christians'. God has *called us with an holy calling* because He Himself is holy. His activities partake of His own character. The same idea is found in 1 Thes. iv. 7 where the call to holiness is set over against uncleanness.

The apostle then makes clear the controlling factor in this calling. It was not on the basis of *works*, as Paul so constantly stressed and as he himself had so poignantly experienced (cf. Tit. iii. 5 for the same negation of works in the Pastorals). It is a process of divine *purpose and grace*, which provides a solid ground for assurance. No words could sum up more characteristically the Pauline approach to Christian calling than this phrase *according to his own purpose and grace*. For the same idea of divine *purpose* see Rom. viii. 28, ix. 11; Eph. i. 11. Easton, who disputes the characteristic Pauline usage of *grace* in all its other occurrences in the Pastorals, nevertheless admits it here. The focus on the sovereign choice of God is unmistakable. This grace is not earned but *given us in Christ Jesus*, another typically Pauline phrase, if we understand the words in the sense that Christ is the medium for the imparting of grace. This gift was determined *before the world began*, or better 'before times eternal' (RV), or 'ages ago' (RSV) (cf. Tit. i. 2). The phrase is introduced to bring into greater relief the historic appearance of Christ (verse 10). This may be a reference to the earliest promise of triumph to the woman's seed (Gn. iii. 15), or to the grace of the pre-existent Christ.

10. The thought moves from eternity to time. Though the idea of God's eternal purposes of grace may be beyond comprehension, at least the fact of the incarnation is capable of being understood. The grace, *now made manifest by the appearing of our Saviour Jesus Christ*, is echoed again in Tit. ii. 11-13, where the same word *epiphaneia* is used for *appearing*. In the Titus passage, however, the word refers to the second, and not the first advent as here. Because of the use of both *epiphaneia* and the title 'Saviour' in the mystery cults, and in the Emperor Cult, Easton (p. 172) claims that 'this verse is a

Christian protest against the pagan doctrine'. But Scott thinks that all that can be concluded is that Christianity 'was freely borrowing ideas and terms from its pagan surroundings'. In any case the use of *epiphaneia* is confirmed as a Pauline expression by 2 Thes. ii. 8. Moreover, the contrast between a mystery once hid but now manifested is the thought of the doxology in Rom. xvi. 25–27, a passage whose language is closely akin to this.

The word *katargeō* used to describe the abolition of death is a favourite with Paul. In 1 Cor. xv. 26 he speaks of death as the last enemy to be destroyed (same verb as here), and although his thought there is clearly future whereas the aorists used here denote a completed event, no contradiction need be assumed. Here the whole range of Christ's work is envisaged as an accomplished fact, but there the attention is focused on its consummation. Although Christians are not absolved from physical death, their approach to it means its virtual abolition since it is no longer to be feared (Heb. ii. 14, 15) and has lost its sting (1 Cor. xv. 55).

But Christ is not only a great destroyer; He is also a great illuminator. *Life and immortality* had been obscured until the gospel, but now are flooded with light. The same thought is found in Eph. iii. 9 where Paul describes the grace given him to bring to light the mystery hidden for ages. By linking *immortality* (*aphtharsia*) with *life*, the apostle defines more closely the quality of *life*. Because Christians possess a life which cannot decay, anticipation of the accident of physical death can do nothing to destroy their confidence.

By *the gospel* is meant the entire revelation of God in Christ. It is noteworthy that nothing is said of the manner in which death is nullified and life illuminated, but since the channel of revelation is the *gospel*, the action must be understood in the light of Christ's life and death and teaching. This verse lends no support, therefore, to the gnostic view of salvation by illumination.

(b) The testimony of Paul (i. 11, 12)

11. For the passive form of the verb *I am appointed* see the comment on 1 Tim. ii. 7, where Paul also expressed his awareness of the divine origin of his commission. The same three designations of his work are repeated here, but without any strong assertion of veracity (cf. 'I lie not' in 1 Tim. ii. 7). It is reasonable to enquire whether such a reminder was necessary for Timothy, who would certainly be well acquainted with Paul's commission. Easton calls it superfluous for the historic Timothy, but it need not be taken that Paul is informing his lieutenant, which would admittedly be inconceivable, but that, as in 1 Tim. ii. 7, his mind is so carried away by the thought of the greatness of the gospel that the wonder of his own call to preach it dominates him here.

12. Timothy is reminded that Paul's present sufferings are entirely due to the fact that he is a preacher of the gospel. The same Greek expression, which is here translated *for the which cause*, is used in verse 6, and again emphasizes the connection with the previous statement.

As Paul contemplates his present unenviable position he is led to make a great personal affirmation calculated to encourage Timothy in his own sufferings for the gospel. He is not *ashamed* of his bonds, even if others are, and this personal claim is probably intended to reinforce the advice given to Timothy in verse 8.

In spite of the constant appeal to sound doctrine in the Pastorals generally and in this context in particular, there is no justification for the view that personal faith has given place to a formulated creed (cf. Easton). It is significant that the apostle's affirmation in this verse is so intensely personal. *I know whom I have believed* draws attention to the intimate relationship between himself and God. The statement would have lost immeasurably if Paul had said 'what' instead of 'whom'. His persuasion here is reminiscent of his persuasion in Rom. viii. 38 that nothing can separate us from the love of God (cf. also verse 5 where the same verb is used in the passive for virtual certainty). The perfect tense used in this context brings out the continuous assurance that the apostle enjoys.

The words translated *that which I have committed unto him* mean literally 'my deposit' (*parathēkē*). The same word, *parathēkē*, is used in verse 14 and 1 Tim. vi. 20, where in both cases it describes the deposit committed to Timothy for safe keeping. But the present verse focuses attention on God's ability to guard. The 'deposit' could be understood either of what God entrusted to Paul or what Paul entrusted to God, but since in the other occurrences in the Pastorals the word *parathēkē* is used in the former sense, it is most probably used in the same sense here. In that case the reference is to the work which the apostle was commissioned to do or the doctrine entrusted to him. White, however, disputes that the word is used here in the same sense as in verse 14, and maintains that it should be interpreted as a reference to Paul's 'soul' or 'himself'. Lock also understands it in this second sense but includes Paul's teaching work, converts, and life—in fact, all the precious things he had put under God's care.

That day, used again in this undefined manner in i. 18 and iv. 8, must be understood of the Parousia as in 2 Thes. i. 10 (cf. also in 1 Cor. iii. 13). Scott sees the possibility of an allusion to the parable of the talents. 'A charge has been committed to Paul as to the stewards in the parable, and he is confident that on the day of account he will not be found wanting.'

(c) The charge to Timothy (i. 13, 14)

13. An interesting word is used to denote *the form of sound words* which Timothy is urged to *hold fast*. *Hupotupōsis* means an outline sketch such as an architect might make before getting down to the detailed plans of a building. The importance of this 'pattern' (as RV, RSV) cannot be over-emphasized. It means that the apostle claims his own teaching to be no more than a starting point. As White puts it, 'It happily suggests the power of expansion latent in the simplest and most primitive dogmatic formulas of the Christian faith.' (Cf. 1 Tim. i. 16 for a discussion of the word *hupotupōsis*.) Timothy is not told merely to repeat what Paul taught, but to follow that teaching as a basis. Its description as *sound words* has been previously noted as characteristic of the Pastorals, but nowhere is the link between sound words and what Paul himself taught so clearly specified as here.

The Greek construction makes clear that what Timothy has heard is *sound words* and not the *form* or 'pattern' underlying it. The content must always be considered of greater importance than the shape. The exhortation calls for some effort on Timothy's part, for he is to *hold fast*; though the AV is probably rather too strong for the Greek word *echō*. It is better therefore to treat 'pattern' (without the article) as a predicate and to understand the words to mean, 'Hold as a pattern of sound words what you heard from me'. In this case *in faith and love* would qualify the act of holding and would not be attached to 'sound words'. The manner in which Timothy maintained his orthodoxy was as important as the orthodoxy itself. Had all loyalty to sound words been tempered by these great Christian virtues, *faith and love*, the bitterness of much ecclesiastical disputation would have been impossible. The two virtues must go together, as Paul eloquently shows in 1 Cor. xiii. The recurrence of the favourite Pauline phrase *in Christ Jesus* shows that an intimate union with Christ is necessary before faith and love are possible. Neither Easton's translation 'in Christian faith and love', nor Moffatt's 'in faith and love of Christ Jesus' does justice to the mystical connotation of the expression. It is true that in Paul's other writings the phrase 'in Christ' is mostly applied to persons and not virtues, but there is no necessity to suppose a discrepancy here. The meaning clearly is that faith and love follow from abiding *in Christ*.

14. This verse is an amplification of the last with special emphasis on guarding the deposit (*thing which was committed unto thee*). The same word (*parathēkē*) is used as in verse 12, but whereas there the deposit is kept safe in God's hands, here Timothy himself must guarantee its security. Although the human element is more stressed, it is immediately recognized that Timothy unaided could never achieve it. It can come only *by the Holy Ghost which dwelleth in us*. The Spirit

dwells (for the word *enoikeō* see note on verse 5) in every
Christian (Rom. viii. 9–11), but a special endowment is given
to those set apart for specific tasks, closely akin to the primitive
charismata (spiritual gifts) mentioned in 1 Corinthians.

There is no support in these verses for the Roman Catholic
doctrine of the ministry as custodian of the Church's traditions (cf. Spicq), for the words *in us* need not mean, as is
widely supposed, that Paul and Timothy are alone intended.
The indwelling Spirit performs the same function in every
Christian, although the degree of operation varies with the
work to be done. This is very different from the view that
'we have now an anticipation of the later doctrine for which
the Spirit was the special endowment of the Church's
ministry' (Scott). It is better to assume the words to mean
that since the deposit must be faithfully guarded, any man
without the aid of the Holy Spirit is attempting the impossible. But although the Spirit of God dwells in Christians
generally, He may certainly be depended on to give gifts of
power to ministers set apart for the work of the gospel.

IV. PAUL AND HIS ASSOCIATES (i. 15—ii. 2)

There is particular point in Paul's earnest exhortations to
Timothy in view of the conduct of certain other of his associates, as he next illustrates.

(a) The Asiatics (i. 15)

15. The defection of the Asiatics is spoken of as a fact well
known to Timothy, and for that reason would provide a
powerful object lesson. The verb *apostrephō* (*turned away*) is
used in Tit. i. 14 of the false teachers who turn away from the
truth, but here the context demands no more than a defection
from the apostle himself. Nevertheless this is painful enough
from whatever cause; and the fact that Phygellus and Hermo-
genes are singled out for special mention suggests that these
were the main cause of the trouble. Nothing more is known
about them, and it can only be surmised that they were
probably opponents of Paul's mission or authority. There

is no need to suppose that Paul speaks of *all they which are in (en) Asia* in a literal sense. The hyperbolical *all* is best understood as what White calls 'the sweeping assertion of depression'. *Asia* is the Roman province comprising Mysia, Lydia, Caria, most of Phrygia and the islands off the coast. Lock suggests alternatively that the reference may be to the failure of Asiatic Christians in Rome to give Paul any assistance at his trial. Yet in that case the Greek preposition *ek* would have been preferred to *en* which implies that the Christians were still in Asia at the time.

(b) Onesiphorus (i. 16–18)

16. In contrast to these *Onesiphorus* is held up as a model of Christian kindness. Both here and in iv. 19, there is mention of *the house of Onesiphorus* which suggests to some commentators (e.g. Bernard, Easton) that Onesiphorus was already dead. But since, as Simpson rightly points out, a man and his household were inseparable, there is no necessity to suppose them to be separated here. It is true that this verse prays for mercy for the household, while verse 18 confines the prayer to Onesiphorus, yet in each case Onesiphorus himself is mainly in mind since it is he who is specially commended for kindness. In the Apocryphal *Acts of Paul and Thecla*, Onesiphorus is spoken of as a convert of Paul's who gave him hospitality on his first visit to Iconium.

The particular help given by Onesiphorus is picturesquely described in the words *He oft refreshed me*, conjuring up the idea that the presence of his friend provided a special tonic. As Moffatt aptly expresses it, 'he braced me up'. Although Onesiphorus' help may have included material assistance, his fellowship was of much greater value. He seems somewhat sensitive to his chains, presumably because they had become an object of shame in the eyes of some (cf. verse 8). But one fellow-Christian at least, Onesiphorus, *was not ashamed*, and his example is probably cited as an indirect hint to Timothy.

17, 18. In strong contrast to being ashamed, Onesiphorus had actually *sought out* Paul *very diligently*. Such earnestness in seeking was necessary because of the difficulties of tracking down prisoners in Rome (cf. Easton).

The prayer in verse 18 is a reiteration of verse 16, but here an eschatological factor is introduced. *That day* is evidently the judgment day of Christ. Bernard suggests that the first *Lord* (with the article) refers to Christ and the second (without the article) to God the Father, to whom the function of judgment is often attributed. This conforms to the LXX practice of applying the anarthrous form to God. Jeremias, with some probability, suggests that the double mention of *Kurios* (Lord) springs from a mixed formula:—(1) The Lord grant him to find mercy and (2) may he find mercy from the Lord (i.e. God). Scott, however, prefers to apply both to God the Father.

Since it is assumed by many scholars that Onesiphorus was by now dead, the question has been raised whether this verse sanctions prayer for the dead. Roman Catholic theologians claim that it does. Spicq, for instance, sees here an example of prayer for the dead unique in the New Testament. Others, such as Bernard and Easton, agree with this judgment, and claim the Jewish precedent of 2 Macc. xii. 43–45. Bernard further cites the support of early Christian epitaphs. Yet it is precarious to base a doctrine, which finds no sanction anywhere else in the New Testament, upon the mere inference that Onesiphorus was already dead. Plummer argued that Onesiphorus must have been dead, on the following grounds: 1. Only the house of Onesiphorus is here spoken of in the present tense. 2. In the closing salutations (iv. 19 ff.) the same phrase is used coupled with the names of individuals. 3. The apostle's prayer for Onesiphorus himself relates to the day of judgment. But if the household was coupled with Onesiphorus in the apostle's warm affections, the difference of tense used would be explained as no more than a reminiscence of past events. Even if he were dead, however, the words need mean no more than that Paul is expressing 'a very natural feeling' (Scott). The eschatological emphasis suggests that he is looking ahead and is keen that Timothy also should stand well in the judgment day.

The conclusion of the verse reminds Timothy of his familiarity with the solid Christian service Onesiphorus had done at Ephesus. The words *unto me* are not well supported except in various ancient versions, and must therefore be omitted. The deletion, however, brings into greater relief the general character of Onesiphorus' ministry. 'The final charity in Rome had been only the climax of a consistent loyalty' (Scott).

(c) Timothy (ii. 1, 2)

1. The personal exhortation to Timothy which follows contrasts with the general defection of the Asiatics, as *therefore* shows, coupled as it is with the emphatic pronoun *thou*. The injunction is reinforced by the splendid example of Onesiphorus. Timothy is to *be strong*, a characteristic Pauline word (*endunamoō*) which occurs in the same sense in Eph. vi. 10.

The phrase *in Christ Jesus* qualifying *grace* shows not only that the grace comes from Christ alone, but also that all Christians possess it and may rely on its enabling power. Easton's view, that grace here means 'power' and not Christ's favour, must be considered arbitrary, for the two ideas are inseparable. In White's words, '*Grace* here has its simplest theological meaning, as the divine help, the unmerited gift of assistance that comes from God.'

2. No doubt exists as to the precise nature of the tradition and doctrine to be transmitted, for Timothy had heard them from Paul's own lips (cf. i. 13). The next statement, *among many witnesses*, is somewhat obscure and has proved a perplexity to commentators.

i. It is sometimes explained by referring it to the occasion of Timothy's ordination, at which many would have witnessed the charges delivered by Paul to his child in the faith (cf. Lock). But in that case the preposition *dia* must be given the unusual meaning 'in the presence of'. Although this Greek usage is not impossible it is better to assign a more usual meaning if possible. Another difficulty in this view is that it appears to presuppose a charge too long to be feasible on a public occasion. In any case there is no supporting evidence for such a practice in primitive Christian records.

2. Bernard claims that no necessity for straining the Greek preposition arises if it is understood in a general sense and not restricted to a single event. It would then mean 'through the intervention of many witnesses'. Presumably by this he means that many witnesses could testify to what Paul had committed to him.

3. Various attempts have been made to identify the witnesses. Lock suggests they are the elders of 1 Tim. iv. 14, while others see a reference to a source of Christian testimony unconnected with Paul, such as Timothy's mother and grandmother and some, perhaps, who had heard or seen the Lord (so Spicq), and this would well fit the context. Such an interpretation reflects greater breadth of mind on the part of the apostle who would not then restrict the deposit to his own transmission. It takes great grace for independent thinkers to acknowledge that truth can flow in channels other than their own.

4. Some have regarded the witnesses as impersonal representations either of the various forms and expressions of Paul's teaching, or, more generally, of all the evidences of apostolic authority. But neither of these interpretations belongs naturally to the context.

Timothy is to *commit* (*paratithēmi*) to others what he has heard. The verb has already been used in 1 Tim. i. 18 for the committal of the charge to Timothy. It occurs in Acts xiv. 23 where Paul and Barnabas appointed elders and then committed them to the Lord, and also in Acts xx. 32 where Paul similarly committed the Ephesian elders to God. The idea is clearly to entrust something to another for safe keeping, and in the present context this notion is of great significance. The transmission of Christian truth must never be left to chance, and is clearly not committed fortuitously to every Christian, but only to *faithful men, who shall be able to teach others also*. Two qualifications are therefore demanded: A loyalty to the truth, i.e. a loyalty which has been proved, and an aptitude to teach (cf. 1 Tim. iii. 2).

Two important considerations arise out of this verse. First, the apostle is depicted as solicitous for the preservation of Christian teaching, and it cannot be imagined that he would ever have overlooked this necessity. He must at the end of his life have conceived of the teaching as being in a form sufficiently fixed to be transmitted, in which case the claim that the stereotyped doctrine in the Pastorals is un-Pauline falls to the ground. Secondly, it is evident that Paul recognized that the manner in which he himself had forged out the doctrines would not continue in the next generation, and that more normal methods of transmission would not only be resorted to, but would be essential. Plummer's comment that we have here 'the earliest trace of a theological school' is suggestive. The passage, however, gives no support for the Roman Catholic claim of a deposit of truth infallibly handed down.

V. DIRECTIONS TO TIMOTHY (ii. 3-26)

(a) The basis of encouragement and exhortation (ii. 3-13)

In verses 3-6 three suggestive illustrations are used to encourage Timothy in various aspects of his work. All three, the soldier, the athlete and the labourer, are taken from common life and are frequent literary metaphors, applied here in a specifically spiritual sense. From the soldier Timothy must learn endurance, from the athlete discipline and from the labourer perseverance.

(i) **Various examples (ii. 3-6).** Military metaphors are great favourites with the apostle Paul (e.g. Rom. vi. 13, vii. 23; 1 Cor. ix. 7; 2 Cor. vi. 7; Eph. vi. 11–18). The soldier served as an admirable illustration of fortitude to Timothy who was probably anything but military in his approach to his unenviable task at Ephesus. The same verb (*sunkakopatheō*) is used here as in i. 8, but *endure hardness* fails to bring out the full sense of the word, which is better rendered 'take your share of suffering' (RSV). It implies that every Christian must expect some measure of ill-treatment, as every soldier does. It may be that Timothy was over-sensitive about the evil treatment which constantly threatened him, but more probably the apostle is particularly burdened with the intensity of the spiritual struggle which he is about to lay down and which would naturally fall heavily on Timothy's shoulders. The allusion in Heb. xiii. 23 to Timothy's 'release' suggests that not long after Paul's decease his successor did, in fact, suffer imprisonment. The term *soldier of Jesus Christ* may well have been a current expression in view of the description of two of Paul's associates as 'fellow-soldiers' (Phil. ii. 25 and Phm. 2).

4. The personal injunction of verse 3 is reinforced by a general principle of soldiering. *No man that warreth* is better rendered as RV, RSV—'no soldier on service'. It is a question of priorities, and when the duties of military service are placed in juxtaposition with civilian life, the call to service takes precedence over *the affairs of this life*. What is meant by this latter phrase is an open question among scholars, and the following suggestions have been made: 1. that ministers of the gospel should not be 'preoccupied' with the things of this world. 2. That ministers should not engage in commerce at all. 3. That in Timothy's case he is not to attempt to emulate Paul in working to maintain himself, if by so doing the more important duties of the ministry are neglected. The first seems the most probable solution. The determining word is *entangleth himself* (*emplekomai*) which envisages a soldier's weapons entrammelled in his cloak. The main point is therefore the renunciation of everything which hinders the real purpose of the soldier of Christ. There is nothing intrinsically wrong, in other words, about the *affairs of this life* until they entangle. Then they must be resolutely cast aside.

The basic reason for such renunciation is added to reinforce the metaphor. A soldier must please his commander, as the phrase *him who hath chosen him to be a soldier* must be understood, for it was he who mustered an army to serve under him. This involves for the soldier a sinking of his own desires in a total effort to please his chief. No more admirable figure of speech could be found to illustrate the extent of Christ's claims upon His ministers.

5. The connecting link between the soldier and the athlete is found in the word *lawfully* (*nominōs*), which must be interpreted in the light of the rules of the Olympic games. RSV renders it 'according to the rules'. Simpson includes also the idea 'in a correct style', citing Galen to show that the metaphor is of 'full-fledged athletes, professionals, not amateurs'. These rules extended not only to the race itself but to the prescribed training. Lock cites instances showing that athletes had to state on oath that they had fulfilled ten months' training, before they were eligible to enter the contest. An athlete who had not subjected himself to the necessary discipline would not only have no chance to win and so be *crowned*, but would lower the standard of the Games. Severe penalties were consequently imposed on all who infringed the rules (cf. Spicq). If Parry is right in suggesting that this second vocation is less serious than the first, it may be claimed as evidence of Roman influence on the apostle's mind. Applied to the Christian ministry, this second metaphor stresses the absolute necessity for self-discipline. There may be a hint that suitable training is essential for the Christian ministry, but that idea can hardly have been in Paul's mind. It is better to assume that the apostle is here exhorting Timothy to keep strictly to the 'rules' fixed by the life and teaching of Christ. There is one important difference between the metaphor and its application; only one athlete may gain the crown but every Christian will be crowned who strives loyally in the contest (cf. iv. 8).

6. The third of this triad of illustrations significantly places the emphasis on toil. *The husbandman that laboureth* is better translated 'the hardworking farmer' (RSV), because of the position and meaning of the word for labouring (*kopiaō* denotes diligent toil). A hardworking man has rights which the indolent man has forfeited. Clearly the right to a share of the crop that his toil has helped to raise is elementary, so much so that Scott calls the illustration far-fetched, merely thrown in because of its occurrence in the passage in 1 Cor. ix. 10 f., which he thinks the writer used. But there is more point in the illustration than Scott allows, for the Lord's teaching that a labourer is worthy of his hire was understood by early Christians to mean that God's servants had the right to remuneration from the people whom they served. It may be that Timothy, emulating the example of Paul, had declined material assistance in the belief that it was more noble to do so, and needed therefore to be reminded of what he might fairly claim for himself.

(ii) Further reminiscences (ii. 7-10). There follows an exhortation to *consider* (*noeō*, to 'understand', 'think over') *what I say*, which can be understood either generally of everything that Paul has taught Timothy (so Easton), or specifically of the teaching contained in the illustrations just quoted. If Timothy seriously attempts to 'grasp the meaning' (White), *the Lord* will supply all needed wisdom. Particularly does the Christian minister need *understanding* from the Lord in problems of self-discipline and a right approach to material matters. *The Lord give* represents an inferior text and contains nothing of the firm conviction of the true text, 'the Lord will grant' (RSV). As the Christian ponders and applies the exhortations to his own life, the Lord will increase his powers of understanding.

8. The apostle next strengthens the appeal to his own teaching by directing attention to his Master. As Bengel says, 'Paul, as usual, quickens (gives life to) his own example by the example of Christ'. It is thought by some scholars that an early Christian formula is here quoted, similar to the statement in Rom. i. 3, 4 (so Easton). Indeed the similarities are so striking that Scott suggests that the writer is closely following the Romans passage. But if Paul is reminding Timothy of the essence of his *gospel* there is no necessity to suppose a literary connection. Dodd[1] is probably right in assuming that in Romans, Paul is citing an existing statement

[1] *The Apostolic Preaching and its Developments* (1936), pp. 21 ff.

of primitive belief and if so there is no reason why he should not do the same here. It is significant that the only other places where Paul uses the words *according to my gospel* are found in Romans (ii. 16, xvi. 25), which may suggest that Paul intentionally used common elements of primitive teaching when appealing to *my gospel*, to show that what he preached was the common gospel. The AV *Jesus Christ . . . was raised from the dead* gives a wrong impression, suggesting that the fact of the resurrection is mainly in mind. But the passive participle 'risen from the dead' (RV, RSV) draws attention to a present experience of the risen Lord, which would be particularly underlined by Paul's own conversion. For him the resurrection of Christ is the most prominent Christian truth, containing as it does the guarantee of all other aspects of the work of Christ. It is strange, however, to find coupled with this the descriptive phrase *of the seed of David*, which although occurring in Rom. i. 3 figures nowhere else in Pauline thought.

9. Having in verse 3 urged Timothy to endure hardship, Paul cites his own case as an example. The Greek construction *en hoi* underlying *wherein* indicates the gospel as the sphere of Paul's sufferings. Simpson, less probably, finds the antecedent in Christ not the gospel, and understands the words to mean that Paul suffers as a member of Christ's mystical body. It is Paul's work 'in the gospel' that has caused him to be ill-treated by the authorities. The RSV translation 'for which' suggests that the gospel itself was the basis of the charge against the apostle. Yet it is more probable that Paul's bonds resulted from disturbances following his preaching than from his Christian beliefs.

The words *I suffer trouble as an evil doer* may possibly throw light on the charge brought against the apostle, for *kakourgos* is the contemporary word for 'criminal' (RSV) or 'malefactor' (RV), and suggests that Paul was being treated as a common criminal. It is worthy of notice that the only other place where the word is used in the New Testament is in Lk. xxiii. 32, 39, where it describes those crucified with Jesus. Ramsay[1] sees in

[1] *The Church in the Roman Empire*, p. 249.

the word a hint of the *flagitia* imputed to Christians in the Neronian persecution, in which case this passing reference would support an early date for the Epistle, for Christianity would not yet have been regarded as in itself a forbidden religion.

In contrast to Paul's own bonds is the absolute freedom of *the word of God*. The apostle's statement applies not so much to his own freedom to preach the gospel in prison, as to the fact that even when he is imprisoned others are carrying on the work of proclamation. The persecution of Christian leaders may hamper the progress of the gospel, but it cannot imprison the Word of God nor prevent its spread.

10. The apostle next states a reason for his endurance: it is *for the elect's sakes,* which seems to mean those who are elect but do not yet believe. They have to be won and every ounce of effort must be put into the present conflict, in which both Paul and Timothy are engaged. This is brought out more forcibly by the concluding clause *that they may also obtain the salvation which is in Christ Jesus.* All Paul's present trials are abundantly worthwhile in view of the priceless benefits to be obtained by those who receive the message of himself and his fellow-labourers. As White aptly points out, 'It would be no paradise to St. Paul "to live in Paradise alone" '. The descriptive *in Christ Jesus* marks out not only the specifically Christian character of the salvation to be obtained, but also its sphere of operation, i.e. a salvation possessed by all who are 'in Christ' (see verse 1). The final phrase *with eternal glory* envisages the consummation of Christian salvation. This linking of *glory* with *salvation* is familiar in Paul's writings (e.g. 2 Thes. ii. 13, 14; cf. Rom. v. 1, 2, viii. 21–25), while the idea of suffering giving way to eternal glory is clearly brought out in 2 Cor. iv. 17.

(iii) A Christian hymn (ii. 11–13). Another 'faithful saying' is added at this juncture, at least if we follow the majority of commentators and attach the formula to what follows. Some have attempted to apply it to the antecedent passage but not convincingly. White, for instance, suggests verses 4–11 are in mind, while others consider the reference is to verse 8 (cf. Spicq for details). But there is so marked a rhythmic pattern in the words that follow, that it must be considered more natural to attach the formula to verses 11–13. A difficulty occurs in the inclusion in the first line of the conjunction *for*, which must be taken to connect with something that precedes. But Scott's explanation that part only of a Christian hymn is being cited, seems satisfactory. Most agree that the words formed part, at least, of a Christian hymn, although there is no general agreement as to how much of these verses should be included.[1]

The connection of thought between the hymn and the preceding passage may possibly be found in the idea of glory. There are great things to look forward to in Christian experience even if hardship is the present lot. Some have seen in this hymn an encouragement to martyrdom (so Bernard), but the alternative view which holds that 'baptismal death' is in mind is much more tenable (cf. Lock, Jeremias). This is confirmed by the close connection between this passage and Rom. vi. 8, in which baptism is used to illustrate the union between the exalted Lord and the believer. The idea is therefore in complete accord with Pauline thought, and seems to be brought in here to illustrate the worthwhileness of enduring *all things for the elect's sakes* (verse 10).

The tense of the verb *sunapothnēskō* rendered *be dead with him* is more correctly translated 'died with him' (RV), or 'have died with him' (RSV). A past event is undoubtedly in view; and if this event was the moment of baptism, the apostle is reminding himself and Timothy of that experience of identification with Christ which forms the basis of Christian living and hence of Christian courage and endurance.

12. The next line follows on the thought of the last, for the believer having risen to new life must face the call to endurance. In the AV the same word *hupomenō* translated *suffer* is rendered *endure* in verse 10, and this idea of patient endurance should also be retained here. It is not so much the suffering as the

[1] e.g. Easton finds verses 12b, 13 'out of place in a triumphant hymn'.

attitude of mind towards it which is most important. Yet if endurance is the Christian's constant duty, much more will partnership in the kingdom be his constant enjoyment (cf. Rom. viii. 17).

The possibility of denying Christ seems so reminiscent of the Lord's own words (Mt. x. 33), that some have supposed that a Pauline church has worked into an existing Christian hymn these words of Jesus.[1]

13. The awful contemplation of being denied by Christ is offset by the concluding emphasis upon His faithfulness. The words *If we believe not* are better rendered 'If we are faithless', to bring out the strong contrast with the answering statement, *he abideth faithful*. Christ's constancy to His own promises provides the believer with his greatest security. It is unthinkable that any contingency could affect the faithfulness of God, for *he cannot deny himself*. Yet as Jeremias points out, these words are not a charter for sin and apostasy, but rather a consolation for a frightened conscience. The main point of this statement, however, may be that God's 'faithfulness makes it impossible for Him to acknowledge those who deny Him' (Horton). Some treat this conclusion as the writer's own addition to the hymn, but the moral impossibility of self-contradiction in God forms the basis of His faithfulness and is therefore necessary to complete the hymn.

(b) Methods of dealing with false teachers (ii. 14–26)
Specific instructions are next given to Timothy to guide him in his unavoidable encounters with false teachers. There is little that is distinctive about the data in this Epistle as compared with false teaching denounced in 1 Timothy and Titus:

(i) Positive action: what to promote (ii. 14, 15). The first necessity is maintenance of right doctrine. Men are to be *put in remembrance* of the *things* contained in the previously cited hymn or perhaps more generally of the teaching in the whole of the preceding part of the Epistle. The same strong word translated

[1] So Swete; cf. the writer's Tyndale monograph, *The Pastoral Epistles and the Mind of Paul* (1956), p. 20.

charging them before the Lord (diamarturomai) is found also in
I Tim. v. 21, where Timothy himself is the object of the solemn
charge. The seriousness of the position is impressive when
viewed *before* or 'in the presence of' *the Lord*.

The description of the futility and harmfulness of the false
teachers is cryptic in the Greek. *That they strive not about words
to no profit* might well be translated, 'not to engage in word
battles, a useless procedure'. The content of these verbal bouts
is immaterial, as is also the attempt to discover in them obscure
allusions to gnosticism. Whenever men waste time on trivialities they merit the same condemnation. But the more serious
aspect is the effect upon others, for these unfounded quibbles
were leading to *the subverting of the hearers*. The Christian teacher
must never forget his responsibility to those who listen. The
word *katastrophē*, used here for subversion, which means literally
'turning upside down', is the antithesis of edification.

15. It is one thing solemnly to charge others and quite
another to take oneself in hand. The danger of self-neglect was
certainly not confined to Timothy, for its symptoms are
universal. Yet the value of self-discipline cannot be too highly
estimated, for the most effective refutation of error is for the
teacher to be the living embodiment of truth, with God's
approval upon him. But this is not easy. The word *spoudazō*
contains the notion of persistent 'zeal' which *study* misses.
Moffatt and Easton render it, 'Do your utmost'. The aim is
to shew (or better 'present' RV, RSV) *thyself approved (dokimos,*
'accepted after testing') *unto God*, as contrasted with the
canvassing of men's approval so evident among false teachers.
It is better to leave all wordy strifes alone and to seek the
approval of God, whose estimate always is infallible.

The shame that any workman feels when the incompetence
or shoddiness of his work is detected is used as a figure for the
Christian ministry. *A workman that needeth not to be ashamed* must,
therefore, be understood in the sense of a Christian teacher
who can unblushingly submit his work for God's approval,
like the men in the parable of the talents who had gained other
talents. This unashamedness is achieved by *rightly dividing the*

word of truth, a phrase in which the verb *orthotomeō* is difficult to define with any precision because it occurs elsewhere only twice in the LXX (Pr. iii. 6 and xi. 5). In the latter instances it means 'to cut a straight road', and this has been applied in the present case to the road of truth, which is to be made so straight that all deviations of heretics will be evident. Bernard objects to this on the grounds that *the word* cannot naturally be understood of a road. Simpson, however, takes the expression quite generally as an exhortation to straightforward exegesis. The idea of cutting which is inherent in the verb is thought to mean the correct analysis of the word of truth, either in its separate parts or in its whole. But it is contended by many that the compound had probably lost the meaning from which it was derived and had acquired the more general sense of right handling (RV, RSV). It was from this sense that the derived noun came later to denote orthodoxy.[1] In this context, however, the main idea seems to be that Timothy must be scrupulously straightforward in dealing with the *word of truth*, in strong contrast to the crooked methods of the false teachers. The term *word of truth* is twice used elsewhere by Paul (Eph. i. 13 and Col. i. 5) and in both cases is defined as 'the gospel'.

(ii) Negative action: what to shun (ii. 16–18). *Profane and vain babblings* (RV 'profane babblings', RSV 'godless chatter') have already been met in 1 Tim. vi. 20. They seem to have constituted a dominant element in the Ephesian heresy. The best way of dealing with this kind of situation is to avoid or *shun (peri-īstēmi)* such teaching, although this is not a *carte blanche* for Christian isolationism, but a piece of sound practical wisdom. As in verse 14, particular attention is paid to the devastating influence of these godless chatterboxes, whose trivialities lead to increasing ungodliness (*for they will increase (prokoptō) unto more ungodliness*). The RSV applies the words to 'godless chatter' and translates 'for it will lead people into more and more ungodliness'. On the other hand the RV 'for they will proceed further in ungodliness' focuses attention on the false teachers' own religious deterioration. Both are pos-

[1] Clem. Alex. Euseb, H.E. iv. 3.

sible, and the ambiguity draws attention to the unenviable progress in ungodliness of both teaching and teachers.

17. The rapidity with which false doctrine spreads is most graphically illustrated from the medical world. *Their word will eat as doth a canker* might be paraphrased 'Their teaching finds pasture (i.e. a grazing ground) as easily as a gangrene spreads in the human body'. Both the expressions *nomēn echein* (to have a pasture) and *gangraina* (gangrene) belong to the current medical vocabulary. The metaphor illustrates insidiousness and nothing could more suitably describe the manner of advancement of most false teaching, whether ancient or modern.

The special case of Hymenæus (see 1 Tim. i. 20) and Philetus is cited to give more point to the general injunction. Of the latter nothing else is known, while of the former the only other reference is in 1 Tim. i. 20, where he is delivered to Satan to learn not to blaspheme, i.e. he is excommunicated. There is no need to suppose that 2 Timothy must have been written before 1 Timothy on this account, since Hymenæus might well have continued his subverting activities, even although he had been officially excommunicated. His sphere of activity had possibly changed, for Paul appears to be informing Timothy of something he did not know.

18. On two other occasions in the Pastorals the verb *astocheō* (lit. 'to miss the mark') is used of the defection of false teachers (cf. 1 Tim. i. 6, vi. 21) from the true path. That these men denied a future resurrection shows the serious extent of their error, for this is a basic element of Christian faith, as Paul so forcibly brings out in 1 Cor. xv. In fact, 1 Cor. xv. 12 shows that at Corinth some were denying the reality of resurrection altogether, and the present allusion must be similarly understood. By treating the resurrection as a spiritual experience, these teachers had planned to dispose of it. No wonder they *overthrow the faith of some*, since Christianity without a resurrection ceases to be a living faith.

(iii) Ultimate certainties (ii. 19). In contrast to the insecurity of the false teaching, the stability of Christian doctrine is brought into focus. The Greek particle *mentoi* (nevertheless) brings out the certainty of this part of the antithesis. The AV rendering *the foundation of God standeth sure* is at fault in treating the adjective *stereos* (firm, sure) as predicate, but this is remedied by RV 'the firm foundation of God standeth'. The emphasis falls on the immovable character of God's solid foundation, even in face of such defection as the false teachers represent.

The metaphor of a building to represent the Christian Church appealed strongly to the apostle (cf. 1 Tim. iii. 15; 1 Cor. iii. 10–15; Eph. ii. 19–23), and in the present case was admirably suited to inspire Timothy with renewed confidence in the ultimate triumph of the Church. The *foundation* may here be the Church as a whole, or the Ephesian community in particular, or the truth of God, or the deposit of faith. The word seems to be used to represent the whole structure, in order to show that the major question was the security of the building as a whole and not the instability of a few isolated 'stones'.

It is generally supposed that the ancient practice of engraving inscriptions on buildings to indicate their purpose is alluded to in the phrase *having this seal* (*sphragis*, a word used twice elsewhere by Paul in the sense of authentication; see Rom. iv. 11; 1 Cor. ix. 2). God has put His own seal on His Church by a double inscription. But White thinks the metaphor is confused and the thought has passed away from the building to the seal received personally by each separate member. This interpretation has the advantage of being closer to the normal use of *sphragis*, but as verses 20 and 21 continue the metaphor of a building or household, the former view seems more probable.

The first inscription comes from Nu. xvi. 5, from the account of the revolt of Korah and his associates, in which the people are reminded that the Lord is well able to differentiate between the true and the false. This knowledge of God's infallible discernment is intended to provide strong encouragement to Timothy and all others perplexed by unworthy elements in the Church. It brings also its own restraint on all who take the responsibility of judgment upon themselves.

Although it is not the primary purpose of this quotation to draw attention to the predestination of God, this thought cannot be entirely absent since the knowledge of God is so inseparable from His purposes. The writer's main intention, however, is to show that God unerringly knows His true children.

The second inscription is not a precise citation although it is possibly intended to express the sentiment of Nu. xvi. 26, from the same context as the first. But Is. lii. 11 is nearer the sentiment and the LXX uses the same verb for *depart (aphistēmi)* as here. Bengel remarks that the imperative, *let every one . . . depart from iniquity* implies the power to depart, and the blessedness of those who depart. The reading of the received text, *the name of Christ*, is certainly not original since all the uncials and versions have the reading 'Lord'. To name the name of the Lord implied for Israel identification with His covenant, and all true Israelites would wish to avoid what He abhors. The thought seems to be that since men like Hymenaeus and Philetus had not departed from iniquity, as was clear from their injurious doctrine, they cannot be God's true children.

(iv) Degrees of honour (ii. 20, 21). There is a close connection between the metaphor of an edifice to describe the Church and the foundation referred to in the previous verse. Yet here it is not the external structure but the contents, particularly the various utensils, which are in mind, and Paul's purpose is to illustrate the variety of people, some good, others unworthy, which is to be found in the Christian Church. The language is certainly Pauline, as a comparison with 1 Cor. iii. 12 and Rom. ix. 21 shows, although Scott, who admits this, explains it as an example of the writer's reproduction of his Pauline patterns. But a simpler explanation assumes that the same association of ideas as in 1 Cor. iii is due to the workings of the same mind.

The train of thought does not follow quite as we should expect, for in a great house both types of vessels would be necessary and the wooden and earthen would never be considered worthless. The illustration in fact digresses in its application. The variety of vessels in the house is intended to show the variety of types in the Church, but the application fastens on the people and the vessels are completely forgotten. The real contrast is between the honourable and dishonourable, the thought imperceptibly having moved back to the case of Hymenæus and Philetus (verse 18). The phrase *to honour* finds an exact replica in Rom. ix. 21, 22 where the contrasting phrase *to dishonour* is more specifically applied to 'vessels of wrath fitted for destruction'. Yet the contrast is evidently not so strong here, for no such description is appended. Since the words form a prelude to a personal exhortation to Timothy, it must be assumed that the word *dishonour* is intended to be understood relatively. Timothy's aim must be to attain the most honourable usefulness, of which there are varying degrees. The focus is upon the cleanliness of each vessel, and this seems preferable to Bernard's contention that the illustration indicates the presence of evil members within the Church.

21. The indefinite subject of the verb *purge* shows that the following injunction is intended for all Christians. The action has been interpreted in two ways. Either the purging relates to the false teachers, especially Hymenæus and Philetus, and the words mean that Timothy is to take strong action against them (Bernard); or else it denotes inward purification (Scott). The latter idea would provide a fit sequel to the warning against *vain babblings* in verse 16. Yet the only other place in the Greek Testament where the verb *ekkathairō* is used is 1 Cor. v. 7, where it combines the idea of cleansing out impurities (typified by leaven), with the need of excommunicating a person.

The *vessel unto honour* is carefully delineated in three ways. First, he is *sanctified*, i.e. set apart for a holy purpose. Secondly, he is *meet for the master's use* (*euchrēstos*, another word used elsewhere only by Paul). Both Mark and Onesimus are described by the same word as being useful to the apostle (see 2 Tim. iv. 11 and Phm. 11), yet the Christian's serviceableness to Christ here is of much greater importance. And, thirdly, he is *prepared unto every good work*, which lays the main emphasis upon readiness for any good work rather than on the good work itself.

(v) The teacher's behaviour (ii. 22-26). This direct injunction to Timothy is closely linked with the general principles stated in verses 20 and 21. There is an implied contrast with the pursuit of good works, which *Flee also youthful lusts* does not fully bring out. The RSV has more correctly 'So shun youthful passions and aim at righteousness'. It need not be supposed that Timothy was beyond the age to need such advice, for as compared with Paul he was still at a stage when adverse influences might lead him astray. Spicq suggests that the apostle was here thinking of such passions as impatience, love of dispute and novelties, ambition, etc. This is supported by the contrasted virtues to be pursued, *righteousness, faith, charity, peace*, the first three of which have already been enjoined in 1 Tim. vi. 11. To live at peace *with them that call on the Lord* is an indispensable requisite of the Christian minister, as indeed of every Christian, although all too often ignored. The secret is to be found in the concluding words, *out of a pure heart* (cf. 1 Tim. i. 5), for peace and purity are never far apart.

23. The apostle again delivers a warning against foolish controversy. He uses the same verb (*paraiteomai*) as in 1 Tim. iv. 7 where the AV renders it 'refuse', although here the weaker term *avoid* is used. Something more than evasive action was required to deal with these *foolish and unlearned* (*apaideutos*, 'ill-educated', hence 'senseless') *questions*. Timothy should know that these questionings *gender strifes* (RSV 'breed quarrels'), and the only sane approach is to refuse to have anything to do with them. The word translated *strifes* (*machē*) is used also in Tit. iii. 9, where it applies to legal contentions (cf. comment there).

24. Whereas every Christian is called to be a *servant of the Lord*, the term is used here in a restricted sense. Anyone called as Timothy was to care for a community of believers has special claim to the title and for that very reason must rule out all striving. It may be that the Servant passages of Isaiah have influenced the apostle's thought, for if Christ did not strive it is incumbent on His followers also to cease from striving. Again the negative is contrasted with the positive virtues enjoined. The first word *gentle* (*ēpios*) expresses the general quality of kindliness, which must be exercised *unto all men*, while the third word *patient* (*anexikakos*) denotes an attitude of patient forbearance towards those who are in opposition. The second quality *apt to teach* has already been met in the qualifications required of a bishop (1 Tim. iii. 2).

25. The right treatment of opponents is an urgent matter for all who hold responsible Christian positions, and the apostle's injunction to *meekness* is calculated to win over these opponents rather than antagonize them. *Instructing* could be understood in the sense of 'correcting' (RV, RSV), since these particular opponents are in mind, but the word *paideuō* may be intended as a contrast to *apaideutos* (ill-educated) in verse 23. Simpson understands it of 'indoctrination of the truth rather than exposure of error'. It is not certain whether *those that oppose themselves* is the best translation, for the verb could be taken as passive instead of middle, in which case it would be translated 'those who are adversely affected' (Bernard). But whichever is correct it is clear that the people intended are the false teachers who are referred to elsewhere in the Pastorals. It must be the aim of the Christian minister to lead them, if possible, to *repentance*, although the apostle implies here that such repentance is a gift from God. It requires a change of mind (*metanoia*) to come to a recognition of *truth* when the mind is already ensnared. The same expression for recognition of truth is found in 1 Tim. ii. 4 denoting the divine desire for all men.

26. Graphic words are used to describe the reclamation of the devil's captives. *That they may recover themselves* (*ananēphō*) means literally 'that they may return to soberness' (RV mg.), a metaphor implying some previous duping by evil influences.

As in the case of intoxication the devil's method is 'to benumb the conscience, confuse the senses and paralyse the will' (Horton). But the metaphor becomes mixed when *the snare of the devil* is introduced (see 1 Tim. iii. 7 for a parallel use of the phrase, and cf. 1 Tim. vi. 9). The devil is portrayed in a double role. He is both intoxicator and captivator of men's minds. The second vivid verb *zōgreō* (*taken captive*) means 'to catch alive'; it is used elsewhere in the Greek Testament only in Lk. v. 10 where it occurs in Jesus' promise to Peter that he would catch men.

Considerable discussion has surrounded the use of two different Greek pronouns in the concluding phrase—*by him* (*autou*) *at his will* (*eis to ekeinou thelēma*), and three different interpretations have been suggested:

1. Both pronouns apply to the devil (as in AV and RSV where no distinction is made between them). This can claim the support of later Greek usage when the distinction between the personal pronoun *autos* and the demonstrative *ekeinos* was often disregarded (see Easton). This rendering certainly makes good sense and fits in well with the context.

2. RV takes the *autou* to refer to an antecedent in verse 24 and the *ekeinou* to verse 25, rendering the words, 'having been taken captive by the Lord's servant unto the will of God'. This is favoured by Lock on these grounds: it gives the full force to the verb *zōgreō* ('catch alive'), it makes 'unto His will' parallel to 'unto recognition of truth' (verse 25), and it ends the passage on a hopeful note. But these reasons do not seem to apply exclusively to this interpretation, for the devil also catches men alive, while the so-called parallel may equally well have been intended as a contrast, and the hopeful note is surely contained in the possibility of escape from the devil's snare after a period of submission.

3. A mediating view is that of the RV margin which has 'by the devil unto the will of God', and is preferred by Bernard and Scott. But this may be criticized on the grounds of its grammatical intricacy, involving as it does the assumption that *ekeinou* relates to the main subject of the sentence. Yet it has

the considerable advantage of differentiating the demonstrative and personal pronouns, which it may justly be claimed was probably intentional, and it avoids the difficulty inherent in the second interpretation of imagining that God takes captive the devil's captives and they, so to speak, merely exchange one snare for another.

VI. PREDICTIONS OF THE LAST DAYS (iii. 1–9)

The apostle now turns his attention to the future and describes a time of general moral decadence. There appears to be a definite connection between the heresy referred to in the last chapter and elsewhere in the Pastorals, and the disastrous corruption of society so vividly described here.

1. *The last days* is a common New Testament phrase denoting the period immediately preceding the consummation of the present age. Yet in the apostle's thought this future time is not unrelated to his own, for from verse 6 onwards he uses the present and not the future tense. The statement that *perilous* (*chalepos*, 'grievous') *times shall come* must not be restricted, therefore, to an eschatological interpretation. The following description is, in fact, so generally applicable that it has been used effectively to denounce many periods of moral corruption throughout the history of the Church.

2–5. The list itself seems to lack any premeditated order as was usually the case in the ethical lists used by the Greek moralists.[1] Spicq, on the other hand, points out that the Pastoral catalogues of vices, and especially this one, show many affinities with Jewish descriptions, and are particularly akin to Philo's lists; while Lock suggests the present list was probably based on some previous apocalyptic. There are many similarities between this catalogue and the vices mentioned in Rom. i, the main difference being that in the latter Paul is describing the contemporary Gentile world, whereas here a future condition is being envisaged.

The first two, *lovers of their own selves* (*philautoi*) and *covetous*

---

[1] Cf. Easton, pp. 197-202.

(*philarguroi*), supply the key to the rest of the list. The assonance of the Greek words is more closely retained in RV, 'lovers of self, lovers of money'. Moral corruption follows from love falsely directed. Self-centredness, and material advantages, when they become the chief objects of affection, destroy all moral values, and the subsequent list of vices is their natural fruit. It is significant that the list ends with a similar pair of words compounded with *philo—lovers of pleasures more than lovers of God* (verse 4). 'Rather than lovers of God' is more expressive of the Greek and implies, as the AV does not, that pleasure was regarded as a substitute for God. Basically, materialism is opposed to piety and is bound to end in irreligion.

A clear connection exists between *boasters* and *proud* (verse 2). The former word *alazōn* includes, according to Simpson, 'the bounce of swaggering', while the other word *huperēphanos*, when used in a bad sense, conveys the idea of haughtiness or arrogance. The word translated *blasphemers* is better rendered 'abusive' (as RSV), because the evil-speaking is directed towards fellow-men, not against God. The last three vices in verse 2 are all specific denials of definite Christian virtues (in the Greek all have the adversative prefix), bringing out forcefully the idea of militant moral perversion. The same evident reversal of moral values is also seen in five of the six vices mentioned in verse 3, the only word without the negative prefix being *false accusers* (*diaboloi*). *Trucebreakers* does not express the force of *aspondos* as clearly as RV 'implacable', for it denotes a hostility that admits of no truce. *Incontinent* is a reversal of self-control and *fierce* (*anēmeroi*) the antithesis of 'tame' or 'civilized', while the word rendered *despisers of those that are good* (*aphilagathoi*) really describes haters of goodness.

The assonance of the first two words in verse 4, which appears to be the only reason for their juxtaposition, cannot be reproduced in English. *Traitors, heady* are better rendered in RSV as 'treacherous, reckless'. Closely allied to the latter word is the next, *highminded* (*tetuphōmenoi*), which describes an unwarranted self-importance.

In verse 5 the apostle examines more exactly the religious

situation. Religion is not entirely denied, but it amounts to no more than an empty shell. There is an outward *form* (*morphōsis*, outline, semblance), but no *power*. Indeed it is not simply a matter of an organized religion which has ceased to function but a religion which is not intended to function. Its adherents are *denying the power thereof* which suggests a positive rejection of its effective power. They have no conception of the gospel as a generating force. It is clear that moral decadents can hardly be expected to pay more than the most superficial lip-service to piety, and then only to maintain a cloak of respectability.

Though the full development of this state of affairs is still future, yet Timothy is even now given the warning *from such turn away*, which apparently means that he must exercise discernment to prevent the admission of such people into membership of the Church. RV brings out the force of the Greek *kai* by including the word 'also' ('from these also turn away') in which case the reference may be to those mentioned in ii. 23.

6, 7. The same influences are seen in the actions of certain men who take advantage of gullible women, as the opening words, *For of this sort* (lit. 'of these', i.e. those mentioned in verse 5) show. Both Moffatt and Easton render the verb *endunō* (*creep*) as 'worm their way', implying insidious methods. The verb is used only here in this sense. Evidently the false teachers, having sought out women of the weaker sort, exerted such powerful influence upon them that the women lost their own freedom of thought, and could be described as taken *captive* (the same word as is used of prisoners of war). The word rendered *silly women* literally means 'little women' which is probably used to denote feebleness (RSV 'weak women'). Scott supposes that these women lacked moral substance rather than brains, but the context does not suggest that their intelligence was very remarkable. These women were *laden with sins* in the sense of being overwhelmed in their consciences. The verb *sōreuō* literally means 'to heap up' and is metaphorically used to express a cumulation of sins which has become so unbearable that any solution offered is clutched at. The last phrase in verse 6 is well translated 'swayed by various impulses' (RSV).

These women apparently desire to listen to other people's advice (*ever learning*), but their minds have become so fickle and warped that they have become incapable of attaining the *knowledge of the truth* (cf. 1 Tim. ii. 4). Their main quest is for sensational rather than serious information, and consequently they fall an easy prey to pseudo-Christian teachers.

8. An example of these teachers is found in *Jannes and Jambres*, two of Pharoah's magicians who withstood Moses, according to a work which probably circulated under their names and is referred to by Origen. While no mention of these names is found in the Bible, they are referred to in the Targum of Jonathan on Ex. vii. 11 and in various early Christian literary works (cf. Lock and Dibelius for details). Timothy would no doubt have been well acquainted with legend and would draw his own conclusions from the allusion. 'Like the Egyptian sorcerers, the false teachers are bound to fail, and like them they act from evil motives' (Scott): some have supposed the word *so* implies the practice of magic on the part of the false teachers, but the word need not be pressed, for the similarity consists rather in a common resistance to *the truth*. At the same time, as Plummer rightly points out, 'the connexion between heresy and superstition is a very real and a very close one', and is as patent in modern times as in ancient. It is noteworthy that both *truth* and *faith* have the definite article, and are therefore used in an objective sense.

The idea of corruptness of mind is found also in 1 Tim. vi. 5, where it even more strongly denotes men destitute of the truth. It is no surprise that they are described as *reprobate* (*adokimoi*), for when put to the test *concerning the faith* they have no hope of being proved acceptable.

9. The same verb expressing advancement (*prokoptō*) is used in ii. 16 of the increasing impiety of the false teachers, and in iii. 13 of their progressive degradation. Here, however, Timothy is assured that their apparent success is severely limited, for their true character *shall be manifest unto all men* (the word *manifest, ekdēlos,* is a strengthened form meaning 'clearly evident'). The thought in this verse appears to be based on the assumption that imposture is always tracked down in the end.

VII. FURTHER EXHORTATIONS TO TIMOTHY
(iii. 10–17)

(a) An historical reminder (iii. 10–12)

10. There is a strong contrast between Timothy and the false teachers as is clear from the emphatic *thou*. The historical allusion that follows is particularly designed to encourage the apostle's rather fearful lieutenant. *Thou hast fully known (parakoloutheō)* does not bring out the precise sense for the meaning is 'to follow up' or 'trace out as an example'. The same verb is used in the sense of 'investigate' in Luke's preface (Lk. i. 3). It need not, therefore, imply that Timothy was an eye-witness of Paul's earliest sufferings as a missionary, as is supposed by Easton, who then cites this as an anachronism because Timothy is not mentioned in Acts until after these early persecutions.

In a catalogue of nine features the apostle cites his own example not for his own enhancement but for Timothy's encouragement. Paul's life had borne rich testimony to God's faithfulness. It is significant that *doctrine* is mentioned first, for throughout the Pastorals it occupies a prominent place. Timothy had been privileged to listen to Paul's expositions on many themes. But doctrine must be linked with life, and so the next six virtues bring out the practical character of the apostle's impact upon Timothy.

The word translated *manner of life (agōgē)* denotes general behaviour, which a man's closest associates can never fail to know in all its aspects. Linked with this is the apostle's *purpose (prothesis)* or 'chief aim' in life, which Easton translates 'firm resolution'. *Faith, longsuffering, charity* and *patience* are essentially Christian virtues, often referred to by Paul, of which all but 'long-suffering' had been enjoined on Timothy himself (1 Tim. vi. 11). The last word *patience* (*hupomonē*) is better rendered 'endurance' or 'steadfastness' (as RSV), as it denotes a quality of fortitude in adverse conditions. If it be felt that the apostle lacks modesty in relating his own Christian graces, it should be remembered that a man, whose own race of life is nearly run, may draw out the main lessons of his experience for the benefit of younger aspirants without the least suggestion of egotism.

11. The appeal to the happenings at Antioch, Iconium and Lystra rather than to more recent examples of Paul's sufferings is prompted by Timothy's vivid recollection of these when he was still a youth at Lystra. The apostle's bearing during these trying events may well have made a deep impression on his mind and may even have been the major factor in influencing Timothy's attachment to the apostle. In any case the reminiscence of the earliest meeting of the two men is very natural for an ageing man in prison. The apostle brings into focus not only his own endurance, but the Lord's deliverances. There may possibly be an allusion to the words of Ps. xxxiv. 17 ('the Lord delivereth them out of all their troubles').

12. After the apostle's visit to the places named in verse 11, it is recorded in Acts xiv. 21 that he exhorted the believers 'that we must through much tribulation enter into the kingdom of God'; so the present reference to the sufferings of those who *will live godly in Christ Jesus* is possibly due to the association of ideas in the apostle's mind. The principle that devoted Christians must expect persecution was explicit in our Lord's own teaching. The phrase *in Christ Jesus* means more than 'Christian' (Easton), for it brings out the mystical sphere in which Christian life is lived and is in close harmony with the use of the expression in Paul's earlier Epistles.

(b) An exhortation to steadfastness (iii. 13–17)

13. A contrast to those who desire to live godly lives is now introduced. A progressive worsening of evil influences is prophesied, the same verb (*prokoptō*) being used as in verse 9 (q.v.). The underlying idea is somewhat ironical—'making progress in the direction of the worse'. Having set the worst possible goal in front of them they will make good headway by means of deception, but on the way they will fall a prey to their own methods. The word translated *seducers* (*goētes*) is literally 'wizards' but should be understood in the sense of 'impostors' (RV, RSV). Its use here was probably suggested by the earlier allusion to the Egyptian magicians (verse 8).

14. But against such a background of militant error, the Christian leader must stand firm on what he knows of the truth, like a rock resisting the increasing fury of the waves. He is to *continue* in the sense of 'abiding' in *the things* he has *learned* and *been assured of* (RSV 'firmly believed'). In contrast to the false teachers with their constant endeavour to advance to something new, Timothy may be satisfied with what he has already received. The basis of this confidence in the tradition is twofold. It is assured by Timothy's knowledge of his teachers and his knowledge of the Scriptures. The character of teachers closely reflects the character of what is taught; and since Timothy knew well the integrity not only of the apostle Paul, but also of his own mother and grandmother and others who had helped him arrive at an understanding of Christian truth, he may rest assured that he has not himself been deceived.

15. An unusual phrase here describes *the holy scriptures*, *hiera grammata*, 'sacred writings' (RV), and the question naturally arises why this form was used. Scott notes three possible answers: 1. It may be used technically to draw attention to the way Timothy learnt to read, hence the significance of the words *from a child*. 2. It may stress the sacred character of Timothy's learning in contrast to the varieties of doubtful literature used by the false teachers. 3. It may be designed to include other literature, such as apocalyptic and even Christian books. But Dibelius cites many instances from early writers where the phrase is used of the Scriptures, apparently without any special significance. It seems reasonable to suppose, however, that the apostle had some specific purpose in using the phrase here in contrast to the more usual phrase in the next verse.

The power of the Scriptures is directed to a particular end, *to make thee wise unto salvation* or, as RSV, 'to instruct you for salvation'. The latter phrase *eis sōtērian* is frequently used in the earlier Epistles of Paul, while the notion of such value attached to the Old Testament is so thoroughly Pauline that Schlatter thinks it is difficult to imagine anyone else speaking of it in such terms (cf. Spicq). That salvation is appropriated only *through faith which is in Christ Jesus* is also thoroughly Pauline. The mere reading of Scripture is ineffective in securing salvation unless faith is in operation, faith centred entirely in Christ. This was evident in the case of the unbelieving Jews.

16. There is a twofold problem in the interpretation of this verse. First, what is the precise meaning of *graphē* (*scripture*)? and second, should *theopneustos* be rendered as a predicate, *is given by inspiration of God*, or as a qualifying adjective, 'Every scripture inspired of God is also profitable' (RV)? The second problem cannot properly be settled until the first is decided, although in some aspects the two problems are inseparable. *graphē* could mean any writing, but the uniform New Testament use of it with reference to Scripture (i.e. the Old Testament) determines its meaning here. But does it mean Scripture as a whole or separate passages within Scripture? The latter meaning is in accordance with the general use of the singular noun, and must therefore be given due weight in the present passage. Yet the determining factor must be the meaning of *pasa, all* (RV 'every'). Bernard decides emphatically for 'every' on the basis of the absence of the article, but Simpson points out analogous cases where *pas* is used in a semi-technical phrase and where the meaning 'every' is ruled out, e.g. Acts ii. 36 where 'all the house of Israel' is clearly demanded (see also Eph. ii. 21, iii. 15; Col. iv. 12). Yet it may well be that in all these exceptions the *pas* draws attention to the partitive aspect of the expression, and, if that is so, the present phrase may mean Scripture as viewed in each separate part of it.

The second problem cannot be decided purely on grammatical grounds for both AV and RV renderings are grammatically possible. It would be more natural for the adjective, if attributive, to precede the noun, i.e. 'every inspired scripture' rather than 'every scripture inspired', but the latter is not impossible. The context itself must decide. Simpson maintains that the adjectival interpretation 'presents a curious specimen of anticlimax'. It is difficult to see why the apostle should need to assure Timothy that inspired scriptures are profitable. On the other hand, it is not easy to see why Timothy should need to be assured, at this point, of the inspiration of the Scriptures. Bernard's explanation is: 'It is the *profitableness* of the Old Testament which St. Paul would press upon Timothy, not its *inspiration*, of which he had been assured from his youth'. The *kai* (*and*) before *profitable* is certainly more intelligible in the AV rendering, for the RV 'also' seems to be pointless (cf. Lock). Bernard defends the ascensive force of *kai* from the similar use in 1 Tim. iv. 4, but Simpson appeals to the same passage to support the conjunctive force of *kai*, and it would seem that Simpson's opinion is here correct. While not ruling out the possibility of the alternative interpretation, it is rather more in harmony with both grammar and syntax to translate 'All scripture is inspired by God and profitable . . .' (RSV). Timothy is not therefore being informed of the inspiration of Scripture, for this was a doctrine commonly admitted by Jews, but he is being reminded that the basis of its profitableness lies in its inspired character.

Four spheres are now mentioned in which the usefulness of Scripture can be seen. The former two relate to doctrine and the latter two to practice. *Profitable for doctrine* refers to positive teaching, while *reproof* represents the negative aspect. On the ethical plane, the Scriptures provide both *correction* and *instruction* (*paideia* is better rendered 'training' as RSV); again both negative and positive elements are stressed. All these uses of Scripture were admitted by Judaism; and the advanced ethics of the Jews was due to its basis in the Old Testament. Since the Christians took over the same Scriptures, the same profitableness applies. But for them each one of these uses became more comprehensive as the Old Testament teaching was illumined by the life and teaching of Christ.

17. There is a distinct objective in this profitableness of Scripture. The verse opens with a clause introduced by *hina* which denotes that purpose or result. The Christian minister has in his hands a God-given instrument designed to equip him completely for his work. The word *artios* (*perfect*, RV 'complete') describes a man perfectly adapted for his task, while the cognate verb *exartizō* (*throughly furnished*) adds further emphasis to the same thought. The RSV well renders the last phrase 'equipped for every good work'. For this use of 'good works' cf. ii. 21.

The phrase *man of God* appears to apply specifically to the Christian teachers rather than to Christians generally (cf. 1 Tim. vi. 11). 'The man of God is before all the man of the Bible' (Spicq). There may be an allusion to the work of the prophets in the use of this title, for it was frequently applied to them in the Old Testament.

VIII. PAUL'S FAREWELL MESSAGE (iv. 1–18)

(a) The final charge (iv. 1–5)

1. The apostle has already used the solemn verb *diamarturomai* (*charge*), with which the verse starts, in urging Timothy to exercise impartiality in dealing with Church affairs (1 Tim. v. 21), and the adjuration here is couched in almost identical terms, yet without reference to 'elect angels' as in the former case. The solemnity of the present charge is doubly impressive as the parting advice of the aged warrior to his younger and rather timid lieutenant. It would be emptied of much of its meaning and dignity if it were no more than a fictitious attempt to represent what the real Paul might have said to the real Timothy. Particularly appropriate to Paul's closing instructions is the reference to Christ as the One who *shall judge the quick and the dead*, which may already have become 'a fixed formula in a baptismal creed' (Lock). As the apostle contemplates his life's end the idea of judgment cannot escape his thought. He had often stressed it before (cf. Acts xvii. 31; Rom. ii. 16; 1 Cor. iv. 5). RSV 'the living and the dead' avoids the archaism of *quick*.

Both the *appearing* and the *kingdom* are regarded as still future, yet they are so much the Christian's assured hope that they can form a basis for adjuration. Such future glories could not fail to inspire Timothy to present fortitude.

2. The five exhortations contained in this verse are as applicable to all Christian ministers as to Timothy. *Preach the word*; the aorist tense of this verb and all the succeeding imperatives adds solemnity and abruptness to the injunctions. The apostle regards Timothy as being at a crisis in which he must make definite resolves towards positive action. He must preach the word, in which he had been nurtured, as never before. *Be instant in season, out of season*; the verb *ephistēmi* means 'to stand by, be at hand', hence the meaning here seems to be that the Christian minister must always be on duty. He must take every opportunity to serve, whether the occasion seems opportune or not. Easton paraphrases 'be at your task whether men will listen or not', but this tends to restrict the application to preaching, whereas the reference is probably to all Timothy's varied tasks. *Reprove*; Timothy and Titus are both strongly urged to reprove (*elenchō*) (cf. 1 Tim. v. 20; Tit. i. 13, ii. 15), and no Christian minister must shirk his responsibility in this respect. Christian discipline in our modern age is so generally lax that the moral status of many communities is greatly weakened. *Rebuke*; this word (*epitimaō*), closely akin to the last, denotes in New Testament usage the idea of censure. *Exhort*; *parakaleō* may mean either 'exhort' or 'encourage', and both these meanings describe aspects of the preacher's work, but if this duty is taken with the preceding two 'involving an appeal to the reason, the conscience, and the will' (Scott), the former meaning is the more probable (as RV, RSV).

All these imperatives must be effected *with all longsuffering and doctrine*. The first qualification denotes the manner and the second the method which Timothy must adopt; *makrothumia* (patience, forbearance, longsuffering) is a favourite Pauline expression, and is generally used of God's forbearance. In Col. i. 11 it is used, as here, of the Christian's patience in trying circumstances. Christian reproof without the grace of long-sufferance has often led to a harsh, censorious attitude intensely harmful to the cause of Christ. But the other requirement is equally essential, for correction must be intelligently understood and hence based on 'teaching'. To rebuke without instruction is to leave the root cause of error untouched.

3. Such attention to *sound doctrine* will become increasingly urgent as the time (*kairos*) comes when there will be open opposition to the gospel. The apostle is looking ahead to times even less favourable than his own, when men *will not endure* (*anechō*, 'bear with') such doctrine. Scott supposes the author is really describing his own day but attributing it to Paul's prophetic insight. But there is no need to deny that the apostle could foresee times in the not too distant future when the conditions he describes would apply, for these future conditions were already present in germ. Christian history can furnish many examples of men's desires to *heap* (*episōreuō*, 'heap together', RSV 'accumulate') *to themselves teachers* who are not renowned for their ability to teach or their authority, but who seek the satisfaction of *their own lusts* (RSV 'suit their own likings'). The emphasis is, as Bernard remarks, on 'personal caprice'. The absence of any serious purpose behind this amassing of 'teachers' is ironically summed up in the description of the hearers as *having itching ears*, which means literally 'having the hearing tickled', as if what they heard merely scratched their eardrums without penetrating further.

4. Those with no more serious intentions than to satisfy their own desires will not only lack sufficient discernment to differentiate between *truth* and *fables* (*muthoi*, 'myths'), but will, in fact, *turn away their ears from the truth*, which suggests a deliberate refusal to hear it. The reason appears to be the superior fascination of fables; but the verb used for *turned unto fables* (*ektrepō*) is used of deviation from the true course, and suggests here a wandering into counterfeits (RSV has 'wander into myths'), with no awareness that truth has been left behind.

5. The opening words bring the thought emphatically back to Timothy. RSV 'As for you' expresses the emphatic pronoun *su* much more definitely than *watch thou in all things*. The verb *nēphō* means 'be sober' and enjoins moral alertness or 'coolness and presence of mind'. The same verb is used in 1 Thes. v. 6, 8 to denote a watchful and alert attitude towards Christ's second coming. The Christian minister must seek to cultivate an unruffled alertness in every aspect of his work. He must also *endure afflictions*, which recalls the previous injunction in ii. 3 where the same verb occurs in a compound form.

The word *evangelist* is used of Philip in Acts xxi. 8, no doubt to distinguish him from Philip the apostle, and also in Eph. iv. 11 where it seems to denote an order of workers midway between apostles and prophets on the one hand and pastors and teachers on the other. There was probably a good deal of fluidity in the use of these terms describing various offices and there is no need to suppose that the terms were uniformly used. The function implied here is preaching the gospel and the term could equally well be used of Timothy and of any other Christian worker. The concluding words, *make full proof of thy ministry*, are not correctly rendered, for the verb *plērophoreō* means here simply 'to accomplish'. Timothy is putting his hand to the plough and must not look back until his *ministry (diakonia)* is completed. The word *diakonia* brings out the many aspects of his service, and Moffatt well renders, 'discharge all your duties as a minister'.

(b) A triumphant confession (iv. 6–8)

6. There is a definite connection between the solemn personal assertions which the apostle is about to make and the last charge just given to Timothy. *For I (ego gar)* contrasts with *but thou (su de)* of verse 5. The words translated *ready to be offered* mean literally 'poured out as a libation'. Paul had earlier used this figure in Phil. ii. 17, where the verb *spendomai* is found in a conditional clause, in which the apostle contemplates the possibility of his being condemned to death. Here the action is in process. Harrison (pp. 112, 113) finds it inconceivable that such a metaphor could have been stored in

Paul's mind during the four or five intervening years, but the idea of a Christian martyr's life-blood being a libation or drink-offering was sufficiently striking when it had once caught the imagination of a man like Paul, to recur to his mind on many occasions.

Closely linked with the preceding statement are the words, *and the time of my departure is at hand,* which also draw attention to the imminence of death. But the word translated *departure* (*analusis*) triumphantly expresses the apostle's view of the end; it is 'a loosing, e.g. of a vessel from its moorings or of a soldier striking his tent' (Abbott-Smith). What might seem the end to Timothy appears to the apostle as a glorious new era when he will be released from all his present restrictions. The noun is used nowhere else in the New Testament, but the cognate verb is used by Paul in the same sense in Phil. i. 23.

7. The three perfects convey a sense of finality; for Paul this is the end. In 1 Tim. vi. 12 the apostle had appealed to Timothy to 'fight the good fight of faith', and now he declares his own fight is over. It is probable that the responsibilities of his apostolic office are here graphically represented by the word *agōn*, meaning 'struggle' or 'contest'. It is generally supposed that *agōn* must be understood of an athletic contest in view of the next phrase, but Simpson strongly argues for the military meaning, which he considers more impressive.

I have finished my course (*dromos,* 'race') draws specific attention to the athletic arena as a metaphor of Christian service. It is significant that Paul makes no claim to have won the race, but is content to have stayed the course. This metaphor is a Pauline favourite and is particularly suited to express the idea of endurance in Christian life and service.

The third assertion *I have kept the faith* has been understood by some writers to refer to the athlete's promise to keep the rules (Easton), or to the military man's oath of fidelity (Calvin). But since the apostle has urged his lieutenants many times to guard the deposit, it is possible that the same metaphor of a steward is here in mind. Deissmann considers the phrase to be no more than a business formula for keeping an engagement;

but even if the apostle borrowed his phrase from contemporary commercial practice, he ennobles it in the process. *The faith* seems to be as objective as *the fight* and *the course*.

8. The apostle continues his thought into the future as is shown by *henceforth* (*loipon*), a word drawing attention to what remains to be realized as contrasted with those things already accomplished (verse 7). *There is laid up* (*apokeimai*) *for me a crown of righteousness* is reminiscent not only of the laurel wreaths of honour awarded to Olympic winners, but also of the awards made to loyal subjects by oriental sovereigns for services rendered (Dibelius cites an example from an inscription of Antiochus I, where similar phraseology is used). There are two ways of understanding this phrase *crown of righteousness*. If the genitive is appositional as in parallel phrases, e.g. 'crown of life' (Jas. i. 12; Rev. ii. 10), then *righteousness* must be the crown. But if the genitive is possessive, the phrase would mean 'the crown which is the reward of the virtues of the righteous man' (White). Most commentators prefer the second interpretation, which is the only one in harmony with Paul's doctrine of righteousness.

There may be an implied contrast between *the Lord, the righteous judge* and the wrong judgments of the emperor Nero under whose perverted sense of justice the apostle is at the moment suffering. The idea may, on the other hand, contrast with the not always impartial decisions of the Olympic umpires (Easton). If the Olympic Games supply the metaphor here there is a marked deviation in the delay between the completion of the race and the receiving of the crown, which for the Christian is not immediate as in the Games, but must await *that day*. Already in i. 12 (q.v.) the apostle has intimated his forward look to that glorious day of Christ's appearing and it is evident that this apocalyptic vision dominated his present reactions and his future hopes.

The apostle hastens to add that this *crown* is not a special reservation for himself alone. He seems sensitive about appearing self-centred and points out, no doubt for the immediate encouragement of Timothy, that a similar crown awaits all

who fulfil the conditions. Those *that love his appearing* probably
describes all those who loved the Lord, for all the early
Christians had an intense longing for Christ's complete
triumph (Scott). As the perfect tense suggests they have loved
His appearing in the past and will continue to do so to the
moment of receiving the reward.

(c) **Some personal requests** (iv. 9–13)

9. The concluding section (verses 9–22) marks the climax of
the Epistle, and shows the great apostle making his final
personal arrangements before his departure. Twice (in verses
9 and 21) he urges Timothy to lose no time to come to him,
and this reiterated desire proves not only the imminence of the
end but also the strong attachment which existed between the
two men. A problem has been raised about the appropriateness
of the present request. It is argued by Easton, for instance,
that the earlier part of the letter has given the impression that
Paul is writing because he does not expect to see Timothy
again, and that this verse and the following section introduce
a startling change. Yet i. 4 seems to suggest a possibility of
reunion. The contents of this letter may be designed not so
much to give Timothy new instructions about what he is to
do after Paul's decease, but to confirm policies already verbally
communicated. The fact that Paul urges haste shows that he
is not too optimistic about the possibility of his request being
fulfilled in time. Admittedly some months would elapse before
Timothy could receive the request and travel to Rome, as
Scott points out, but this does not justify the conclusion that
the request must be out of place in the present letter.[1]

10. The request for Timothy's presence is all the more
significant in view of the defection of Demas. There is a note
of solitariness as well as sadness in the statement *For Demas hath
forsaken me, having loved this present world*, for Paul clearly regards
his action as related to him personally and not to the Church
at large. He is mentioned in Col. iv. 14 as one of Paul's close
associates, but by this time he had perhaps found the apostle's

[1] See the Introduction, pp. 22 ff., for a discussion of this point.

demands too rigorous. There is, however, nothing to suggest that Demas became an apostate, although there was a later tradition to this effect.

The contrast between those who love Christ's appearing and *Demas* who loved *this present world* (*aiōn*) is brought out not only by the use of the same verb (*agapaō*, 'love'), but also by the fact that *aiōn* denotes the world under aspects of time, thus emphasizing the difference between the present and future time sequences.

There is no other reference to *Crescens* in the New Testament, but there is a tradition which connects him with the churches of Vienne and Mayence in Gaul. The reading *Galatia* is changed in some MSS to 'Gaul', and this may have arisen either from the similarity of the two names in the Greek or from the fact that Gaul was widely called Galatia among first-century Greek writers (cf. Bernard's discussion). Since, however, the apostle's use of the term 'Galatia' elsewhere applies to Asiatic Galatia this seems the most probable here.

The despatch of *Titus* to *Dalmatia* would seem to indicate the cessation of his work in Crete. His new sphere was on the eastern shore of the Adriatic Sea.

11. *Luke* is also mentioned in Col. iv. 14, where he is styled 'the beloved physician' and probably remains with Paul to minister to his weakness. The position of the word *only* in the AV suggests an emphasis which is absent from the Greek. Moffatt well renders it 'Luke is the only one who is with me'. It need not be supposed that the others had forsaken Paul as Demas had done, but that Paul had himself sent them on various missions, retaining only Luke. As in Col. iv. 10 *Mark* appears as a member of the Pauline circle, and, in striking contrast with the dissension he created by his early association with Paul (Acts xv. 37 f.), he is now commended for his usefulness (*euchrēstos*, 'serviceable', not *profitable*) for *ministry* (*diakonia*, a quite general term expressing any form of service). Scott suggests the meaning 'he can turn his hand to anything'. Timothy is asked to *take* and *bring* him with him, which presumably means that Mark was somewhere along Timothy's route.

12. The many references to *Tychicus* in Paul's Epistles indicate that he was a reliable associate. He was the bearer of the Epistles to both Colossians and Ephesians, and it is not improbable that he took the present letter to Timothy, if *apesteila* (*have I sent*) is regarded as an epistolary aorist. The most likely explanation of Tychicus' mission to *Ephesus* is that he was to relieve Timothy during the latter's absence in Rome while visiting Paul (cf. Tit. iii. 12).

13. The references to the *cloke*, the *books* and the *parchments* are so incidental that they bear strong marks of authenticity, and this fact is acknowledged in the various fragment theories, which all number this verse among the genuine passages. The word used for cloak is *phailonēs* or *phelonēs*, which represents the Latin *paenula*, an outer garment of heavy material, circular in shape with a hole in the middle for the head (cf. Easton). Paul had evidently left it on a recent visit to Troas, when Carpus, unknown elsewhere, was apparently his host. This cannot be the visit to the same city mentioned in Acts xx. 6 for several years had now elapsed.

It is impossible to say what either the books or the parchments (*membranai*) were, but the latter word suggests documents of some value, since vellum was too expensive to replace the common papyrus for general purposes. Some have suggested these latter were Paul's legal papers, e.g. his certificate of Roman citizenship. Another suggestion is that they contained parts, at least, of the Scripture. But though there can be no more than speculation about their identity, the desire to receive them throws interesting light on Paul's literary pursuits, even while on missionary journeys. It is not impossible, at least, that Paul had in his possession some written account of the Lord's doings and sayings and that he wished to have them to hand in his present critical situation.

(d) A particular warning (iv. 14, 15)

14, 15. The mention of the opposition of *Alexander the coppersmith* may be occasioned by the previous reference to the cloak and the books. There may have been some association of ideas which caused the revival of the memory. The words *did me* *much evil* mean literally 'showed forth many evil things against me'. The nature of this evil is further defined in verse 15, *for he hath greatly withstood our words.* Whether we take words (*logoi*) as the Christian doctrine which Paul preached (RSV has 'our message'), or Paul's defence at his trial, at which Alexander may have been a witness for the prosecution, it is clear that the evil was in the realm of mental and not physical violence. The use of the plural *our* for the singular is thoroughly Pauline.

Two other references to an Alexander are found in Acts xix. 33, 34 and 1 Tim. i. 20. In the latter case Paul links Alexander with Hymenæus in a temporary excommunication and some have identified the coppersmith with this man, and then have proceeded to argue that 2 Timothy must have preceded 1 Timothy. But even if the two Alexanders are the same person there is insufficient evidence that the present verse must describe an event prior to the excommunication. The aorist tenses point to a specific act of opposition, but no indication is given as to how long ago the action happened. The other Alexander mentioned in Acts has some claims for consideration, for he attempted on that occasion to make a defensive speech but was prevented from doing so. It is possible, therefore, that on some later occasion he sought to revenge at Paul's expense the humiliation he suffered at the hands of the mob. Harrison thinks it inconceivable that Alexander would have nursed his grudge for so many years, but personal grievances have been known to survive a great deal longer than this theory necessitates. Even if we cannot with certainty identify this coppersmith, he was evidently well known to Timothy, who is urged *be thou ware* of him, or more literally 'be on your guard against', 'keep yourself away from him' (*phulassou* being used in the middle voice).

The apostle curbs his natural resentment by citing the words of Ps. lxii. 12, which reads 'for thou renderest to every man according to his work'. Compare Paul's injunction in Rom. xii. 19.

(e) The first defence (iv. 16, 17)

16, 17. *At my first answer* (verse 16) should read as RV 'at my first defence' (*apologia*). Evidently the reference is to the preliminary investigation preceding the formal trial, which was sometimes delayed for a considerable period. There are three factors to be taken into account in attempting to reconstruct the historical situation. At this defence *all men forsook* Paul; the defence provided an opportunity for the preaching of the gospel; and it resulted in some form of deliverance. There are many points of resemblance with Paul's defence at Caesarea, and some have claimed on the basis of this that Paul is here calling to mind this earlier trial. But there is no mention of his being generally forsaken in Acts xxiv, and the situation there seems much less hostile than here. On the other hand, if these words describe the preliminaries to the second Roman trial, a serious difficulty has been imagined because of the alleged contradiction with verses 6–8. There the end is imminent and Paul sees no hope of any release. He is, in fact, already in process of being offered up. But here he speaks of a deliverance, *and I was delivered out of the mouth of the lion.* The aorist tense of the verb suggests that the apostle is thinking of an historic occasion on which his defence was successful. Many solutions have been offered to account for the apparent contradiction. Some who deny Pauline authorship of the Pastorals as a whole have recourse to one of two alternatives. Either verses 9–22 were part of a genuine fragment which belonged to a totally different context from verses 6–8; or the personal details were composed by a later author to give the conclusion of the letter a thoroughly Pauline flavour. The second alternative seems inconceivable for the whole section contains incidental personal notes such as no later admirer of Paul would ever have thought of inventing. Would such a Paulinist portray all men forsaking his hero in the hour of his greatest need? And would the cloak and parchments ever have occurred to a writer wishing to append a characteristic Pauline conclusion? The first alternative raises the problem of the author's apparent unawareness of the alleged conflicting statements which he places in such close juxtaposition.[1]

[1] Cf. Introduction pp. 21 ff. for further difficulties in the Fragment Hypothesis.

Those who maintain the Pauline authorship of the whole of 2 Timothy have generally supposed that verses 16, 17 refer to an earlier examination which appeared to turn out favourably for the apostle and at least gave him the opportunity for witnessing in Rome, but that the position had since deteriorated, verses 6–8 representing the position at the time of writing. The alleged conflict between verses 6–8 and 18 is apparent only if the words of verse 18, *the Lord shall deliver me from every evil work*, are understood to imply that the apostle optimistically expects release. But these words seem more intelligible if understood in a spiritual sense.

It was the custom for a defendant's friends to appear with him to give moral support, but Paul complains that *no man stood with me* (*paraginomai*, to 'stand by', 'support' or 'second' (cf. Simpson)). The RV and RSV 'no one took my part' brings out this technical sense. It may therefore mean that no one officially acted the part of *patronus*, or that the Roman Christians, knowing nothing first hand of Paul's missionary journeys, were not in a position to assist. Yet Paul is not bitter against the desertion of either the local Christians or his closer associates as his words 'may it not be laid to their account' (RV) show. The words *I pray God* are not expressed in the Greek.

The desertion of his friends is mentioned to bring into greater prominence the divine assistance. *Notwithstanding* probably brings out the contrast too strongly, but the Greek *de* is certainly adversative and warrants the translation 'But the Lord stood by me' (RV, RSV). The word *paristēmi* is here used in the same sense as in Rom. xvi. 2 where it has the sense 'stand by for help'. This help is further described as a strengthening (for the verb *endunamai* see 1 Tim. i. 12), the meaning clearly being that the apostle received great moral courage to proclaim the gospel to his judges. *That by me the preaching might be fully known* does not rightly represent *plērophoreō*, which means 'fully performed, hence completed', the reference being to the apostle's preaching commission. He regards his mission as incomplete until he has preached at Rome.

A difficulty arises over the next words, *and that all the Gentiles might hear*, for if the words are understood literally the reference cannot be to Paul's defence before his judges. Scott argues that these words show that Paul hoped for release and consequently for a further period of missionary activity. But even then it would be necessary to understand *all* in a very general sense. Bernard supposes that the words must be understood metaphorically. 'The opportunity given to St. Paul of pleading his cause in the official centre of Rome, the mistress of the nations, was in a sense the "fulfilling" of the preaching of the Gospel.' Spicq takes the same view, maintaining from Mt. x. 17–33 that witness before tribunals was one of the greatest forms of the preaching of the gospel. At the same time it should be noted that *all the Gentiles (panta ta ethnē)* is a phrase used in Rom. i. 5 of the scope of Paul's apostleship, and in Rom. xvi. 26 of the extent of the revelation of the mystery of the gospel. In each case the phrase is used generally in a sense equivalent to 'cosmopolitan'. If this is the meaning here the apostle is contemplating the cosmopolitan character of the audience he addressed on the occasion of his first defence.

When he adds *I was delivered out of the mouth of the lion* Paul is using a common metaphor to express deliverance from some extreme danger (cf. Dn. vi. 20 and Ps. xxii. 21). This is more reasonable than to suppose that the lion is metaphorical for the Emperor Nero, or is an allusion to the amphitheatre, or symbolic of Satan, the roaring lion (1 Pet. v. 8).

(f) **The forward look (iv. 18)**

18. The key to the understanding of this verse lies in the obvious associations in thought between the aorist, *I was delivered* of verse 17 and the future, *the Lord shall deliver*. If these two verbs are both taken in a literal sense of deliverance in this life, there can be no doubt that Paul had a firm conviction that he would be released. But this seems contrary to the resignation to his fate in verses 6–8. The deliverance in this verse is reminiscent of the Lord's prayer, which is clearly intended in a spiritual manner, and it seems most reasonable, therefore, to suppose that a similar meaning is attached to the words here. The past physical deliverance reminds him of constant spiritual deliverances and raises his confidence for the future.

Not only is he confident that the Lord will deliver, but He will also *preserve* him *unto his heavenly kingdom*. The verb used is *sōzō* usually 'to save' but here in the more specific sense of 'keeping safe'. The use of the adjective 'heavenly' (a characteristic Pauline expression) draws attention to the emphatic contrast between God's kingdom and the present earthly circumstances of sorrow and suffering. It is strongly reminiscent of the Lord's teaching about the kingdom of heaven. It is no wonder the contemplation of it raises in the apostle's mind a doxology in which he ascribes eternal glory to Christ. His mind is clearly centred more on eternal realities than any hopes of further release.

IX. CONCLUDING SALUTATIONS (iv. 19–22)

19. It is interesting to note that *Prisca* (otherwise called Priscilla) is mentioned before her husband as in Rom. xvi. 3; Acts xviii. 18, 26, although the reverse order is found in Acts xviii. 2 and 1 Cor. xvi. 19. These facts are hardly sufficient to support the suggestion that Priscilla was either of higher rank or of stronger personality than her husband. All the references to them show a strong attachment to the apostle. The same is true of *Onesiphorus* whose *household* is so warmly commended in i. 16, 17.

20. There is an *Erastus* mentioned in Rom. xvi. 23, described as the city treasurer (presumably of Corinth). Another person of the same name, referred to in Acts xix. 22, was an associate of Timothy when both were sent by Paul into Macedonia. Although no certainty can be established, it is more likely that this helper of Paul is to be identified with the Erastus mentioned here. Timothy may have been unaware of his location and if they were old associates would naturally be interested in his whereabouts.

The reference to *Trophimus* has occasioned difficulties, for it is evident from Acts xx. 4 that he was with Paul when he went to Miletus during the closing stages of his third missionary journey and from Acts xxi. 29 that he went with Paul to

Jerusalem, for he was seen with him in the city. The present intimation that Paul left him ill at Miletus cannot, therefore, refer to this visit. It must relate to a subsequent visit after the apostle's release from his first Roman imprisonment. Some scholars (e.g. Harrison) find difficulty in believing that history would repeat itself and that Paul would twice visit Miletus with Trophimus, but this does not seem a major difficulty when it is remembered that Trophimus was an Ephesian (Acts xxi. 29). It is not impossible, therefore, that on Paul's last journey from Asia to Rome Trophimus was to accompany him, but had to be left at Miletus due to illness, a fact of which Timothy could easily have been unaware.

21. The urgent request of verse 9 is repeated with the addition of the words *before winter*. For a period of some weeks the Adriatic would be closed to shipping and the apostle is therefore anxious that Timothy should hasten to reach Italy before transport delayed him. This is another intensely human touch which suggests the imminence of the apostle's trial.

The four whose greetings are coupled with Paul's are all unknown elsewhere in the New Testament, although there is a tradition that identifies *Linus* with the Roman bishop of that name.

The inclusion of *all the brethren* in the salutation need not be thought to be in conflict with verse 16, 'all men forsook me', for these latter words relate to the lack of support at the trial. This would not prevent these timid Roman Christians from sending greetings to the apostle's lieutenant.

22. The closing benediction is in two parts. Part one is directed personally to Timothy and the words used are reminiscent of Gal. vi. 18 and Phm. 25. But a significant change is made. There it is 'the grace of our (the) Lord Jesus Christ be with your spirit', but here the prayer is more directly personal. Bernard's comment is worth repeating, '*there* the presence of "the grace of the Lord", *here* the presence of "the Lord of grace" is invoked'. Part two is directed to the Christians generally for the pronoun used is plural, as in the similar benedictions in 1 Timothy and Titus.

TITUS: ANALYSIS

   I.   SALUTATION, i. 1–4.

  II. QUALIFICATIONS OF CHURCH OFFICIALS,
      i. 5–9.

 III. THE CRETAN FALSE TEACHERS, i. 10–16.

 IV. REGULATIONS FOR CHRISTIAN BEHAVIOUR,
     ii. 1–10.
      (a) The aged people, ii. 1–3.
      (b) The younger people, ii. 4–8.
      (c) Slaves, ii. 9, 10.

  V. THE THEOLOGICAL BASIS FOR CHRISTIAN
     LIVING, ii. 11—iii. 7.
      (a) The educating power of grace, ii. 11–15.
      (b) The Christian attitude in the community, iii. 1, 2.
      (c) The superiority of the gospel over paganism, iii. 3.
      (d) The appearance and work of the Saviour, iii. 4–7.

 VI. CLOSING ADMONITIONS, iii. 8–11.
      (a) About good works, iii. 8.
      (b) About false teachers, ii. 9–11.

VII. PERSONALIA AND CONCLUSION, iii. 12–15.

TITUS: COMMENTARY

I. SALUTATION (i. 1-4)

This salutation is much longer than that of either 1 or 2 Timothy, and its formal character, addressed to so close an associate as Titus, has been considered a stumbling-block by many exponents of non-Pauline authorship. Easton, for example, thinks this introduction is more formalized than 2 Tim. i. 1, 2, and the suggestion is therefore made that the writer strives to give as impressive a Pauline flavour as possible. But the difficulties of construction and slight obscurities of thought are more in favour of Pauline authorship than against it; and in the view of some the formal character of the introduction is due to the semi-official character of the contents.

1. On no other occasion does Paul describe himself as *a servant* (*doulos*, slave) *of God*, although 'servant of Jesus Christ' is twice used in salutations (i.e. Romans and Philippians). The more usual *apostle of Jesus Christ* is also appended to draw attention to the official character of his service.

The words *according to* (*kata*) *the faith of God's elect* suggest that Paul's apostleship was somehow regulated by the faith of others (Lock, Simpson); but many scholars think such a meaning to be improbable and therefore suggest for *kata* the sense of 'for, in regard to' (Bernard). RSV has 'to further the faith of God's elect'. Twice elsewhere the apostle Paul employs the phrase 'God's elect' (Rom. viii. 33 and Col. iii. 12), but no other New Testament writer uses it. Lock shows it to be a well-known Old Testament phrase, especially describing Israel as the Lord's servant. As used by Paul it stresses the idea of God's choice of His Church. Faith must be linked with knowledge (the noun *epignōsis*, *acknowledging*, means 'recognition') of the truth in a genuine apostleship, and this the writer claims for himself. God's servants are not intended to be ignorant in the field of truth, nor is their knowledge to be out of keeping with their religious profession (*kat' eusebeian, which is after godliness*; Moffatt 'that goes with a religious life').

2. An apostleship, as any sphere of service for God, is not dominated by present circumstances alone, but has a distinct future reference *in hope of eternal life*. The preposition *epi* suggests that such hope is the basis on which the superstructure of Christian service is built. This Christian hope is rooted in God's promises made *before the world began*, or more literally 'before times eternal'. There would seem to be a reference here to the same truth that John expresses in his Logos doctrine, the profound recognition that God's promises are grounded in His eternal purposes. The apostle applies to God the unusual epithet *that cannot lie* (*apseudēs*, 'free from falsehood'), in order to bring out the absolute trustworthiness of the hope just mentioned. Even if it is true that Christians (and Jews) would take such a characteristic for granted, as Easton claims, there is special point in its mention here to mark the validity of the Christian's hope (cf. Paul's language in Rom. iii. 4).

3. The *due times* (*kairoi idioi*) of the manifestation are in contrast to the eternal times (*chronoi aionioi*) of the promise, and point to the appropriate events appointed by God for His self-revelation in Christ. The word *kairos* denotes a suitable opportunity as compared with *chronos* used for duration or succession of time.[1] The plural may either represent various points in the Lord's life, or is more probably used in the sense of the singular to describe the historic life of Christ as a whole (cf. Lock's discussion).

The *word* made known *through preaching* must be the message of the gospel, which forms the content of Christian preaching. The idea of having such ministry *committed* to him (*episteuthēn* means 'to be entrusted with') was a constant source of wonderment to Paul (e.g. Gal. i. 1, ii. 7), and is reiterated in all the Pastorals (cf. 1 Tim. i. 11; 2 Tim. i. 11). The phrase *according to the commandment of God our Saviour* is exactly paralleled in

[1] See Lightfoot's *Notes*, p. 70.

1 Tim. i. 1, and draws attention once again to the divine character of Paul's commission.

4. The description of Titus as 'genuine' (*gnēsios*, AV *own*) is also exactly paralleled in 1 Tim. i. 2. It is exclusive to Paul's writings in the New Testament (cf. Phil. iv. 3). No mention is made of Titus in the Acts of the Apostles but it is clear that he was a stalwart member of the apostle's entourage, to whom, in fact, he refers several times in his letters (Gal. ii. 3; 2 Cor. ii. 13, viii. 23, xii. 18). It may be gathered from the Corinthian correspondence that Titus was selected for a particularly difficult and delicate mission and since the outcome appears to have been a happy one, it is clear that Titus was a man of unusual tact who possessed high qualities of leadership. His allotted task in Crete certainly demanded much wisdom and strength of character, and the apostle's confidence in him accords completely with what is known of him elsewhere.

After the common faith has a rather different emphasis from 'in the faith' in 1 Tim. i. 2. It brings into prominence the catholicity of the gospel. The words of the salutation are almost identical with 1 Tim. i. 2 and 2 Tim. i. 2 except for the interesting variation of *Jesus Christ our Saviour* for 'Christ Jesus our Lord' and the omission of *mercy*, which although included in AV should be deleted on the grounds of inadequate MS support. It is particularly significant that, whereas in i. 3, ii. 10, iii. 4 the apostle applies the term 'Saviour' to God, here and in ii. 13 and iii. 6 the same title is applied to Christ. The apostle evidently uses it indiscriminately of Father and Son.

II. QUALIFICATIONS OF CHURCH OFFICIALS
(i. 5–9)

After this rather formal salutation the apostle moves directly to Titus' specific commission.

5. Paul had presumably visited Crete and left Titus there to carry on the work. But it is generally admitted that no room exists in the Acts framework for such a mission, and recourse must be had to one of two alternatives; either this visit occurred during a release period after the Roman imprisonment, or else this Epistle cannot be genuine. It has, however, been shown in the Introduction,[1] that there are no intrinsic reasons for rejecting the release hypothesis.

The Church in Crete was in a more disorganized state than at Ephesus, and Titus has therefore two important duties. He has to complete what Paul had left incomplete, *set in order the things that are wanting*, and to *ordain elders*. It has often been assumed that the appointment of elders shows an ecclesiastical organization too advanced for the time of Paul, but in order to maintain this view it has been necessary to regard Acts xiv. 23 as an anachronism. While there does not appear to be any uniformity in Paul's practice, there is no reason to doubt that he ordained elders on his earliest missionary journeys where occasion arose. It is essential for Christian churches to possess some orderly scheme of government and the apostle had previously impressed this on his close associates. In the phrase *as I had appointed thee* (RSV better 'as I directed you') the *I* is emphatic, bringing out not Paul's egotism, but his authoritative endorsement of the elder-system. The close link between *elder* and *bishop* in this context seems to show that the terms are virtually synonymous.

6. There is a measure of agreement between the list of qualifications required of a *bishop* as given to Titus and to Timothy. While these similarities betray a common author, the divergencies reflect different but genuine historic situations. The same Pauline word *anenklētos* used to describe the blamelessness of the Cretan *elders* is applied in 1 Tim. iii. 10 to the Ephesian *deacons* reflecting the need for an irreproachable moral standard in all types of Christian office. For the phrase *husband of one wife* see the comment on 1 Tim. iii. 2. Whereas in 1 Timothy the *bishop* must maintain an orderly discipline over his children, in Titus a further requirement is added. The children must be 'believing' (as *faithful* must here be understood), and must not lay themselves open to the charge of prodigality or insubordination. The former of these two words

---

[1] See pp. 20 ff.

(*asōtia*) means literally 'inability to save', hence metaphorically 'wasting money on one's own pleasures' (cf. Lock's lexical comment). As in 1 Timothy, the home is regarded as the training ground for Christian leaders. Although Scott argues that by referring to Christian children the author inadvertently lets us know that he belongs to the second generation of Christians, there is no need to suppose that Christianity had been long established. Bernard is nearer the truth when he understands the point to be that elders who have children are expected to have a Christian household.

7. Because the list of qualifications appears to begin all over again, Easton supposes that some secular ethical list underlies the text, and that this verse preserves its official beginning. But the repetition is not redundant for it gives the reason why a *bishop* must be *blameless*; he is *the steward of God*, a metaphor drawn from contemporary life and picturing the manager of a household or estate (cf. Paul's use of it in 1 Cor. iv. 1 and Gal. iv. 2). Whoever holds a position of Christian responsibility must similarly be beyond reproach in order to serve as a true example to others.

The subsequent list appears to set extremely moderate standards, to such a degree that Easton claims that the author has not been careful about the appropriateness of the ethical list he has used. But, as in the case of the Ephesians, great care would be needed in selecting officers in Crete, where the character of the people is seen to be generally unstable. To our modern age the vices denounced may seem too obviously non-Christian to require mention in the description of a Christian minister, but many parallels to the contemporary Cretan situation could be furnished from modern missionary enterprise among primitive peoples. That the Christian minister must not be arrogant (*selfwilled*) or hot-headed (*not soon angry*) is timely, for such moral deviations have all too often wrecked the healthy progress of the Church. The three prohibitions *not given to wine, no striker, not given to filthy lucre* probably had greater point in first-century Crete than in modern times (cf. 1 Tim. iii. 3).

8. The more positive qualities are closely akin to those in
1 Tim. iii. 2, but it is noteworthy that here there is no prohibition of novices. This suggests that the Cretan communities
were more recently founded than the Ephesian church. The
bishop must be both a *lover of hospitality*, which implies a real
devotion to the welfare of others, and a *lover of good men*, or
perhaps less definitely 'of good', the word *philagathos* including
things as well as persons. This word occurs in early Hellenistic
inscriptions as exemplifying a quality singled out for special
honour (cf. Dibelius). Calvin renders the word 'devoted to
kindness' as a contrast to niggardliness. The absence here of
any unusual or exceptional qualities shows again the realistic
approach of the apostle (cf. 1 Tim. iii). Honest, upright, clean
living, social men are all that is demanded on the moral
side, but it is significant that two specifically religious words
just and *holy* are included here but not in 1 Tim. iii. To the
word *sober* used in 1 Tim iii is added the parallel virtue
temperate (*enkratēs*), which, according to Lock (pp. 148–150)
involves more deliberate effort at self-control than the former
word.

9. Further qualifications are demanded on the doctrinal
side, for a Christian official must cleave to the true message,
as he hath been taught, i.e. 'according to the teaching', as RV. By
faithful must be understood 'reliable, trustworthy'. The minister
must have clear convictions and an understanding of the
'teaching' (presumably that which was passed on by oral
tradition, although it may possibly refer to some written
records; cf. Sim on), and he must be prepared to cling to the
truth even in face of opposition. Only so will he be able
to perform the double task of exhorting others and correcting
those who contradict the truth. *By sound doctrine* should probably
give place to RV 'in the sound doctrine', by which is meant
a body of teaching in which the Christians are to be instructed.
The three words in this verse describing teaching all presuppose in the original some objective and authoritative
system of doctrine. In a primitive community like Crete such
authoritative doctrine was indispensable.

III. THE CRETAN FALSE TEACHERS (i. 10–16)

10. The apostle proceeds to describe the contradictors or *gainsayers*. They are apparently numerous and are characterized by three undesirable qualities. They are *unruly* (or better, as RSV, 'insubordinate', *anupotaktoi*) flouting the official rule of the church. Second, they are emptyheaded in their teaching, doing much talking but saying nothing (the word *mataiologoi*, *vain talkers*, may contain the idea of worthlessness associated in the Jewish mind with heathen idols; cf. Lock). Third, they are self-deceived and consequently *deceivers* of others. Such characteristics are dominant in all heresies, but were particularly evident among the Jewish teachers then active in Crete, as the mention of the *circumcision* party shows.

11. Strong medicine is prescribed for such teachers. Their mouths must be *stopped* (*epistomizō*, meaning 'bridled', or 'muzzled') to prevent their doing damage. This imagery would seem to be particularly suggestive in the light of the description of the Cretans in the next verse. It is significant that no question of expulsion from the Church arises provided the false teachers are silenced, presumably by the skilful presentation of the true doctrine mentioned in verse 9.

By affecting one or two members of a family the false teachers were able to *subvert* or upset *whole houses*. Presumably these families were Christian, and any movement which causes rifts in such family life must be most carefully watched.

By *teaching things which they ought not* (RSV 'what they have no right to teach') these men are opposing the *sound doctrine* of verse 9. There is also a prominent mercenary element about them which merits the apostle's strong condemnation. *For filthy lucre's sake* (RSV 'for base gain') vividly brings out the sordid character of these empty religionists. Wherever mercenary considerations dominate a religious movement the same strong condemnation is deserved.

12. The apostle supports his argument by appealing to a venerated Cretan critic of the Cretan character. The lines quoted are from Epimenides, a sixth-century philosopher

whom his fellow countrymen had raised to mythical honours.
Many ancient writers (e.g. Aristotle and Cicero) mention him
as a prophet and the apostle therefore cites him by this well-
known description. There is some question whether the lines
quoted are correctly assigned to Epimenides, although many
early Christian writers regarded the lines as coming from an
ode *Concerning Oracles*. Since part of the citation occurs in
Callimachus' *Hymn to Zeus* (c. 270 B.C.) some scholars attribute
the statement to him. But Lock is of the opinion that the hymn
was probably earlier than Callimachus. Because a well-known
Cretan condemns his own people the apostle cannot be
charged with censoriousness for his exposures.

That Cretans were notorious for untruthfulness is strikingly
confirmed by the Greek language containing a word *crētizō*,
meaning 'to lie'.[1] The accompanying elements in their unenviable reputation give the measure of their sensuousness.
Evil beasts represents a maliciousness akin to the more savage
animal creation, while *slow bellies* (RV 'idle gluttons') describes
their uncontrolled greed. The inclusion of such a lashing
criticism of the Cretan character in this letter to Titus would
seem to rule out the idea that the letter was semi-official. The
apostle is about to urge Titus to take a strong hand with the
unruly element in the Church, and is first priming him on the
well-known characteristics of the people with whom he is
dealing. This principle has constant relevance, for every
minister of the gospel must of necessity be cognizant with the
character of his people, however distasteful the facts may be.

13. The apostle endorses the veracity of the proverbial
saying. It may have been the result of personal experience, or
else by common report, that he knew the Cretans were a
difficult people with whom to deal. The sharp *rebuke* is, of
course, to be directed against the false teachers, not the
Cretans generally. It is noteworthy that the adverb *sharply*
occurs elsewhere in the New Testament only in 2 Cor. xiii. 10.

---

[1] Rendle Harris maintained that a particular lie was in mind, i.e. the
claim that Zeus was buried in Crete. It was, therefore, mainly a religious
accusation. *Expositor*, VII (1906) II, pp. 305-311.

Such severe reproach has a saving purpose, *that they may be sound in the faith*, which may either refer to the accepted body of doctrine, or their personal loyalty to Christ. The former would seem to be preferable in view of verse 9. Much vituperation would have been saved had Christians always had this saving purpose in mind when dealing with those erring from the faith.

14. There was a double strand in the false teaching. The *Jewish fables* were no doubt akin to those mentioned in 1 Tim. i. 4, and probably consisted of useless speculations based on the Old Testament. Since these fables are here specified as Jewish as distinct from the general reference in 1 Timothy, it is a fair assumption that the Cretan heretics were more Judaistically inclined than their Ephesian counterparts.

The other strand, termed *commandments of men, that turn from the truth*, is strongly reminiscent of the ascetic tendencies in the Colossian heresy which are also described as 'commandments of men' (Col. ii. 21, 22). That some ritual is involved is apparent from verse 15, which raises the problem of what is clean and unclean. False teaching and false practice are usually close companions, and find willing allies in men occupied in turning others away from the truth.

15. In the true Pauline manner, an answer is given to the latter point raised in verse 14 by the enunciation of general principles. It is an echo of Jesus' own words in Lk. xi. 41 (cf. also Mk. vii. 15), and Paul has partially expounded the same idea in Rom. xiv. 20. Many scholars suggest that these words form part of a current proverb (cf. Lock and Scott). Christianity exalts purity to the realm of the spirit, which automatically obviates lesser ceremonial purity. A pure mind cannot be contaminated by physical contact, and the purest minds will have no relish in seeking unnecessary defilement.

No stronger condemnation of the would-be 'purifiers' could be made than the assertion that there *is nothing pure* to those *defiled and unbelieving*. Calvin argued that those defiled could touch nothing without defiling it, hence to them nothing could be pure. The *unbelieving*, as Lock suggests, could refer either to weak Jewish Christians, who did not believe that Christ was the end of the law, or to those who, like the later Gnostics, refused to admit the divine creation of matter. Paul is in effect repeating our Lord's teaching that it is what comes out of a man that defiles him, not ceremonial impurity. The real seat of purity is the *conscience* and if defilement has entered there, *mind* and action are alike affected.

16. Those who make a false profession of religion often strongly avow their knowledge of God, and this was particularly true of those with Judaistic tendencies. Some scholars (e.g. Dibelius, Easton) see in this profession to *know* God a sure indication of gnosticism, but Weiss cites it as sufficient in itself to deny second-century gnosticism. Since the Cretan heresy was strongly Jewish, it is more reasonable to suppose that Judaistic pride in monotheism is here in mind. Where profession and practice are as clearly conflicting as in the case of these Cretan claimants (*in works they deny him*), words of strong condemnation are richly deserved and the apostle uses three such terms to characterize their conduct. The first, *abominable*, is an expression of disgust at their hypocrisy. This word may here be used ironically, in the sense that those who claim to track down detestable things are themselves detestable. The second, *disobedient*, follows from their virtual denial of the true character of a holy God who also demands holiness. The third, *reprobate* (*adokimoi*, 'rejected after testing'), is in striking contrast to the constant call to good works in the Pastorals, for in these cases good works are not even possible. All who profess must be tested, but these will be shown to be 'unfit for any good deed' (RSV).

IV. REGULATIONS FOR CHRISTIAN BEHAVIOUR
(ii. 1-10)

Attention is now drawn to problems arising from the pastoral care of the churches, and the various classes of people with which Titus must deal are separately considered. Much of the apostle's advice is as instructive for modern times as for the contemporary situation.

(a) The aged people (ii. 1-3)

1. This verse is in contrast to the last. Whereas the false teachers are making empty professions, Titus is to be solicitous to speak *the things which become sound doctrine*. The word for *become, prepei*, which means 'to be suitable, fitting', is characteristic of Paul, who had a special sense of the fitness of things (cf. Eph. v. 3; 1 Cor. xi. 13; 1 Tim. ii. 10). The notion of sound doctrine has already been met in i. 9, and once again 'soundness' or 'healthiness' is set over against the disease of heresy which was troubling the Church. The pronoun *thou* (*su*) is intended to emphasize that Titus belongs to a very different category from the trouble-makers. It is hardly correct to claim, as many scholars do, that the writer merely denounces heresy, for in this case he clearly believes that truth is the best antidote to error.

2. The first practical outworking of such sound doctrine will be an insistence that behaviour should tally with belief. Older men are to act as becomes senior members of the community. The first three qualities are those generally expected from men in advancing age, and may be paralleled, as Easton points out, in contemporary secular usage. The word *sober* (*nēphalios*) is used in the sense of 'temperate' (RV), including not merely restraint in the use of wine but general moderation. The adjective *grave* (*semnos*) has already been met in 1 Tim. iii. 8, 11, where it relates both to deacons and to their wives. A seriousness of purpose particularly suits the dignity of seniors, yet gravity must never be confused with gloominess. The next quality, *temperate*, is more correctly rendered 'sober-minded' in the RV. The Greek *sōphrōn*, pointing to self-control (Moffatt, 'masters of themselves'), has previously been applied to bishops (cf. 1 Tim. iii. 2 and Tit. i. 8).

But not only is self-restraint required of elderly Christians, as of all elderly men; they must exhibit also a triad of Christian virtues. The linking of *faith, charity* (*agapē*, RV 'love') and *patience* (*hupomonē*) is found not only in 1 Tim. vi. 11, 12; 2 Tim. iii. 10 but also in 1 Thes. i. 3. Scott claims, however, that for Paul 'the cardinal Christian virtues are faith, hope and love'; but patience is not so far removed from hope to constitute a difficulty. In fact Scott's own comment on the use of *hupomonē* supplies an adequate justification for the apostle's special inclusion of it here. He says, 'Or perhaps he (i.e. the writer) sets patience in the place of hope because he is thinking specially of old men, whose attitude to life is now one of resignation'. At the same time endurance is a quality highly to be prized at any time of life. It is interesting to note that the Greek word *hugiainō* (to be sound) used of elderly men's pursuit of these Christian graces, is used in verse 1 to describe doctrine. Both heart and mind for the Christian must function in a healthy manner. While this soundness is most applicable to faith, it may have an application to charity and patience, 'in the sense that each quality may degenerate into weakness' (Lock).

3. In introducing the subject of elderly women the apostle uses the adverb *hōsautōs*, *likewise*, a favourite expression in the Pastorals, bringing out the closeness of the comparison with what precedes. *In behaviour as becometh holiness* is a phrase containing two words unique in the New Testament; *katastēma* means 'demeanour', describing a state of mind, while *hieroprepēs* means 'suited to a sacred character'. The two ideas are well expressed by RV 'reverent in demeanour'. Dibelius gives parallels of *hieroprepēs* meaning 'consecrated as priestesses', an idea well captured by Lock, who gives the meaning, 'they are to carry into daily life the demeanour of priestesses in a temple'.

The two prohibitions which follow, *not false accusers* and *not given to much wine*, again vividly portray the contemporary Cretan environment. The first has already been met in 1 Tim. iii. 11 and the second in 1 Tim. iii. 8. Evidently in Crete the liability to these excesses was more severe than in Ephesus, especially among the women, for the verb (*doulō*) used here signifies 'bondage' (RSV 'slaves to drink'), a much stronger expression than the corresponding phrase in 1 Timothy.

To bring out the required Christian characteristics the apostle uses a unique compound expression, *kalodidaskaloi*, *teachers of good things*. Since elderly women in general are included in this category, the word cannot refer to public teaching, which was in any case mainly the responsibility of elders, but must refer to ministry in the home. Within this sphere experienced Christian women have throughout the history of the Church performed invaluable service in the cause of Christ by their example and teaching.

(b) The younger people (ii. 4–8)

4. Something of the nature of this service is now indicated. The senior women are to *teach the young women to be sober*, though the RV and RSV 'train the young women to love their husbands' does more justice to the Greek construction (*hina sōphronizōsi*). In other words, Christian matrons are to assist the younger women in the discipline of family love, not of course as interfering busybodies, but as humble advisers on problems of married life. It seems hardly necessary for Christian women to be trained in loving their own *children*, but again the exhortation may pinpoint some special weakness in the Cretan character. It would have a particular significance in view of the home-disturbing tactics of the false teachers mentioned in i. 11 (cf. Spicq). Even our modern age is not without instances of professing Christian women lacking true maternal affection. For women who put their careers before the welfare of their own children are displaying a significant symptom of this weakness.

5. The same quality *sōphrōn* is used of young women as of old men in verse 2, although in the one case AV renders *discreet* and in the other *temperate*. In both cases there is the same idea of self-control.

This is particularized in the next quality, *chaste* (*hagnos*), which in all its New Testament occurrences is indistinguishable from 'pure' (as RV has here). Timothy is exhorted to covet the same quality (1 Tim. v. 22).

A question arises about the correct reading of the next word. *Keepers at home* would be a fair translation of *oikourous*, but the better supported reading seems to be *oikourgous* which apparently denotes 'workers at home'. But the latter is an extremely rare word, and its exact connotation is uncertain. Perhaps the best solution is to adopt Moffatt's rendering 'domestic' which would cover both alternatives. In any case, the apostle merely underscores what he has stated in principle in the previous verse, that a young married woman's sphere is the home.

Agathos (*good*) should be understood in the sense of 'kind' as in Mt. xx. 15, and be taken independently. That wives should be *obedient to their own husbands* is a sentiment expressed elsewhere by the apostle Paul (Eph. v. 22; Col. iii. 18), and in all three instances he uses the verb *hupotassō*, which properly means 'to be submissive to' (RV 'in subjection to').

Such care about behaviour, especially in home-life, has for the Christian a specifically religious purpose, i.e. *that the word of God be not blasphemed*. The substitution of *word* for the more usual 'name' gives the phrase a special significance. Contravention of these Christian qualities would be a denial of the *word* or 'gospel', which they professed to believe. It would be an affront to the Christian message, suggesting that some women, emancipated by the gospel, were abusing their new-found liberty in ways which were not approved in contemporary society.

6. Attention is now focused on the *young men*, in whose case the special exhortation is once again directed towards self-mastery. Titus is to *exhort* (*parakaleō*) them *to be sober minded*, a much stronger directive than 'speak' in verse 1. RSV has 'urge the younger men to control themselves', thus emphasizing the need for constant moral reminders. Because of the prevalence of this thought of self-mastery in the Pastorals and its dominance in Greek ethics, it has sometimes been supposed that there is nothing distinctively Christian about such advice as is given here. But as Scott points out, the self-mastery of the Christian has an element of humility lacking in the Greek moralists. It is, in fact, an essentially religious conception in the New Testament.

7. Titus, as a Christian minister, must be *a pattern (tupos) of good works*. This word, which is also applied to Timothy in 1 Tim. iv. 12, literally means an impress of a die, and hence in a metaphorical sense an 'example'. The exhortations of Titus would carry no weight unless backed by the pattern of his life, a principle which has been amply illustrated in the history of the Christian ministry. It is a high demand to show an example *in all things*,[1] but no less than this suffices for the Christian minister.

Whereas the spotlight so far has been turned mainly on Titus' actions, it is next transferred to his teaching. The order is significant; example comes before precept, but the precept which accompanies it must be of the noblest kind. Bernard argues for an active meaning for *didaskalia*, i.e. 'act of teaching' and not 'the content of the teaching' as *doctrine* tends to suggest. Such teaching is described in a twofold manner as consisting of *uncorruptness* and *gravity*. The first word, *aphthoria*, unique in biblical Greek, denotes 'untaintedness' in teaching as a direct contrast to the false teaching currently in vogue. The second word *semnotēs* has already been met in its adjectival form in the description of deacons and their wives (1 Tim. iii. 8, 11) and here the same note of seriousness is introduced. The Christian teacher must teach in a serious manner if his words are to earn respect. The final word *sincerity* is insufficiently supported by MS evidence, and is rightly dropped in the RV.

8. As the manner of teaching must be untainted, so must the matter be *sound*, i.e. wholesome. A different word, *logos*, is used to denote the content of what is said as compared with verse 7 where *didaskalia* is used. This teaching must be irreprehensible (*akatagnōstos, that cannot be condemned*, is another unique word); Titus must ensure that he gives no occasion for these gainsayers to level an accusation against himself or his teaching. By exemplary life and speech Titus can make those opposed to him *ashamed*. The concluding words, *having no evil*

---

[1] Some scholars (e.g. Dibelius, Jeremias) attach *peri panta* to the previous verse, as setting out the sphere in which soberness must be exercised.

thing to say of you, are a little misleading, as they suggest that opponents will find no words with which to abuse the Christian minister; the idea, however, is that the Christian minister should present no opportunity for his opponents legitimately to use an evil report against him. The word used for *evil* (*phaulos*) means literally 'worthless', and is twice used by Paul in opposition to what is morally commendable (Rom. ix. 11; 2 Cor. v. 10). Bernard shows that in the New Testament it is regularly applied to deeds rather than words and for this reason Titus' actions are particularly in mind.

(c) Slaves (ii. 9, 10)

As in writing to Timothy (1 Tim. vi. 1), so now in advising Titus the apostle finds it necessary to deal with the problem of slavery. He lays down the same principles governing their relationship with masters, but the injunctions are slightly varied.

9, 10. It is significant that, whereas in Ephesians and Colossians Paul urges servants to obey (*hupakouō*) their masters, here alone he uses the verb *hupotassō*, meaning 'to be in subjection'. The latter word is rather the stronger, perhaps suggesting a greater tendency on the part of Christian slaves in Crete to abuse their new-found emancipation in Christ. Presumably the injunction applies primarily to slaves with Christian masters as in 1 Tim. vi. 2, for no Christian slave could agree to submit to heathen masters if questions of conscience were at stake, as the Christian Church recognized at an early age.

Slaves are to *please* their masters *well* in everything, or as Moffatt translates, 'to give them satisfaction all round'. The word *euarestos* is exclusively Pauline, apart from Heb. xiii. 21, but is elsewhere always used of what is well-pleasing to God. If Christian slaves could introduce into their lives so high a principle as this, it would do much to lessen the evils of the system and to show the power of Christianity to transform the most diff ult relationships. The prohibition against *answering again* should probably be understood in the wider sense of 'opposition'. RV captures this with 'gainsaying', which would involve the thwarting of their master's plans.

The third requirement is little more than a straight demand for honesty. *Nosphizō* (*purloining*) 'is the regular term for petty larcenies' (Simpson), a vice to which slaves would be particularly tempted. *Shewing all good fidelity* presents the positive side of honesty, which must always include an element of good faith. The verb *endeiknumi* ('show forth') is, apart from two occurrences in Hebrews, an exclusively Pauline word expressing the idea of providing proof.

The concluding statement in verse 10 gives the dominating principle which raises these injunctions to slaves to a much higher level than contemporary Greek ethics. Slaves must act in such a way as to *adorn the doctrine of God*. The verb *kosmeō* translated *adorn* is used of the arrangement of jewels in a manner to set off their full beauty (cf. Bernard's comment), and that idea is emphasized here. By exemplary Christian behaviour a slave has the power to enhance the doctrine and to make it appear beautiful in the eyes of all onlookers. Such a principle as this is by no means confined to slaves. It is applicable to Christians in all walks of life. The words *en pasin*, translated *in all things*, could possibly be masculine with the sense 'among all men', and this would illustrate the opportunity for slaves to permeate every part of society with their witness.

V. THE THEOLOGICAL BASIS
FOR CHRISTIAN LIVING (ii. 11—iii. 7)

The close connection of this section with the preceding bears out the general relationship between theology and ethics in the New Testament. This imposing statement not only contains an epitome of Christian doctrine but also emphasizes the impossibility of giving practical advice apart from the eternal verities of the Christian faith. The appeal to a theological basis for action is the new factor in Christian ethics.

(a) The educating power of grace (ii. 11–15)

11. The connecting particle *for* proves that this verse leads on

directly from the last. The mention of *God our Saviour* directs
the thought to *salvation* and results in a concise statement
explaining both the incarnation and the atonement (cf.
Bernard). The expression, *the grace of God*, may fairly be said to
be the key word of Paul's theology, and there is no reason for
denying here its most characteristic Pauline sense. He cannot
think of Christian *salvation* apart from *the grace of God* (cf. Eph.
ii. 8), and when he dwells on the divine intervention in human
life he can find no more adequate term than this, expressive
as it is of God's free favour in Christ in dealing with man's sin.
It is this which gives the incarnation its significance.

The verb *epiphainō* (appear) is used only twice in the New
Testament outside Titus (Lk. i. 79, a striking parallel to the
present usage, and Acts xxvii. 20). Its use in iii. 4 is similar to
the statement here, although applied there to the kindness and
benevolence of God. The cognate noun (*epiphaneia*) is in the
Pastorals a characteristic description of the second advent.

It is doubtful whether the AV is correct in attaching *to all
men* to the verb, thus asserting the universality of the manifestation, which in any case presents a difficulty in view of the
fact that many people still have not heard. As Simpson points
out, *sōtērios* (*salvation*) followed by the dative as here is a
classical expression meaning 'bringing deliverance to'; *to all men*
should therefore naturally belong to the noun (as RV), showing
the universal scope of Christian salvation. Lock understands *all*
in the sense of 'all classes of men, even slaves'.

12. Grace is here almost personified in its task of educating
us in the art of living, and, as so often in the Pastorals, attention
is drawn to both negative and positive aspects of a Christian's
'education'. There must be a double denial, first of *ungodliness*
(*asebeia*, the antithesis of the frequently repeated call to godliness), and secondly of *worldly lusts* (*kosmikai epithumiai*), i.e. of
all desires entirely centred in the present world system. While
the Greek word *epithumia* (desire) is morally neutral, in the
New Testament its context generally impregnates it with a
moral stigma. In itself *kosmikos* has no moral significance, but
takes its ethical connotation from the New Testament use of

the noun *kosmos* to describe the world apart from God (e.g. Jn. vii. 7; 1 Cor. i. 21).

The positive elements, self-control, righteousness and a religious disposition have already been emphasized. Self-mastery (*live soberly*) has been demanded of leaders, old men and young women (Tit. i. 8, ii. 2, 5), and no less a standard could be required of Titus. To live *righteously*, i.e. in conformity to God's requirements, is an ideal which Paul earlier claimed for himself and his companions when writing to Thessalonika (1 Thes. ii. 10). The third requirement is the exact counterpart of the first denial. It is not enough to renounce ungodliness; life must be lived in a *godly* manner (*eusebōs*). Possibly this triad of adverbs expresses the Christian's ideal behaviour towards himself, his neighbour and his God (cf. Bernard, Scott).

13. The last verse closed with a reference to *this present world*, but the Christian looks also to the future. In the New Testament *hope* does not indicate merely what is wished for but what is assured. It is a particularly joyful possession for the Christian, hence the description *blessed*.

The content of the hope is given as *the glorious appearing of the great God and our Saviour Jesus Christ*. The AV has here weakened the sense, for the Greek demands 'the appearing of the glory' (as RV). The word *epiphaneia* (*appearing*) was commented on in verse 11, but its use here requires further discussion. Easton thinks the whole expression is 'almost certainly a citation from a (Greek) Christian credal formula or hymn'. He further agrees with Dibelius that the Emperor Cult terminology is followed in this whole section (i.e. from verse 11). But the fact that such terms as 'Saviour of all men', 'grace', and 'appearing' were all part of the technical language of Emperor-worship proves nothing in this context, which echoes sentiments which formed part of the very texture of primitive Christianity. In fact a difficulty here confronts exponents of a late date for the Pastorals, for the apocalyptic hope reflects a very early stage in Christian development, and Scott's solution of this problem is not convincing. He admits that the hope still hovers, but holds that 'the writer is able to speak of it in the language familiar to the previous generation'.

The final words of the verse have perplexed commentators. There are two possible renderings—that of the AV and RV mg., *of the great God and our Saviour Jesus Christ*, and that of the RV and RSV, 'of our great God and Saviour Christ Jesus'. The decision between these two renderings rests on a variety of considerations: Grammatically, the absence of the article before *Saviour* supports the second, although the tendency to omit articles in technical terms and proper names lessens the weight of this consideration. The early Versions all understand the words in the sense of the first, while the majority of Greek Fathers keep to the second. Of this double stream of evidence, the former is probably more reliable than the latter, but neither can decide the matter. Doctrinally, it is to be noted that only here is the adjective *great* applied to God, and for that reason the whole ascription must be regarded as unique. It may be considered more applicable to Christ than to God, since the greatness of God was assumed. Nor would it detract from the supreme greatness of God the Father if the adjective were applied to Christ. There is, moreover, no reason to suppose that the apostle would not have made such an ascription to Christ if the most reasonable interpretation of Rom. ix. 5 is followed (cf. Sanday and Headlam, ICC, *ad loc.*), or, indeed, if the general tenor of his teaching on the person of Christ is borne in mind. The use of the word *appearing*, which is never used of God, further supports the ascription of the entire phrase to Christ. Another factor which has influenced some commentators is the contemporary usage of 'God and Saviour' for heathen objects of worship. J. H. Moulton[1] cites a similar ascription applied to the Ptolemies, where one not two deities is meant. This, at least, shows how the words would probably have been understood in contemporary Hellenistic circles. On the whole, therefore, the evidence seems to weigh slightly in favour of the RV rendering.

14. A direct reference is now made to the self-sacrificial

[1] *Grammar of New Testament Greek*, VOL. I, p. 84.

example of Christ and the words used are reminiscent of Christ's own words in Mk. x. 45, where He speaks of Himself as a ransom (*lutron*) (cf. note on 1 Tim. ii. 6). The verb used here is *lutroō* (*redeem*), which literally means 'to release on receipt of a ransom' (Abbott-Smith). It seems most probable that the language is borrowed from Ps. cxxix. 8 (LXX), where not only the same verb but the same phrase *from all iniquity* is found although in the plural. In the qualifying clause *who gave himself for us*, which is thoroughly Pauline (cf. Gal. i. 4, ii. 20, etc.), the use of the preposition *huper* (as in 1 Tim. ii. 6) brings out the sacrificial character of Christ's act. It may also suggest a substitutionary aspect in view of its connection here with *lutroō* and the close parallel in 1 Tim. ii. 6.[1] It is on the basis of this self-giving that He delivers His people from sin, not merely 'out of' (as the *ek* of Ps. cxxix. 8) but 'from' (*apo*) in the fullest sense (cf. Bernard).

Another metaphor, that of cleansing, is used to express the effects of the Redeemer's work. This is interpreted variously of sanctification (Bernard), or baptism (White, who explains it in the light of iii. 5). But the former seems the most probable in the context, since the act of purification is performed by Christ Himself. In fact, Eph. v. 25, 26, which also connects Christ's self-giving with His sanctifying work, contains the phrase 'cleanse it with the washing of water by the word', which, although using the language of baptism, clearly refers to an inner rather than an outer purification.

For *peculiar people* RV has 'people for his own possession'. The underlying Greek phrase *laos periousios* first occurs in Ex. xix. 5, and means 'a peculiar treasure', i.e. something that belongs in a special sense to oneself. The words in this context are particularly choice as expressing the attitude of the Redeemer towards the redeemed, whose main characteristic is said to be zealousness for *good works*. Paul uses the word *zelōtēs* (*zealous*) in Gal. i. 14 of his own eagerness to maintain the traditions of his ancestors; and although this zeal was misplaced, he never

---

[1] Although it generally means 'on behalf of', *huper* may on occasion have the more restricted sense of 'in the place of' (as *anti*). Cf. Simpson's note on classical instances of this limited meaning, pp. 110-112.

lost his enthusiasm and envisages here a whole people noted for a rightly directed zeal.

15. This verse connects the present doctrinal section with what follows. Titus is to 'declare these things' (RSV), by which is presumably meant all the practical exhortations contained in chapter ii. In addition to speaking, the Christian minister must engage in exhortation and reproof (cf. 2 Tim. iv. 2). Some will require encouragement and others censure, but whatever the need Titus is to exercise *all authority* (*epitagē*). This word is found elsewhere in the New Testament only in the Pauline Epistles and always in the sense of a divine command. Here Paul no doubt means that the Christian minister is endowed with nothing less than a divine authority. Titus need not fear, therefore, to exercise jurisdiction over those entrusted to him. Some would no doubt attempt to *despise* him, but he is to demonstrate the seal of God upon his ministry (cf. 1 Tim. iv. 12).

(b) The Christian attitude in the community (iii. 1, 2)

1. Christian behaviour in contemporary society was of utmost importance for the furtherance of the gospel. No new advice needs to be given to these Cretan Christians for Titus is to *put them in mind to be subject*. This latter verb, which in Simpson's opinion implies 'loyal' subjection, shows clearly the Christian's duty towards the civil administration. The same descriptive words, *principalities and powers*, are combined several times in Paul's writings, and generally refer to spiritual agencies. But here the apostle evidently fears that the turbulent Cretans might too readily implicate the Church in political agitation which could only bring the gospel under suspicion. The words are, therefore, better translated 'rulers and authorities' (as RV, RSV). The Greek verb *peitharchō* translated *to obey magistrates* expresses generally conformity to the regulations of the civil authorities.

The Christian should *be ready to every good work*, in the community in which he lives. Where good citizenship demands communal action, he must always be cooperative, provided no question of conscience is involved. The slight awkwardness of *ready to* is remedied in RSV 'ready for'.

2. To refrain from 'slander' (to *speak evil of no man*) requires considerable grace, but does much to commend the gospel. Christians must be *no brawlers, but gentle*, two words which are also coupled in the qualifications of a bishop in 1 Tim. iii. 3. The phrase *shewing all meekness (prautos)* is well rendered by RSV 'to show perfect courtesy toward all men', although *prautos* literally means 'gentleness'.

(c) The superiority of the gospel over paganism (iii. 3)

As in chapter ii. 11–15, a theological statement is made to support the practical exhortations just given.

3. If Titus should despair of the Cretan character he should remember his own past experience, for retrospect is often salutary in helping us to understand the magnitude of God's grace. The past is described by means of a list of vices which may at first sight seem exaggerated, yet Paul, elsewhere, uses similar language of his converts' pre-Christian experience (cf. 1 Cor. vi. 9–11, Eph. iv. 17–24). When the apostle says *we ourselves also were sometimes foolish (anoëtos)*, he means that we were 'without spiritual understanding'. Next in the list are disobedience, which is directed towards God, and deception, which is related to man. The Greek word for *deceived (planaō)*, suggests a false guide leading astray. The metaphor of slavery is then used to illustrate the Christian's former servitude to *lusts and pleasures*. This combination is well known in Greek ethics, but for the Christian looking back on his pre-conversion state it would have greater meaning than for the Greek moralists (cf. the similar combination in Jas. iv. 1, 2). Only the freed man can appreciate to the full the abjectness of his former state of slavery. *Living* (or spending time) *in malice and envy* reflects the essentially anti-social nature of the former life, for both words emphasize malignity. The climax is reached in *hateful, and hating*. The former of these two words in the Greek is found only here in biblical Greek and means 'odious'.

Coupled with the idea of hating one another it marks the last 'stage of degradation before it becomes hopeless' (White).

(d) The appearance and work of the Saviour (iii. 4-7)

4. Against this dark background shines God's love in the gospel, which is described in a twofold way. The first, *chrēstotēs* (*kindness*), an exclusively Pauline word in the New Testament, is often used to describe the benignity of God, although it is also used of man (cf. 2 Cor. vi. 6). The second descriptive word, *philanthrōpia* (*love*, RV 'love towards man'), was normally used of love towards individuals in distress, but when predicated of God it denotes love to mankind at large (cf. Bernard). In Acts xxviii. 2 it is used of human kindness. Lock mentions its special application to the ransoming of captives, and thinks this idea may be included here.

Easton claims that the language of this verse is borrowed from the Emperor-cult and that *God* is specified as *our Saviour* in contrast to the false claims of the Roman emperors. But the application of the same title to Jesus Christ in verse 6 suggests that the ascription springs directly out of the Christian's experience of salvation. Cf. ii. 11 for the use of the same verb, *epiphainō* (*appear*).

5. The apostle next seems to quote from a Christian hymn as is suggested by the opening formula in verse 8. Jeremias thinks it may have formed part of a baptismal hymn, and this is not improbable in view of the reference to the *washing of regeneration*. The negative statement *not by works of righteousness which we have done* is intended to bring out by way of contrast the absolute character of the divine *mercy* in the next phrase. RSV has a better rendering of the Greek, 'not because of deeds done by us in righteousness'. The word *dikaiosunē* (*righteousness*) here denotes observance of the Mosaic Law, in complete agreement with Paul's general usage. The apostle was deeply conscious of the impossibility of attaining salvation by means of human effort. It is God Himself who has brought it about *according to his mercy*. This is a theme of which the apostle never tired.

The phrase *by the washing of regeneration* has been considerably discussed by commentators. The word *loutron* has been variously rendered *washing* (AV, RV, RSV) or 'laver' (RV mg.), but support for the latter rendering is slight and was probably 'coloured by the dogma of baptismal regeneration' (Simpson). In the LXX the word, which occurs three times only (Ct. iv. 2, vi. 5 and Ecclesus. xxxi. 25), on each occasion seems to represent not the receptacle but the washing itself. This is also the sense in the only other New Testament occurrence, Eph. v. 26, 'the washing of water by the word'. Most commentators take this washing to refer to baptism and connect the *regeneration* with Jn. iii. 5. The Greek word *palingenesia* was current in Stoicism for periodic restorations of the natural world, a sense approximated in the only other use of the word in the New Testament (Mt. xix. 28) where it is used eschatologically of the new birth of the whole creation. But here it takes on a new meaning in view of the Christian new birth, which is applied not cosmically but personally (cf. Lock). It accords with the idea of the new creation (2 Cor. v. 17), each believer being conceived of as a possessor of powers previously unknown. The *renewing of the Holy Ghost* specifies the resultant renovation accompanying the *regeneration*. The one points to the act of entering, while the other marks the quality of the new life. 'Making new' rather than *renewing* is implied, since the latter might erroneously suggest the restoration of former powers (cf. Easton), whereas through the work of the Spirit the believer lives on a higher plane than before (cf. Rom. xii. 2 for the same idea of spiritual renewal). There is an instructive parallel to the present statement in 1 Cor. vi. 11, although Scott, who admits this parallel, draws a distinction between Paul's conception of baptism as a seal on the act of faith and the writer of the Pastorals' view of it as efficacious by itself. He sees here a step towards a sacramental religion in which the Church has 'a magical estimate of baptism'. Yet this view is open to dispute since the whole passage is designed to exhibit the grandeur of the grace of God and many details, such as faith-appropriation, are omitted to serve that end. In the 1 Corinthians passage there is also no mention of faith, but in that case Scott rightly does not suppose that Paul has substituted baptism for faith, because of the contrary teaching of Rom. vi. 2-4. There seems no more reason, therefore, for supposing that the present reference to 'washing' has no relation to faith.

There are two possible ways of construing this second half of the verse. The *regeneration* and the *renewing* may be regarded as distinct operations, or both may be dependent on *washing* and therefore would describe different aspects of one operation. But since regeneration must always precede the process of renewal and since renewal is never described elsewhere as a washing, the former interpretation is to be preferred.

6. The outpouring of the Holy Spirit is directly reminiscent of the historic occasion at Pentecost (Acts ii. 33) since the same verb *ekcheō* (to *shed*) is used in each case. The aorist tense of the verb also points back to this historic event, but it clearly refers more directly to Paul and his associates' experience of the Holy Spirit, as *us* indicates. The apostle uses the word *abundantly*, which literally means 'richly' (RV, RSV; cf. Col. iii. 16 and 1 Tim. vi. 17), to show that God's gift of the Spirit is never niggardly. The mediator of this priceless gift is *Jesus Christ our Saviour*, in conformity with the primitive Christian belief (Acts ii. 33).

7. There is no denying the characteristic Pauline flavour of the next words—*being justified by his grace* (cf. Rom. iii. 24). Nevertheless both Scott and Easton dispute that either *justified* or *grace* are here used in a Pauline sense. Easton, for instance, considers the former to denote 'the fruit of baptism', while the latter he takes to mean 'power'. But in so concise a statement of the gospel as is found here, it is gratuitous to suppose that the writer meant to say that justification followed baptism, for this is bringing the allusion to washing into unwarranted prominence. It is much more intelligible to suppose that *being justified* is an amplification of the previous statement *he saved us*, (verse 5), on which the telic clause introduced by *hina* (in order that *we should be made heirs*) must depend. The point of this reference to justification is that none who is not justified can hope for an inheritance, and there is no doubt Paul would have consented to such a statement (cf. Gal. iii, which begins with justification, iii. 11, and ends with inheritance, iii. 29).

The *heirs* are not yet possessors in the fullest sense, as *according to the hope* clearly shows. The phrase conveys the idea of solid assurance (cf. the comment on ii. 13), on the basis of which the justified believer may look forward towards the full appropriation of his inheritance. The words do not exclude any present possession of *life*, but rather anticipate its complete realization (cf. note on the similar phrase in i. 2). The genitive *of eternal life* may be taken with either *hope* or *heirs*. In the former case it gives the content of the hope, and in the latter describes the inheritance. The former seems to agree better with the context.

VI. CLOSING ADMONITIONS (iii. 8-11)
(a) About good works (iii. 8)

8. The *faithful saying* must relate to the previous theological statement (verses 4–7), which may be regarded as an epitome of Pauline theology. As Simpson puts it, 'not a programme of "work and win", but of "take and have" constitutes its very keystone'. *These things*, which Titus is to *affirm constantly*, are not baptism and its consecration as Easton supposes, but all that has been included in the previous part of the letter. The injunction that believers should *maintain good works* supports this judgment. The verb *diabebaioomai* (RV 'affirm confidently') is used of the false teachers with whom Timothy had to deal (1 Tim. i. 7). They were affirming what they did not understand, but the same is not to be true of Titus or any minister of the gospel.

These affirmations are particularly to be directed towards those *which have believed in God,* for a true belief is an indispensable basis for the right ordering of conduct. Their specific purpose is to encourage believers to *be careful,* i.e. have a thoughtful approach to the maintenance of good works. The most usual meaning of the verb *proistēmi*, translated *maintain*, is 'to put before', which in the middle voice, as here, means 'to be forward in', but it could possibly bear the sense of the RV mg. 'profess honest occupations'. This alternative, however, requires a different meaning for *good works* (*kala erga*) than

elsewhere in the Pastorals and is therefore less probable (cf.
Lock's valuable lexical note on this word).

(b) About false teachers (iii. 9-11)

9. Since the apostle has already dealt with the Cretan false
teachers in i. 10-16, his return to the theme may indicate his
particular concern over this aspect of Cretan Christianity.
He does the same in 1 Timothy (cf. i. 4 ff. and vi. 4). The
Jewish character of the Cretan heresy is brought out as clearly
here as in the earlier reference. In spite of this Scott claims that
the teaching is gnostic in character, but he is no doubt unduly
influenced by understanding the reference to 'genealogies' (cf.
note on 1 Tim. i. 4) in a gnostic sense.

The combination of *questions* and *genealogies*, found also in
1 Tim. i. 4, shows that there was a marked similarity between
the Cretan and Ephesian situations. The adjective *foolish*, also
attached to *questions* in 2 Tim. ii. 23, again emphasizes the
stupidity prevalent among these so-called teachers. Two other
words are here used which are common to both situations;
contentions (*ereis*) as in 1 Tim. vi. 4, and *strivings* (*machas*) as in
2 Tim. ii. 23, where it is shown to be the product of the
questionings. The subject matter of these 'quarrels' (RSV) is
the law, which must refer to the Mosaic Law.

These things Titus is *to avoid*, the word *periïstēmi* literally
meaning to turn oneself about so as to face the other way (cf.
2 Tim. ii. 16 where it is used in a similar manner). The basic
reason given for such avoidance is the essential unprofitable-
ness and uselessness of the false teaching. This consideration
might well be borne in mind by all who undertake the pastoral
office.

10. The Greek word *hairetikos* translated *heretick* does not
mean what the word 'heretic' means today. It designates one
whom Simpson describes as 'an opinionative propagandist who
promotes dissension by his pertinacity'. In later times the
word acquired a more technical meaning of 'one who holds
false doctrine'. A different verb *paraiteomai* (*reject*) is now used
for avoidance. It is a vague term (cf. 1 Tim. iv. 7) which does

not convey the idea of excommunication, but means merely 'to leave out of account'. The first approach to these false teachers is to be by means of admonition (*nouthesia*, a word used only by Paul in the New Testament, cf. 1 Cor. x. 11 and Eph. vi. 4). The lenience advocated is striking, for it is only on the third occasion of admonition that the more serious action of avoidance is to be taken.

11. If this action, however, should seem rather harsh, Titus must recognize that the stubbornness of the man is evidence of a perverted mind. The sinning referred to must be understood in the light of the previous verse, i.e. the desire to promote dissensions. It is useless to contend with men of twisted minds, and there is no need to condemn them for they are self-condemned. The reference, however, seems to be not so much to a deliberate act of condemning oneself, which is admittedly rare, but to the fact that perverted and sinful action in the end automatically condemns the doer.

VII. PERSONALIA AND CONCLUSION (iii. 12–15)

As so often in his letters, the apostle ends with personal allusions. In fact it is so much in the style of Paul that Harrison regards the whole section as one of the Pauline fragments incorporated in the Pastorals.[1]

12. Evidently *Artemas* or *Tychicus* was to replace Titus in Crete during the latter's absence. We know nothing of Artemas, but Tychicus appears to have been a close associate of the apostle, and according to 2 Tim. iv. 12 the apostle sent him to Ephesus to relieve Timothy (cf. note on 2 Tim. iv. 12).

It is not certain which city of *Nicopolis* is meant, but it is generally assumed it was the city of that name in Epirus, although no other evidence that Paul went to Epirus exists. Both here and in 2 Tim. iv. 21 there is a reference to Paul's plan for the winter and in each case he urges his close associates to *be diligent to come*.

---

[1] See Introduction, p. 23.

13. *Zenas the lawyer* is unknown apart from this reference, but we meet with *Apollos* in several situations (both in Acts and I Corinthians). The word *lawyer* (*nomikos*) may be used of an expert in either Hebrew or Roman law. The Gospels would seem to support the former (i.e. the Mosaic Law), but since *Zenas* has a Greek name Scott considers that the latter reference is more probable.

Titus is *to bring* these two *on their journey*, the word *propempō* meaning to 'speed . . . on their way' (as RV). There is no necessity to suppose that Zenas and Apollos were both in Crete, although that would be the most natural assumption. Titus might be expected to meet them on his way to Nicopolis. But since he is to see *that nothing be wanting unto them*, which suggests he was in a position to provide material assistance, it is better to assume that Zenas and Apollos are paying a visit to Crete and that the apostle is anxious to secure adequate hospitality for them.

14. After these specific instructions to Titus, a general exhortation is added directed to *our's* ('our people' RV). Clearly the Cretan Christians generally are intended, for these people are to *learn to maintain good works*. Moffatt has 'practise honourable occupations', taking *good works* in the same sense as in verse 8. But the meaning seems better brought out by Scott— 'Our people must really learn to make themselves practically useful'.

The practical side of Christianity is here brought into vivid focus. The words *for necessary uses* can be understood either as necessitous cases or as wants. The more probable interpretation is the former, as RSV 'so as to help cases of urgent need'. All who engage in such works of mercy need never fear that they will be *unfruitful*.

15. There is no means of identifying the *all* who were with Paul. This linking of fellow workers with him in the conclusion is thoroughly characteristic, although the exact form of the words is not found elsewhere.

The description *them that love us in the faith* brings a most intimate touch into the otherwise rather vague greetings. The absence of the article before faith may mean that *en pistei* should not be understood as a reference to the Christian faith, but perhaps, as Simpson renders it, 'faithfully'. Easton has 'who love us as Christians'.

The final benediction is identical with those of 1 and 2 Timothy, except for the insertion of *all*, which is parallel to the same word in the beginning of the verse.

AN EXAMINATION OF
P. N. HARRISON'S LINGUISTIC ARGUMENTS

The linguistic problem consists of four different aspects. 1. The problem of the Hapaxes. 2. The problem of the other non-Pauline words shared with other New Testament writings. 3. The problem of Pauline words or groups of words missing from the Pastorals. 4. The problem of grammatical and stylistic differences. Before examining the mass of evidence which Harrison ably collates under these heads, a brief indication must be given of his conclusions. By first making a comparison between the linguistic phenomena in the Pastorals with the other ten Pauline Epistles, he considers that the differences are so great as to exclude the possibility that they proceeded from one mind. He then compares the Pastorals with second-century literature drawing mainly on the Apostolic Fathers and the Apologists, but also including the available secular writers, and concludes that the evidence proves a second-century vintage for the Pastorals. The criticism is, therefore, two-pronged, and any adequate assessment of it must deal with both lines of attack.

I. THE PROBLEM OF THE HAPAXES

This much discussed problem has fittingly been described as 'the Battle of the Hapaxes', and however much a commentator may desire to say as little as possible about them he cannot by-pass the problem in view of the great emphasis that Harrison has placed upon it. It is merely a matter of mathematics to show that the number of Hapaxes per page in the Pastorals is considerably greater than in any other Pauline Epistle. All the other ten Paulines range between 3.3 and 6.2 per page, whereas the Pastorals range from 12.9

to 16.1. Harrison claims on the one hand that such an unexpected increase is inconceivable for one mind, and on the other that the Pastorals figures can be paralleled in the Apostolic Fathers and that the Epistles must therefore belong to the second-century period. But there are grounds for criticizing both Harrison's deductions and his method of procedure.

(a) The words per page method
This was first used in the Pastorals discussion by Workman,[1] who made a comparison with Shakespeare's plays. These show a Hapax variation from 3.4 to 10.4 words per page, but Harrison uses the data to prove that Shakespeare's plays, when arranged in sequence of ascending Hapaxes, form a general progression parallel in shape to that of the 'accepted' Paulines. But Harrison does not point out that the lowest and highest extremes occur in plays which, according to Dowden's dating (which Harrison cites) were separated by only one year. Evidently Shakespeare's vocabulary could show considerable variation in a very short space of time. It should further be observed that allowance must be made for the considerably greater number of Shakespeare's extant works (thirty-seven plays), which makes 10.4 per page occurrences of Hapaxes in Hamlet rank considerably higher in proportion than the figures quoted above for the Paulines and the Pastorals. For the greater the number of extant writings with which comparison is made, the greater is the probability that unusual words will be duplicated.

Other literary analogies could also be quoted to show the fallacy of any deductions from such a method. Cicero's Hapaxes, for instance, have been shown to possess remarkable variation in the different types of his extant works, ranging from four per page in his oratorical works to twenty-five in his philosophical. In this case[2] subject-matter clearly affects range of vocabulary and no prediction could possibly be

---

[1] 'The *Hapax Legomena* of St. Paul', *Expository Times*, vii (1896), pp. 418, 419.
[2] These figures are the result of Dr. Purser's calculations cited by Montgomery Hitchcock (*J.T.S.*, xxx, 1929, p. 278).

made from one group of writings to show the vocabulary variation which might be expected in the others. In short, literary art cannot be reduced to a mathematical equation.[1]

(b) Second-century parallels

Attention must now be given to Harrison's contention that the writer of the Pastorals not only differs from Paul's vocabulary, but speaks the language of the second century. If Harrison's point is proved, authenticity is clearly impossible. Now the presupposition with which Harrison commences his study,[2] is that all non-Pauline and non-New Testament words used in the Pastorals and found also in the Apostolic Fathers and Apologists show that the writer is lapsing into the language of his own time, i.e. the second century. But this involves an extraordinary assumption. It assumes that the Pastoral Hapaxes cannot have been current in the first century because no other New Testament writer happens to use them. While it is true that some of these words were used by the Apostolic Fathers, Harrison gives insufficient attention to the possibility that the Pastorals influenced the vocabulary of these later writers even where there is no indication from the context that they are citing the Pastorals.

To offset this possibility Harrison takes refuge in the number of words and Pastoral Hapaxes common to second-century secular writers like Epictetus, Appian, Galen and Marcus Aurelius, and argues that these latter cannot have enriched their vocabulary from the former.[3] But the two cases are clearly not analogous for there is a presumption in favour of the Pastorals influencing second-century ecclesiastical writers, but none whatever in the case of secular writers. It is not a matter of enriching vocabulary so much as using words in common ecclesiastical usage for similar purposes.

Out of the total of 175 Hapaxes, sixty are found in the Apostolic Fathers, and this forms the basis of Harrison's argument that the Paulinist author belonged to this period.

[1] Dibelius admitted that the statistical method for determining authenticity has been largely discounted, *op. cit.*, p. 3.
[2] Cf. *op. cit.*, pp. 67, 68.
[3] *Op. cit.*, p. 82.

Yet several considerations reduce the weightiness of this evidence. 1. There is a high percentage of these Hapaxes which are absent from the Apostolic Fathers (1 Timothy 74 per cent, 2 Timothy 58 per cent and Titus 60 per cent).[1] This hardly supports the idea that the author lapsed into current second-century speech when departing from his Pauline model. 2. Of the sixty shared with the Apostolic Fathers, twenty-eight occur in the latter writings once only, and cannot therefore constitute evidence of common language.[2] 3. Only seventeen of the Hapaxes occur in more than one writer of the Apostolic Fathers, which shows the extent of their frequency during this period.

When the evidence from the Apologists is combined with that from the Apostolic Fathers it is found that a further thirty-two may be added to the list of common Hapaxes, although as many as half of these occur once only. During the period A.D. 95–170, there happens to be no more than forty-five of the Pastorals Hapaxes which occur in more than one author. The great majority of the Hapaxes, therefore, are either absent from or else very rare in the entire range of second-century Church writers. Harrison, however, in further support of his claims states, 'We find more than a few of the Pastoral Hapax Legomena recurring again and again in one writer after another'.[3] The seventeen words he then cites are the only words (with one exception) which occur in three writers or more in the second-century period under review, (i.e. A.D. 95–170). He omits to point out that all but one of these words occur in the LXX.

The validity of Harrison's deductions is also affected by the total known vocabulary in the two periods he is comparing. He gives the vocabulary of the Apostolic Fathers as 4,020 words, while the Pauline figure is only 2,177.[4] There are, therefore, almost twice as many words to form a quarry from which to dig out parallels. Before such parallels can prove

---

[1] Calculated from Harrison's lists, *op. cit.*, pp. 137 ff.
[2] Cf. Harrison, *op. cit.*, p. 73.
[3] *Op. cit.*, p. 69.
[4] *Op. cit.*, p. 68.

common vintage, it is necessary to show that the words in question could not have been used in the first century. But Montgomery Hitchcock[1] showed that all but twenty-eight of the non-Pauline words in the Pastorals were known before A.D. 50, while Harrison himself admits that the number unknown before A.D. 90 is less than a score.[2] Such a small group of words is hardly enough to prove second-century vintage, since their non-appearance in first-century literature may be due to the small amount of such literature still extant.

In addition to the search for parallels among ecclesiastical writers, Harrison brings in a wide range of non-Christian second-century writers. Of the eighty-two Hapaxes not found in the ecclesiastical writings, fifty-seven are paralleled in the non-Christian writings from Josephus to Marcus Aurelius.[3] Some of these occur with great frequency.[4] But this does not mean that they were not current in the first century. Harrison works on the assumption that the Paulinist writer, when lapsing from his master's vocabulary, reverted partially to the current ecclesiastical vocabulary (using many rare words), partially to the secular literary vocabulary and partially to a vocabulary all his own. In the latter case, Harrison appeals to cognates and analogies with words used in the secular group in justification for these unique words, although such a procedure is rejected for proving a first-century vintage.[5]

(c) Parallels in the LXX

No New Testament word-study is complete without examination of LXX influences. In the case of the Pastorals, there are about eighty of the Hapaxes which are paralleled in the LXX.[6] Indeed, no less than forty-two of the sixty shared with the Apostolic Fathers are LXX words, and a further eighteen of those shared with the Apologists. There are, in fact, twenty-

---

[1] *J.T.S.*, xxx (1929), p. 278.
[2] *Expository Times*, lxvii (Dec., 1955), p. 79; cf. also the discussion in Falconer, *op. cit.*, pp. 5-11 and Badcock, *The Pauline Epistles and the Epistle to the Hebrews in their Historical Setting* (1937), pp. 115-133.
[3] *Op. cit.*, pp. 82 f.
[4] Cf. Harrison, *Expository Times*, lxvii (Dec., 1955), p. 79 for details.
[5] Cf. *op. cit.*, pp. 65, 83, 84.
[6] See the writer's *The Pastoral Epistles and the Mind of Paul* (1956), pp. 39, 40.

two LXX words among those not found at all in the second-century ecclesiastical writers. Harrison summarily dismisses this LXX evidence[1] on the grounds that the words in question cannot be shown to be in vogue. But as many of the words which he claims as proof that the writer belonged to the second-century ecclesiastical group are found in the LXX, it is a much more reasonable assumption that these words were as current in the first as in the second century. Another factor not considered by Harrison is the influence of the LXX on the Apostolic Fathers and Apologists, which clearly affects the value of his linguistic deductions. The writings of the apostle Paul show so rich an acquaintance with the Greek Scriptures, on which it would seem his mind had been nourished since childhood, that parallels with the LXX must carry far greater weight in discussions on the authenticity of the Pastorals than any accidental parallels with second-century secular writers.

(d) New Testament cognates and analogies

It is impossible to discuss at any length in our present compass, the fascinating subject of the apostle's word-building propensities. But no just appraisal of the Pastoral Hapaxes can be arrived at without some attention to this. If many of the Hapaxes are cognates of Pauline words and many of the new compounds have analogies in Paul's other Epistles, there is a strong presumption in favour of Paul's use of them.[2] Cognates cannot, of course, prove that the Hapaxes in question were current in the time of the apostles, but they can contribute to the contention that the absence of such words from other New Testament writers is no proof that they could not have been known.

Word formation on the basis of analogy is one of the most fruitful sources of language development, and the Pastorals show many new forms which may be paralleled in Paul's

---

[1] Cf. *op. cit.*, pp. 65, 66 and *Expository Times*, lxvii (1955), p. 78.

[2] Paul, for instance, uses *opheleo* and *opheleia*, and it is difficult to see why he should not have used *ophelimos* in the Pastorals, especially as all but one of the other New Testament words with a similar ending are used by him. Such an example could be multiplied many times.

other writings. Consider, for instance, a form such as *kenophonia* (not found in the Apostolic Fathers or Apologists), which has only two analogous New Testament forms, *kenodoxos* and *kenodoxia*, and since both of these are Pauline Hapaxes, this prefix appears to have made a strong appeal to the apostle. He clearly had a great love of compound expressions, and this may provide a reasonable explanation for some, at least, of the Pastoral Hapaxes.

Harrison counters this approach by maintaining that cognates and analogies are a greater assistance to his theory than to Pauline authorship, reducing 'almost to the vanishing point those elements in the vocabulary of the Pastorals which cannot be shown to belong to the current phraseology of the period to which our criticism assigns them'.[1] But a radical weakness vitiates Harrison's contention, for he assumes an exact parallel exists between the attempt to show that Paul was acquainted with these words, and the attempt to prove that a second-century Paulinist could have known them. No one disputes that a postulated Paulinist could have used the words in question, but this does not prove that he wrote the Epistles. On the basis of Harrison's argument from cognates it would be possible to assign the Pastorals to any period.

(e) Comparison with Pauline Hapaxes

As Harrison's argument is based on the number of Pastoral Hapaxes in the Apostolic Fathers and Apologists, a corresponding investigation is necessary for the Hapaxes in the other Paulines. If the numbers of these Hapaxes which occur also in the second-century writers is expressed as a percentage of the total number of Hapaxes in each Epistle, the results are as follows—Romans 25.2 per cent, 1 Corinthians 34.7 per cent, 2 Corinthians 21.7 per cent, Galatians 34.4 per cent, Ephesians 25 per cent, Philippians 37.8 per cent, Colossians 24.2 per cent, 1 Thessalonians 30 per cent, 2 Thessalonians 50 per cent and Philemon 60 per cent. When these figures are compared with the 34.9 per cent for the Pastorals, the fallacy of Harrison's linguistic argument is immediately

[1] *Op. cit.*, p. 65.

apparent. Moreover, of the 137 Hapaxes in the ten Paulines which are shared by the Apostolic Fathers, forty-three occur in more than one of these latter writings, a higher percentage than for the Pastorals.

Such mathematical calculations can never prove linguistic affinity, yet this is the basis of much of Harrison's evidence. When the ten Paulines are compared with the second-century ecclesiastical language, it is found that they have 46.8 per cent of Hapaxes in common as compared with the Pastorals 53.1 per cent. It is instructive to notice that 1 Corinthians (55.1 per cent) has a higher percentage than 1 Timothy (50.6 per cent) or Titus (50 per cent). Since it is inadmissible to assign 1 Corinthians to a second-century date, the only alternative is to suppose that this Epistle had a greater influence on second-century writers than others of Paul's Epistles,[1] but the same explanation would be valid for the Pastorals.

Since Harrison claims that the Pastoral Hapaxes occur with increasing frequency in the second-century writers,[2] it is significant to compare the frequency with which the Pauline Hapaxes are used. There are 899 occurrences, including repetitions, of the 220 Pauline Hapaxes in the second-century writings, an average of 4.1 times per word, but the ninety-two Pastoral Hapaxes have only 319 occurrences, an average of 3.5 times per word. Again, the comparison is not favourable to Harrison's theory.

Hitchcock[3] has further shown that there is a greater concentration of Hapaxes in the ethical sections in Paul's Epistles than in the doctrinal, suggesting some correlation between these practical sections and the need for new words. Parry[4] has shown that in the case of the Pastorals new subject matter is responsible for a great majority of the new words, and since their purpose is essentially practical this is no more than we should expect.

[1] Cf. Hitchcock's argument in *J.T.S.*, xxx (1929), p. 279.
[2] Cf. *op. cit.*, pp. 69, 70.
[3] *J.T.S.*, xxx (1929), p. 279.
[4] *The Pastoral Epistles* (1920), pp. cxi–cxxvi.

APPENDIX

(f) Conclusion

The preceding examination of Hapaxes has provided various grounds for criticizing Harrison's claim to have established the date of the Pastorals on the basis of the occurrence of some of these in second-century writings. The major fallacies in his argument may be summed up as follows: 1. It is based on an arbitrary opinion on the length of time during which words may be current. 2. It proceeds on the basis of heterogeneous evidence, using a wide variety of second-century writings and an even more heterogeneous selection of secular writers.[1] 3. It is capable of different applications, for it is difficult to determine in cases of linguistic affinity which of two sets of writings has been influenced by the other.

None of the evidence from the Hapaxes compels the conclusion that the writer reflects second-century working vocabulary, and there is no reason on this basis for denying that the Pastorals belong to the mid-first century, or for asserting that it is impossible to attribute them to Paul.

II. OTHER NON-PAULINE WORDS

Another linguistic problem is the 130 words shared by the Pastorals and other New Testament writers, but missing from the ten Paulines. Of these 117 occur in the second-century groups of ecclesiastical writings, most of them in both groups. The words in question were not, therefore, confined to any particular era, and are no more characteristic of the second than the first century. Their absence from the ten Paulines is problematic only if these ten Epistles are regarded as representing the apostle's total working vocabulary.

That the prevalence of these words in the second-century writings cannot indicate the date of writing is apparent when similar tests are applied to the ten Paulines. Each of these Epistles has a number of words not found elsewhere in Paul, although paralleled in other New Testament writers, and in the majority of instances the words in question are found in the Apostolic Fathers and Apologists. Romans, for

---

[1] It is noteworthy that a greater number of Hapaxes is shared by Justin than by any other, but Harrison does not assign the Pastorals to his period.

instance, has 148 such words, of which all but eight are in the second-century writers, while 2 Corinthians has 100 with only eight missing from the later writers. The other Epistles show similar percentages of words common to the second century. This investigation suggests that similar results would be obtained from any group of writings we might submit to the test, and any deductions based on such evidence must, therefore, be pronounced valueless.

If further demonstration is necessary, attention is drawn to the fact that whereas 78.3 per cent of the Pastorals vocabulary is found in the Apostolic Fathers, two at least of the ten Paulines (Colossians 85.6 per cent and Ephesians 86.2 per cent) show a considerably higher percentage.[1] If the Apologists are included, the percentages for the separate Paulines range from 87.6 per cent to 96.2 per cent, and for the Pastorals 86.7 per cent.[2] No other conclusion is possible but that the major part of the Pauline and Pastorals language is current language in both first and second centuries.

III. PAULINE WORDS MISSING FROM THE PASTORALS

Another strong criticism of Pauline authorship is the absence of many characteristically Pauline expressions. To Harrison this fact involves 'a change of perspective, a shifting of horizons, a profound modification of the whole mental and spiritual outlook'.[3] The difficulties may be analysed briefly under the following headings.

(a) Characteristic Pauline words

Harrison[4] cites a list of eighty words, in five or more Pauline Epistles, which are absent from the Pastorals, and claims that Paul could not have written letters without using some of these words. But all of the words occur elsewhere in the New Testament, all but seventeen are, in fact, in Luke/Acts,

---

[1] See the writer's *The Pastoral Epistles and the Mind of Paul*, p. 11, for further details.
[2] See the writer's *The Pastoral Epistles and the Mind of Paul*, Appendix D for details.
[3] *Op. cit.*, p. 34.
[4] *Op. cit.*, pp. 31, 32.

and all but three in the Apostolic Fathers. They appear to be equally 'characteristic' of both first and second centuries, and of various writers within the New Testament period. The number of times these words occur both in the other New Testament writers and in the Apostolic Fathers exceeds that of the Pauline writings, which weakens the contention that they are specially characteristic of Paul. Difference of subject matter would again seem to offer the most reasonable solution of the problem of these terms.

It should be noted that Harrison's own theory is not without difficulty here, for the Paulinist, who set out to imitate Paul, not only missed so many of his characteristic expressions, which would have suggested a Pauline imprimatur, but also avoided expressions characteristic of his own age. Of the eighty words under review, fifty-six occur in i Clement and fifty-three in Hermas.

(b) *Characteristic groups of words*

An even stronger emphasis is placed by Harrison on groups of cognate words which occur in five or more Paulines but are absent from the Pastorals. He cites twenty-seven such groups.[1] It may certainly seem strange that Paul has not used them in the Pastorals and due weight must be given to this fact. But it is not immediately apparent that Paul must have used them. The use of groups of words cannot be mechanically determined in this manner, for expressions are called to mind more by the nature of the subject in hand and the indefinable reaction of the human mind towards a given situation, than by previous usage. Yet even if Harrison's line of argument possessed validity some difficulties would confront the fragment theory, for the Paulinist would again have omitted groups of words so characteristically Pauline, and at the same time occurring with great frequency among his ecclesiastical contemporaries. All but five of the twenty-seven groups are used with as great or greater frequency among the Apostolic Fathers than in the ten Paulines. Moreover, if the Paulinist, purposing to give his writings a

[1] *Op. cit.*, p. 33.

'Pauline' appearance, could omit so many, there is more reason for Paul himself, with no such necessity, to have done so.

(c) Similar words with different meanings
There are a number of Pauline words in the Pastorals which are not used in the same sense as in the ten Paulines. Harrison cites several examples of this,[1] e.g. *analambanō, antechomai, grammata,* etc. In many of the cases mentioned the antithesis between the Pauline and Pastoral uses is rather forced (cf. the use of *morphōsis (form)* in Rom. ii. 20 and 2 Tim. iii. 5), but in any case Harrison admits not only that no writer can be expected to use every word in exactly the same sense but also that Paul uses words in different senses.[2] It is difficult to see, therefore, what importance can be attached to this evidence. A significant feature of Harrison's list is that, in almost every case, the usage found in the Apostolic Fathers agrees with the Pauline and not the Pastoral meaning.

(d) Different expressions for similar thoughts
Where the same ideas are expressed in different ways in the ten Paulines and the Pastoral Epistles, there may appear some justification for regarding the latter with suspicion. But again full allowance must be made for unconscious changes in expression which are not only psychologically possible but even desirable if monotony is to be avoided. Harrison cites twelve instances, of which two examples will be given to illustrate his type of argument. In 1 Cor. xvi. 11, *exoutheneō (despise)* is used with reference to Timothy, whereas in 1 Tim. iv. 12 the verb used is *kataphroneō.* But since Paul uses the latter word elsewhere, the objection is clearly invalid. Harrison points out that Paul describes the second advent as *parousia,* whereas the Pastorals (1 Tim. vi. 14; 2 Tim. i. 10, iv. 1, 8 and Tit. ii. 13) use *epiphaneis (appearing).* But this objection is considerably weakened not only by Paul's use of the latter word in 2 Thes. ii. 8, but its double occurrence in one of Harrison's 'genuine fragments' (i.e. 2 Tim. iv. 1, 8). Most of

[1] *Op. cit.,* pp. 27 ff.
[2] *Op. cit.,* p. 28.

the other variations are of a similar character, although the use in the Pastorals of such expressions as *charin echō* for *eucharisteō* (*I thank*), *di hēn aitian* for *dio* (*wherefore*), and *despotai* for *kurioi* (*masters*) is admittedly unexpected.

IV. GRAMMATICAL AND STYLISTIC PROBLEMS

Most scholars agree that stylistic considerations form a more formidable obstacle to Pauline authorship than vocabulary,[1] and these must therefore be carefully examined.

(a) The particles, pronouns, prepositions, etc.

According to Harrison's list,[2] there are 112 of these forms occurring in Paul's ten letters but missing from the Pastorals. These, he maintains, make it most improbable that Paul wrote the Pastorals, since the writer has not used 'a single word in all that list—one or other of which has hitherto appeared on the average nine times to every page that Paul ever wrote'.[3] But Harrison's statement is misleading on two counts. He assumes that all that Paul ever wrote must be restricted to the ten Paulines, and he suggests these particles, pronouns, etc. are spread with some regularity over these Epistles.

Of the 112 particles, etc. fifty-eight occur in only one or two Epistles and cannot therefore be considered a major obstacle. Of the rest, twenty-four occur in five or more Epistles and thirty in three or four, and these two groups might reasonably be claimed as characteristic of the apostle's style. Yet from Harrison's own figures it will be seen that considerable variation exists among the ten Paulines, for whereas Romans, 1 and 2 Corinthians have more than fifty, Colossians, 2 Thessalonians and Philemon have less than twenty. An interesting feature about the list is that nearly all occur in other New Testament writings, while all but twenty-one are

---

[1] See A. M. Hunter's cautious statement, *Interpreting the New Testament* (1951), p. 64.
[2] *Op. cit.*, pp. 36, 37.
[3] *Op. cit.*, p. 35.

used by the Apostolic Fathers. The absence of these twenty-one suggests to Harrison a corresponding tendency 'to dispense with that same series of Pauline particles, etc.'.[1] Now all but four of these words occur in only one or two Pauline Epistles and are, therefore, not the most characteristic of Paul. Moreover, it might as logically be claimed that there is a tendency to dispense with these particular words within the Paulines themselves, since the four captivity Epistles contain only seven between them.[2] The same Epistles, furthermore, lack between them no less than fifty-nine of the 112 particles, etc.

An even more obvious weakness about Harrison's list is the exclusion of all those which occur in the Pastorals. A parallel list can be compiled showing some ninety-three additional particles, pronouns and prepositional forms, of which all but one are found in the Pastorals and all but eight in the other Pauline group.[3] Romans has seventy-three, 1 Corinthians seventy, 2 Corinthians sixty, Galatians sixty-four, Ephesians fifty-four, Philippians fifty-seven, Colossians forty-six, 1 Thessalonians forty-six, 2 Thessalonians forty-five and Philemon thirty-two. When these are added to Harrison's figures for the separate Paulines, it is found that the Pastorals compare favourably with the captivity and Thessalonian Epistles.[4] It seems a reasonable deduction that 'connective tissue' cannot be mathematically computed in this way, and cannot be cited as conclusive proof against Pauline authenticity. No allowance can be made in such word counts for fluctuations of mood or purpose, and no one would expect a similar style in a theological treatise as in a private letter or general circular.

If Harrison further appeals to the frequency with which these particles, etc. occur in Pauline writings as indicative of

[1] *Op. cit.*, p. 75. Harrison cites twenty-two words missing but *tou'nantion* occurs in the *Martyrdom of Polycarp*.

[2] Cf. Newport White, *op. cit.*, p. 71, for twenty-four characteristic particles mostly absent from the captivity Epistles.

[3] See the list given in the writer's monograph *The Pastoral Epistles and the Mind of Paul*, Appendix E, pp. 41-44.

[4] See the writer's monograph, pp. 12-15.

a predominant characteristic,[1] it is strange that he excludes from his list the words that do appear in the Pastorals on the grounds that they occur too often to remain significant. But if some words occur frequently in all Paul's Epistles, including the Pastorals, it is surely arbitrary to exclude these from a list of characteristic words, and yet include thirty-five words occurring in one only of Paul's Epistles.

(b) *Different uses of the article*

In addition to the particles, etc. Harrison appeals to the absence of many characteristic uses of the article, and this objection deserves careful study.

1. The articular infinitive is used 106 times by Paul in all his writings except Colossians and Philemon. The exceptions weaken the force of the contention, but in any case the Paulinist theory is in difficulties here since this usage occurs 208 times in the Apostolic Fathers and is used by all the writers.

2. The article with the nominative in place of the vocative. Although occurring twenty-five times, this usage is found in only four Pauline Epistles and is obviously dictated by the subject matter.

3. The article with the numeral. In all the eleven instances (in six Epistles) cited by Harrison the context demands the article, but in the three instances of numerals in the Pastorals (1 Tim. ii. 5, v. 9 and v. 19) the article would have been entirely inappropriate. Moreover Paul's more frequent usage is the anarthrous form.

4. The article with an adverb. Harrison cites twenty-three instances for the ten Pauline Epistles, but 1 Tim. iii. 7 contains a similar construction. The anarthrous adverbial form *loipon* (*henceforth*) is used in 2 Tim. iv. 8, one of Harrison's genuine fragments, although Paul often uses the same form with the neuter article. The fourfold adjectival use of *ontos* with the article in the Pastorals (e.g. 1 Tim. v. 3 *widows indeed*) admittedly cannot be paralleled in Paul's other Epistles, but the adjectival use of *exō* and *anō* in 2 Cor. iv. 16 (*our outward man*) and Phil. iii. 14 (*the high calling*) furnish close analogies.

[1] *Op. cit.*, p. 35.

5. The article with whole sentences. Of the seven instances of this mentioned by Harrison, four introduce citations, though this is clearly not Paul's normal way of introducing literary allusions. The sole objection possible among those mentioned is the supposed contrast between 1 Thes. iv. 1 where *to pōs dei* (*how ye ought*) is used and 1 Tim. iii. 15 where the article is dropped, but even this falls to the ground in view of the anarthrous use of the same words in Col. iv. 6.

(*c*) *The use of* hōs

There are three Pauline but non-Pastoral uses of *hōs*, eleven instances with a participle, five with an adverb and six with *an*. The absence of the first may be paralleled by its absence from Galatians, Ephesians, Philippians, 2 Thessalonians and Philemon. The latter two are absent from six of the ten Paulines, which means they are practically valueless as support for non-Pauline authorship. This data, in fact, only corroborates what has already been amply demonstrated, that Paul's style was much more flexible than many scholars allow.

In summing up the stylistic position, the two main criticisms of Harrison's mass of statistics may be stated in the following way. It has been shown in the first place that the same arguments could equally well prove the non-Pauline character of undisputed Pauline Epistles, and secondly that these statistics take no account of mood and purpose. Even where two Epistles such as Romans and Galatians deal with allied themes they share only twenty-five of Harrison's 112 particles etc., whereas the closely connected Colossians and Ephesians have only six in common. The apostle clearly allowed himself, consciously or unconsciously, a considerable amount of variation in his 'connective tissue'. Lock's[1] opinion that the Pastorals style is closer to Paul than to any other New Testament writer would seem to be amply justified.

V. CONCLUSION

It has been shown in the preceding discussion that nothing

[1] *Op. cit.*, pp. xxvii, xxviii.

in the linguistic evidence demands the abandonment of Pauline authenticity, and it remains now only to summarize the variety of suggested solutions to the phenomena of linguistic differences from the earlier Paulines.

1. Dissimilarity of subject matter undoubtedly accounts for many new words.[1] Themes not previously dealt with unavoidably produce a crop of new expressions.

2. Variations due to advancing age must be given due weight, since style and vocabulary are often affected in this way.[2]

3. Enlargement of vocabulary due to change of environment may account for an increased use of classical words.[3]

4. The difference in the recipients as compared with the earlier Epistles addressed to churches would account for certain differences in style in the same way that private and public correspondence inevitably differs.

---

[1] Cf. Parry, *op. cit.*, pp. cxi-cxxvi. Cf. also W. E. Bowen, *The Dates of the Pastoral Epistles* (1900).

[2] Cf. Spicq, *op. cit.*, p. xci and Simpson *op. cit.*, pp. 15, 16.

[3] Cf. Montgomery Hitchcock, 'Latinity in the Pastorals', *Expository Times*, xxxix (1927-28), pp. 347-352, and Simpson, *The Pastoral Epistles* (1954), pp. 20, 21.